IMAGES
of America

MONTICELLO

ON THE COVER: The W.W. Vick store on Monticello's town square specialized in men's and women's hats, dressmaking materials, and clothing accessories. This picture was taken during the store's big fall sale in October 1914. (Courtesy of Drew County Historical Society.)

IMAGES
of America

MONTICELLO

Mary Heady and
Mark Spencer

ARCADIA
PUBLISHING

ISBN 978-0-7385-8789-9

Published by Arcadia Publishing
Charleston, South Carolina

Printed in the United States of America

Library of Congress Control Number: 2011924922

For all general information, please contact Arcadia Publishing:
Telephone 843-853-2070
Fax 843-853-0044
E-mail sales@arcadiapublishing.com
For customer service and orders:
Toll-Free 1-888-313-2665

Visit us on the Internet at www.arcadiapublishing.com

To the people of Monticello—past, present, and future.

Contents

ACKNOWLEDGMENTS

This book was only made possible because of the cooperation and assistance of the Drew County Historical Society, University of Arkansas at Monticello (UAM) library director Sandra Campbell, UAM provost David Ray, and UAM chancellor Jack Lassiter.

A heavy debt is owed to the many local historians who have, over the years, researched, organized, and analyzed records of the past and written eloquently of their conclusions and findings. Special recognition is owed to Dr. Donald Holley, Dr. William F. Droessler, Sheilla Lampkin, Beth Thurman, Bettye Kellum, Claudia White, Kathy Davis, Annette Vincent, Shay Gillespie, Helen Guenter, Mary Tomlinson, and Connie Mullis.

Thanks to Joshua Pettigrew of the UAM Graphic Design & Copy Center for his assistance in scanning and uploading images.

We also wish to thank Amy Perryman, our editor at Arcadia Publishing, for her patience, expertise, and guidance.

Introduction

Monticello's roots go back to the formation of Drew County in 1846 and the village of Rough and Ready—an appropriately named community, given its reputation for personal feuds that led to brawls and killings. Established as the county seat and located less than a mile from Rough and Ready, Monticello derived its name perhaps in part from local residents' desire for a cultivated elegance to replace the less-than-civilized reputation of Rough and Ready, and what better symbol of culture and elegance than the Virginia home of Thomas Jefferson? The first courthouse, that quintessential symbol of order and civilization, was built in 1851. In 1872, it was replaced by Monticello's famous "French castle" courthouse, which majestically towered over the businesses and residences of the continuously growing and prospering town until it was razed in 1932.

In the late 19th century, dense timberlands, rich soil, the railroads, cotton gins, an entrepreneurial spirit, and the recognition of the value of education made Monticello the premier community of southeast Arkansas. The town's schools have been at the center of its prosperous history. In 1857, Rodger's Female Academy opened to provide guidance to the young ladies of Monticello. Although the school closed during the Civil War to serve as a hospital for Confederate soldiers wounded in nearby skirmishes, it reopened afterward as the Wood Thompson School for Boys. Eventually, the school became coeducational and ultimately evolved into W.C. Whaley Elementary School, located on North Main Street. Monticello Academy was established for African American students in 1888 and operated until 1933. Hinemon University School was founded as a high school in 1890 and evolved into Monticello High School. In nearby Wilmar, Beauvoir College began conferring degrees in 1903; its programs in music and elocution were considered particularly prestigious. The national economic crisis of 1907 forced its closing, however, and half its structures were disassembled and moved to Monticello. In 1909, the Fourth District State Agricultural School (SAS) was created by an act of the state legislature. In the years to come, SAS would evolve into Arkansas A&M College and eventually the University of Arkansas at Monticello.

In 1876, a desire to repudiate the "Rough and Ready" days led to the forming of the first Arkansas chapter of the Women's Christian Temperance Union in Monticello. Hannah Hyatt embodied a calling to community service as she began taking orphans into her home in 1887; her charitable nature led to the establishment of the Arkansas Baptist Home for Children. In 1910, Monticello native Lulu Williamson started a day nursery for the children of women working in the cotton mills, as well as a home for women unable to continue working. This generosity led to the founding of the Vera Lloyd Presbyterian Home for Children in 1923.

The desire for elegance was well established with the construction of the "French castle" courthouse, and from 1890 to 1920, Monticello saw many elegant churches and homes constructed during its "gilded age." A Chicago-trained architect named Sylvester Hotchkiss had made his way south at the advice of his physician and designed many structures in Monticello, including private homes, churches, and schools, some of which still stand today. Hotchkiss designed the mansion of Joe Lee Allen, whose rise from an impoverished farm boy reared by a widowed mother to a leading entrepreneur and bank president—achieved through hard work, perseverance, and integrity in the context of the opportunities afforded by Monticello—epitomized the American dream.

In the early years of the 20th century, with relatively easy access via railroads and riverboats, residents of Monticello were always connected to the styles and commerce of large cities like Memphis, St. Louis, and New Orleans. Prosperous citizens sent their daughters to finishing schools in places like Nashville, Tennessee; and Lexington, Kentucky, and their sons to colleges like Baylor and Harvard.

Although a skirmish was fought between Confederate and Union troops six weeks after the Civil War ended because word of surrender had not yet reached the community, Monticello's isolation greatly diminished in the later years of the 19th century. By the time of the Roaring Twenties, the ease of rail travel, two local newspapers, and the arrival of the telephone (in 1897) and radio (in 1920) helped Monticellonians stay connected to the news, fashions, and philosophies of the rest of the world.

When America sobered up during the Great Depression, Monticello became the home of many looking for a new start and its population rose significantly. During World War II, a prisoner-of-war camp for Italian soldiers was established in the community, and the Navy's V-12 program made the college a training ground for many young Americans preparing to shield America from the nefarious ambitions of Hitler and Hirohito. The optimism and prosperity of the 1950s made its way to Monticello and shaped a new generation that is still active in community affairs in the early 21st century. In the midst of the cultural and social revolution of the 1960s, Monticello shed prejudices and removed barriers and its opportunities became available to all.

As many small businesses and industries came and went through the decades, a stable and ever-expanding presence was "the college," as many people still refer to the University of Arkansas at Monticello, which has always provided not just educational opportunities but also concerts, plays, and athletic events for the general public. Legendary in collegiate sports, the Wandering Weevils football team brought national attention to Arkansas A&M College. The Weevils, unconcerned with winning games, travelled America from 1939 to 1941 in a dilapidated bus and became known as the Marx Brothers of college football because of their comedic antics on the field.

The authors acknowledge that no history is complete, that inclusion is a matter of availability of information and space limitations. Of course, in all communities, folklore and fact blur together. Imagination, faulty memory, politics, prejudice, and pride keep history in flux. But whether fact or fiction, the idealizing of Confederate soldiers, the antics of colorful local personalities, and numerous ghost stories enliven Monticello's history.

Although commerce has largely shifted in the last couple of decades from the historic downtown square to Highway 425—the site of Walmart, Walgreens, fast-food chains like McDonalds and Sonic, and hotels like Hampton Inn and Holiday Inn Express—efforts are under way to revitalize the historic district. For example, the Ridgeway Hotel, which was built in 1930 and played host to big band acts like Count Basie and Glenn Miller, is being renovated to become residential housing for retirees, and the square itself is receiving a face-lift for its fountain and sidewalks. While the new businesses on Highway 425 represent progress and continued growth, Monticellonians also recognize the importance of preserving the past as a source of knowledge and pride. The authors hope that this book will contribute to that knowledge and pride, as well as entertain, in part through the manifestations of the old paradoxical saying that "everything changes and everything stays the same."

One

Monticello's Golden Age 1890–1920

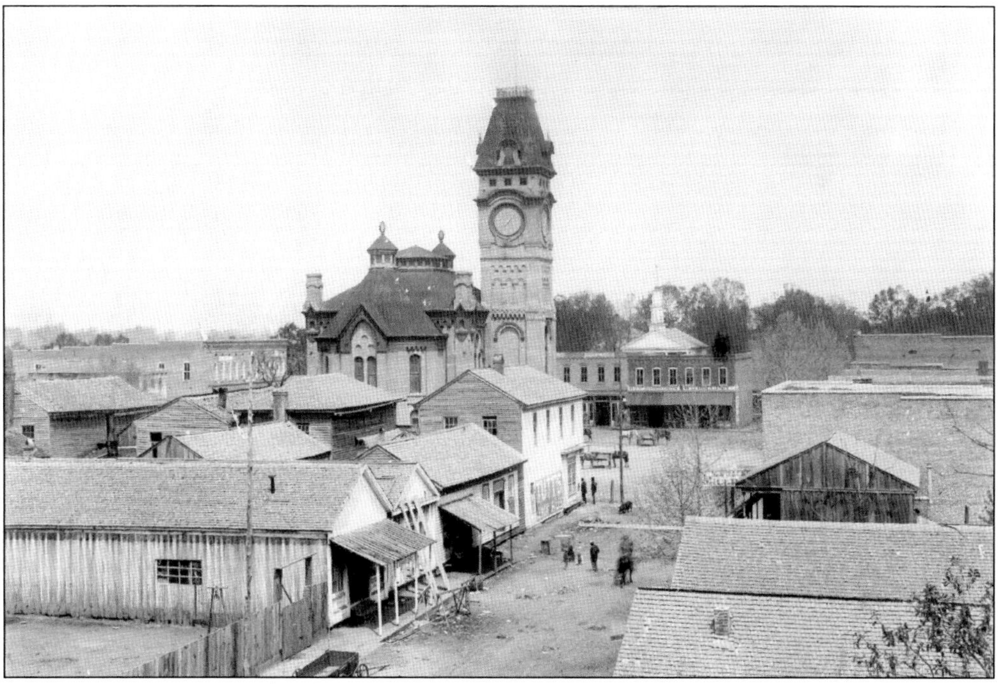

With construction completed in May 1872, the "French castle" Drew County courthouse on Monticello's town square replaced the original courthouse, which was a simple two-story frame building erected when Monticello was founded. (Courtesy of Drew County Historical Society.)

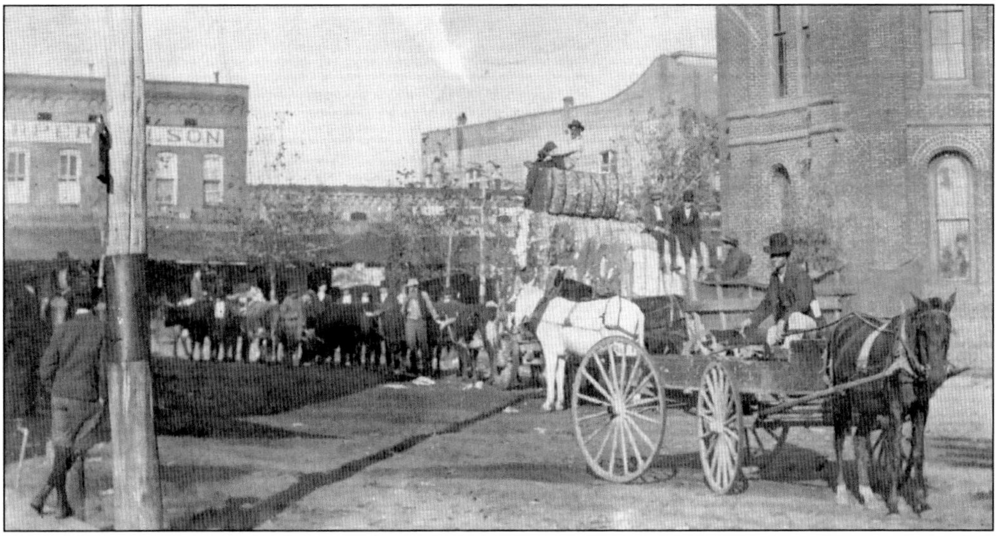

This 1907 photograph shows a bustling downtown, with the Drew County courthouse at the center of the activity. It is important, perhaps, to note that Drew County's population hit its peak in 1910 at 21,960, a number that exceeds the 2010 population by more than 3,000. (Courtesy of Drew County Historical Society.)

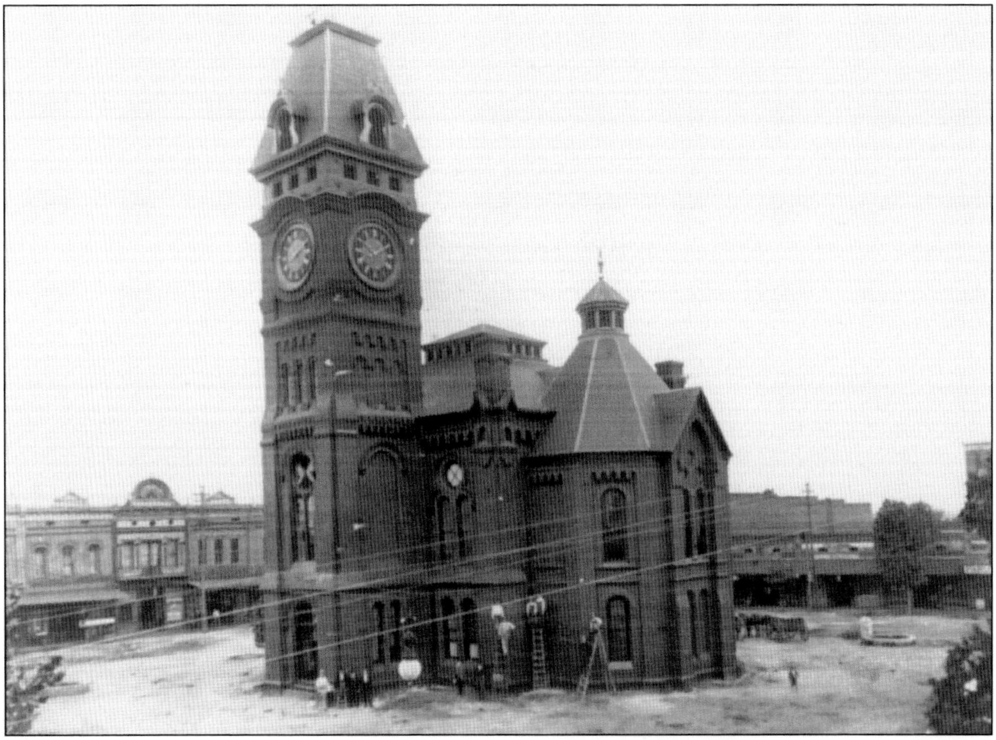

The red bricks of the courthouse receive a cleaning in this photograph taken in the 1890s. Designed by the Memphis architectural firm of Jones and Baldwin, the style of the courthouse was consistent with the popularity in the early 1870s of Second Empire architecture, a reference to the Second French Empire of Napoleon III—hence the "French castle" nickname. The construction costs totaled approximately $36,000. (Courtesy of Drew County Historical Society.)

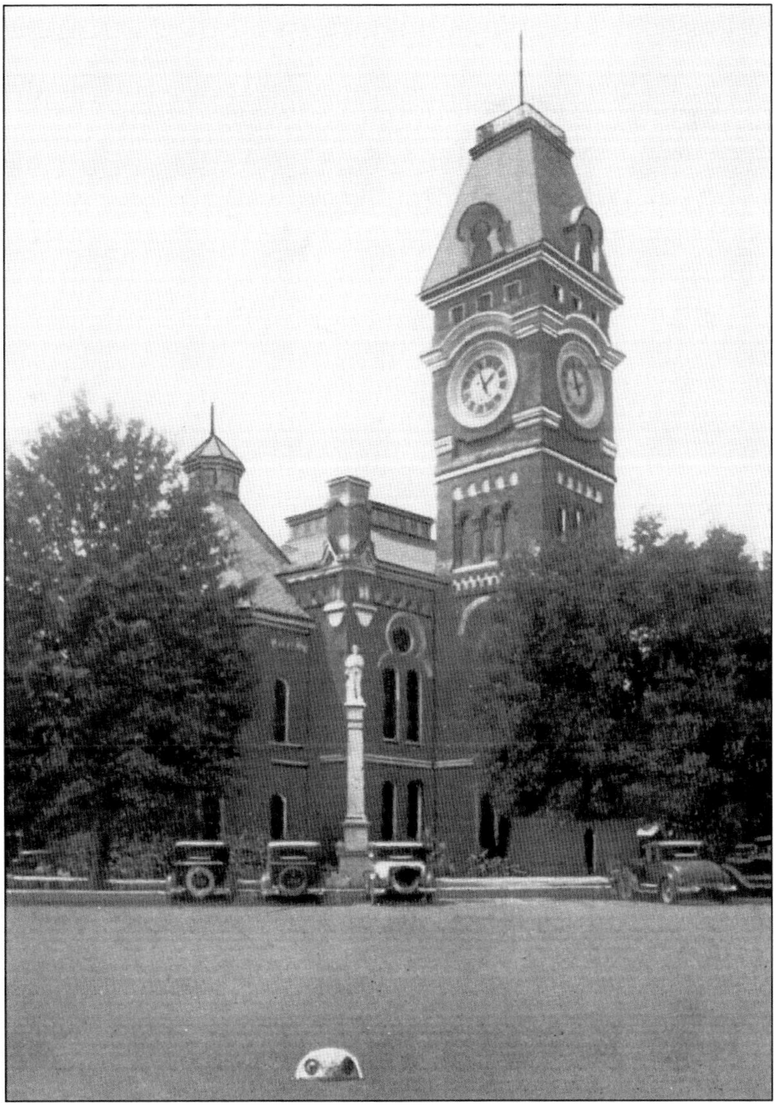

This 1920s image of the courthouse shows that the trim was painted at some point to emphasize architectural details. When the building's cornerstone was laid in October 1870, there was much fanfare and the local newspaper *The Monticellonian* predicted that construction of the new courthouse would raise property values as much as 50 percent. Wanting to ensure that this symbol of a new era for Monticello kept its fresh, elegant appearance, the County Court enacted ordinances threatening fines for any individual caught spitting or writing on the courthouse walls. Over the course of its 60-year existence, the courthouse was the gathering place for a variety of activities. In 1934, a resident reminiscing in the local newspaper wrote that it was the "temple of justice, town hall, community house, theater, and grand ballroom all in one." As the building aged, county officials became concerned about its safety, and with the accumulation of government documents over the years, its size became inadequate. After the completion of the new courthouse on South Main Street in 1932, there was some debate about the fate of the "French castle." However, interest in historical preservation was modest at that time and the building was razed. Also visible here is the Confederate monument, erected on the square in 1914. (Courtesy of Drew County Historical Society.)

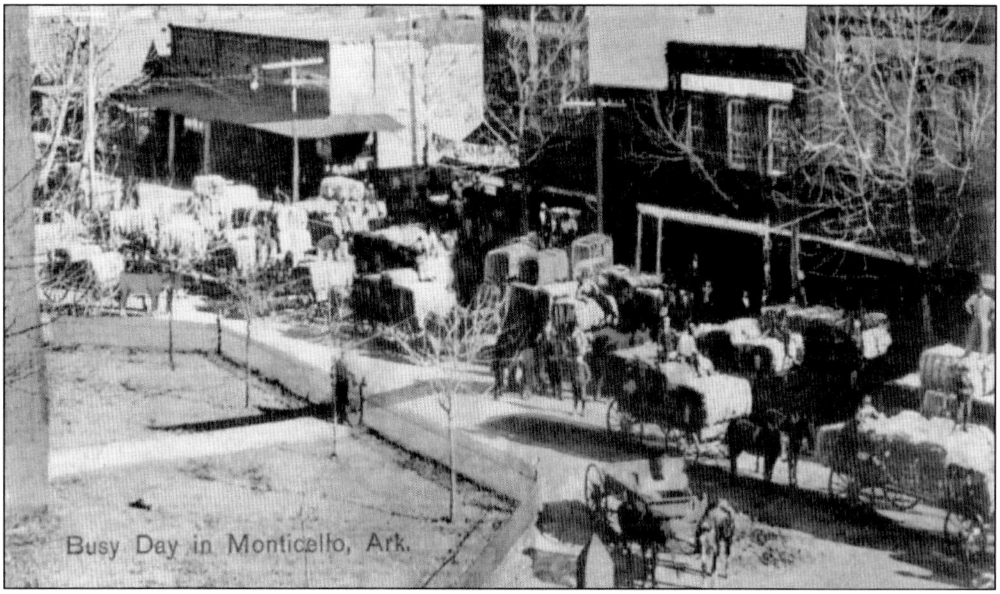

The caption of this 1909 postcard image is "Busy Day in Monticello, Ark." The postcard was printed for Bordeaux's Drug Store, of Monticello. One of the thriving businesses of the time, the McCloy-Trotter General Mercantile Store, is visible on the right. (Courtesy of Drew County Historical Society.)

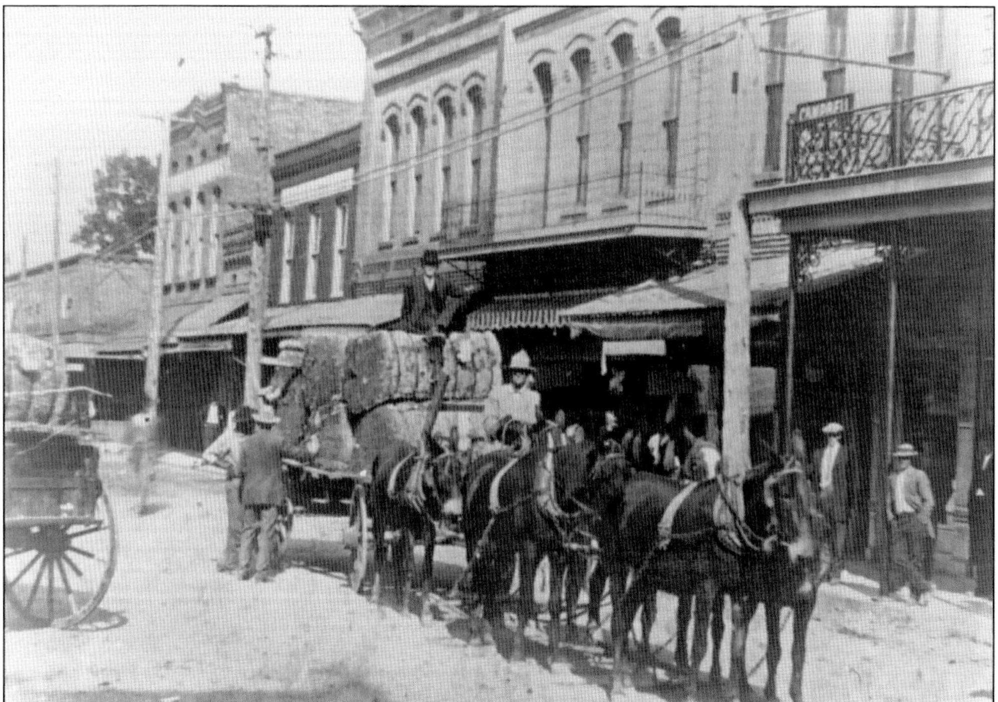

In this c. 1913 image taken on the east side of the town square, prominent businessman John McCloy sits on top of the cotton bales while another successful businessman, Guy Burks, drives the mules. (Courtesy of UAM Library.)

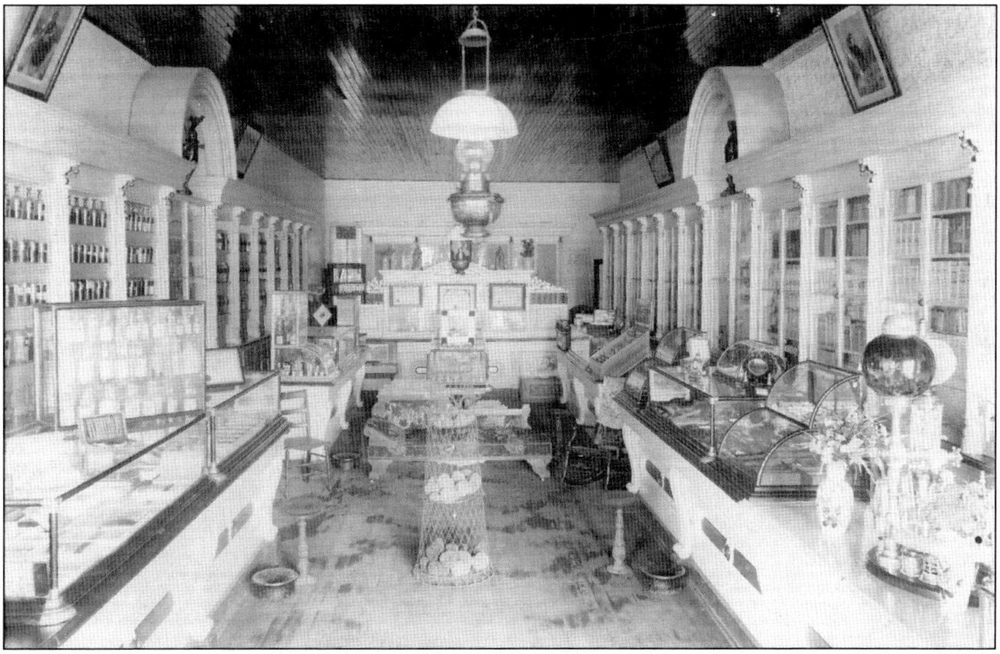

Dr. W.A. Brown and Will McQuiston operated a drugstore in the Masonic building on the west side of the town square, the subject of this photograph taken around 1892. As in the 21st century, drugstores in the 19th century were critical to the health and quality of life of Monticello's citizens. Throughout America, many pharmaceuticals such as morphine, heroin, and cocaine were misunderstood and made available over the counter. (Courtesy of Drew County Historical Society.)

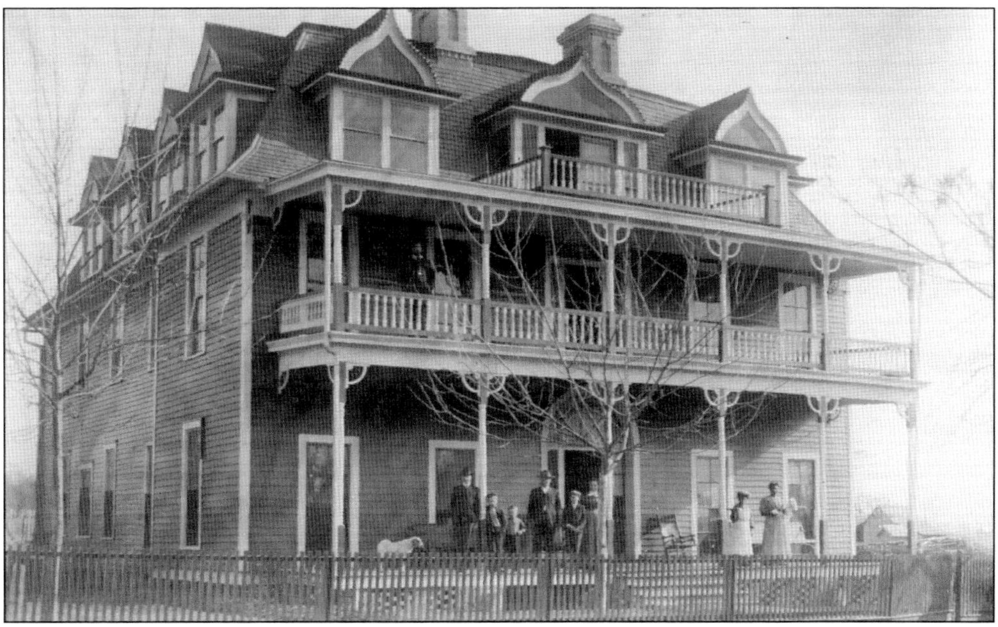

Pictured here is the Terra Cotter Hotel on the north side of East Trotter Street. It was owned and operated by Zeph Wood and his wife until it was torn down in 1914. The Allen Hotel, built in 1912, significantly diminished the number of patrons for the Terra Cotter. (Courtesy of Drew County Historical Society.)

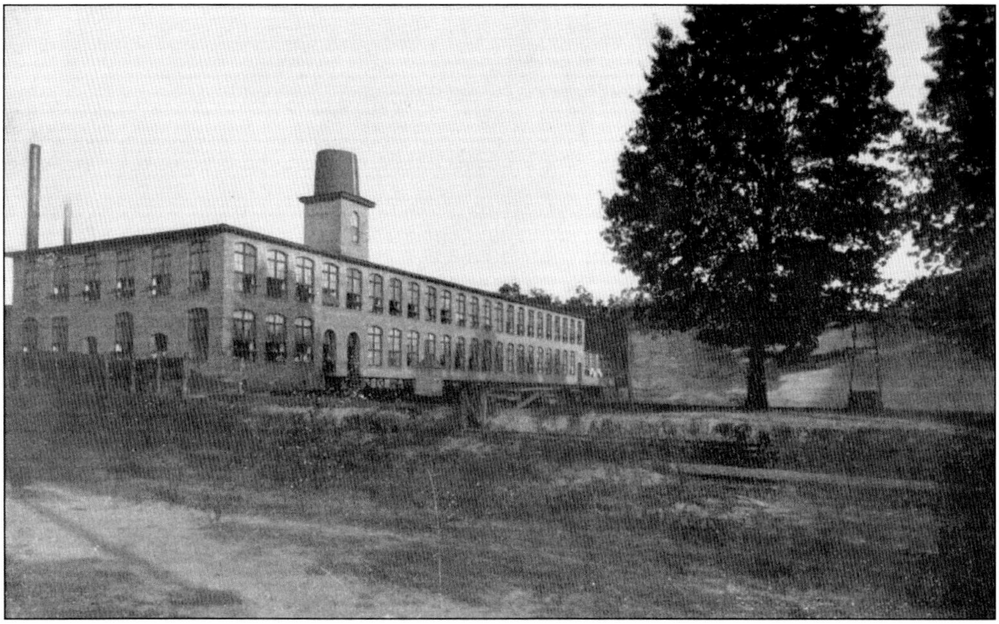

In the early 20th century, many residents—both men and women—made a living at the Monticello Cotton Mill. (Courtesy of Drew County Historical Society.)

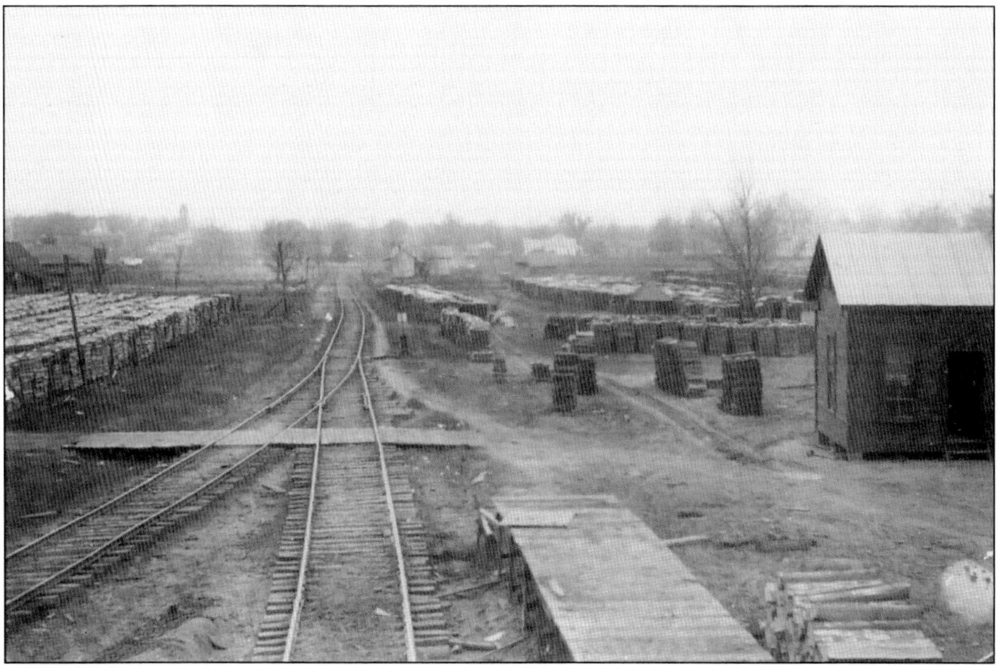

Established in 1913 and representative of Monticello's bustling commerce, the M.L. Sigmon Stave Mill was located in the Willis Street area. This photograph looks north toward the Monticello square. The courthouse and the First United Methodist Church are visible on the skyline. (Courtesy of Drew County Historical Society.)

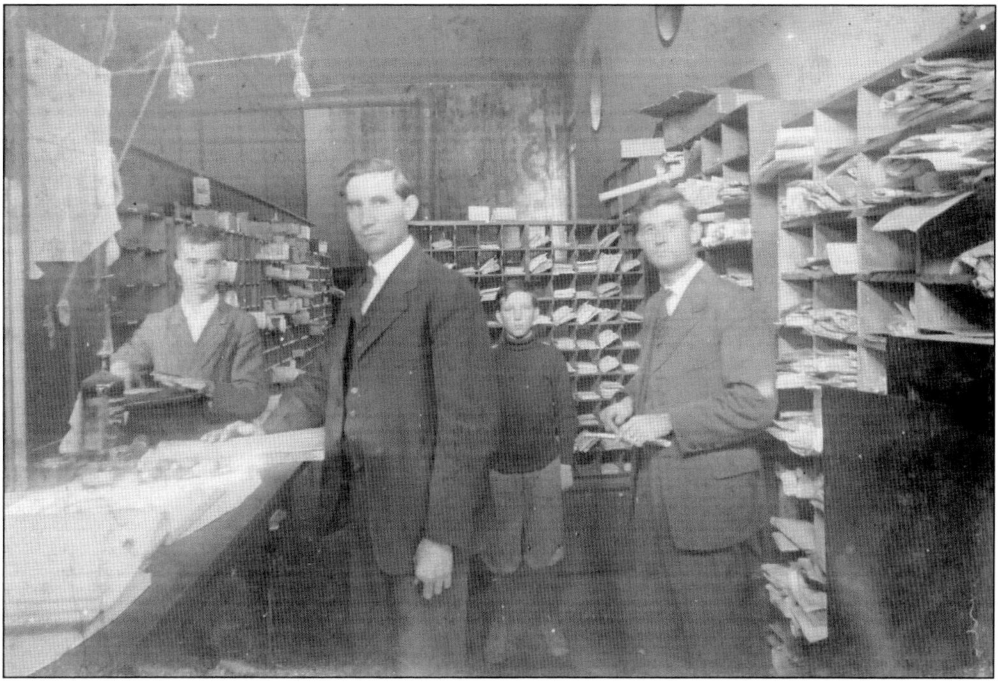

This image of the Monticello post office is from 1911 or 1912. Pictured from left to right are Howard Bishop, postmaster E.T. Lucky, Carl Lucky, and Henry Lucky. (Courtesy of Drew County Historical Society.)

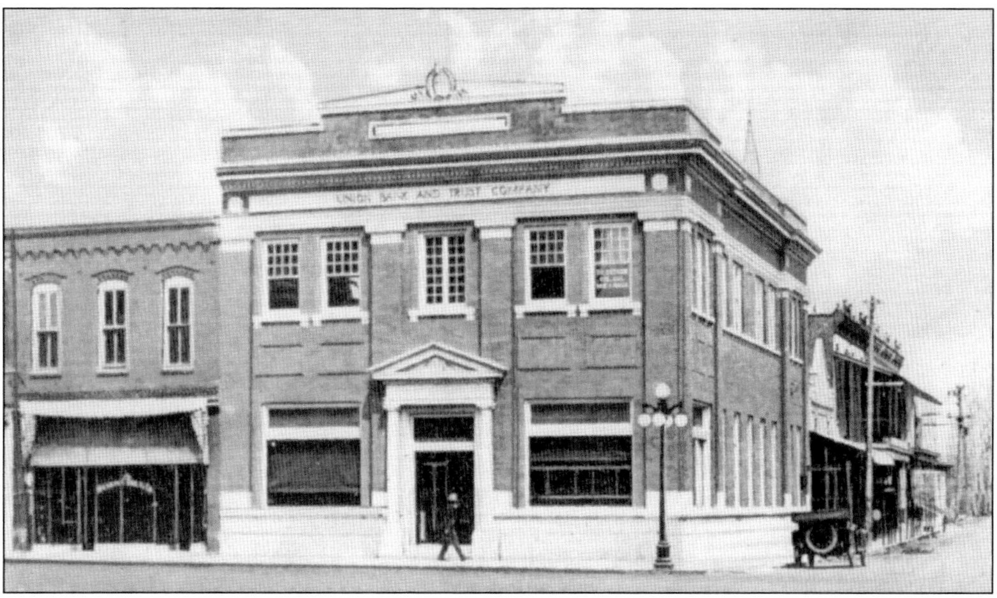

The Union Bank and Trust Company came into being after the September 1915 merger of Monticello's two oldest banks, Citizens Bank and Monticello Bank. The old Union Bank building on the square is shown here as it appeared around 1920. (Courtesy of Drew County Historical Society.)

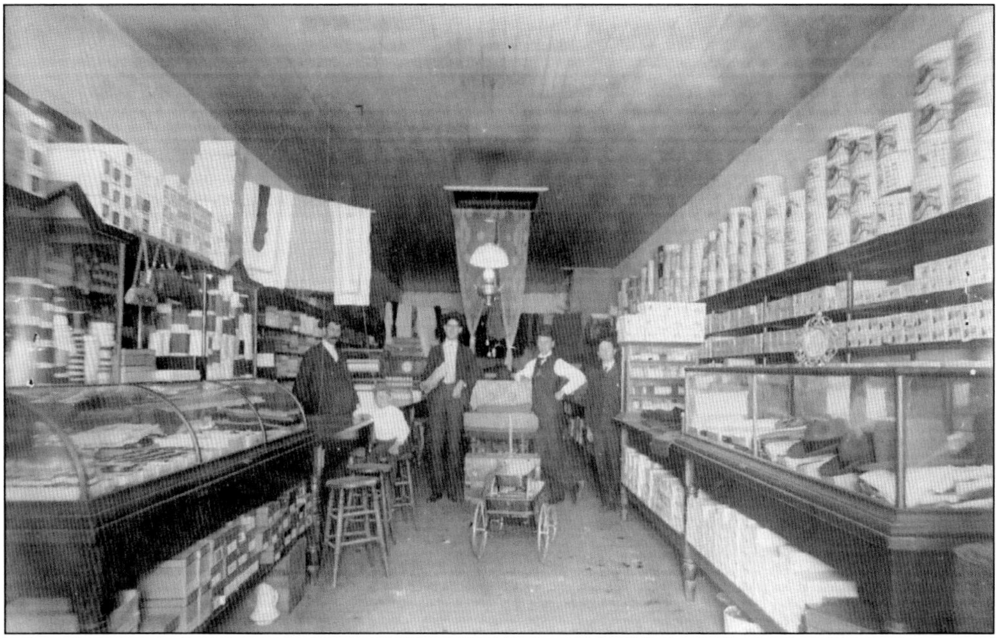

The A.T. Cotham and Harris Nunn General Mercantile Store was one of the businesses on the square in the first decade of the 20th century. The store's site was later occupied by the Union Bank building. (Courtesy of Drew County Historical Society.)

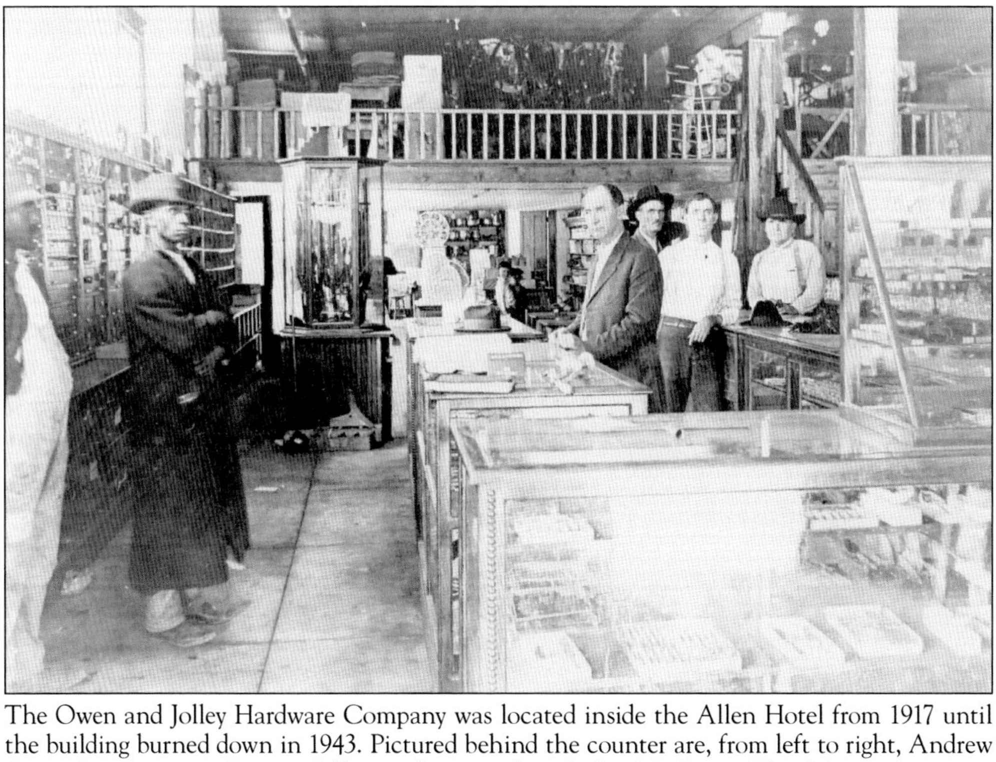

The Owen and Jolley Hardware Company was located inside the Allen Hotel from 1917 until the building burned down in 1943. Pictured behind the counter are, from left to right, Andrew Owen, Jim Cavaness, Preston Jolley, and a man identified as Mr. Berry. The African American men are unidentified. (Courtesy of Drew County Historical Society.)

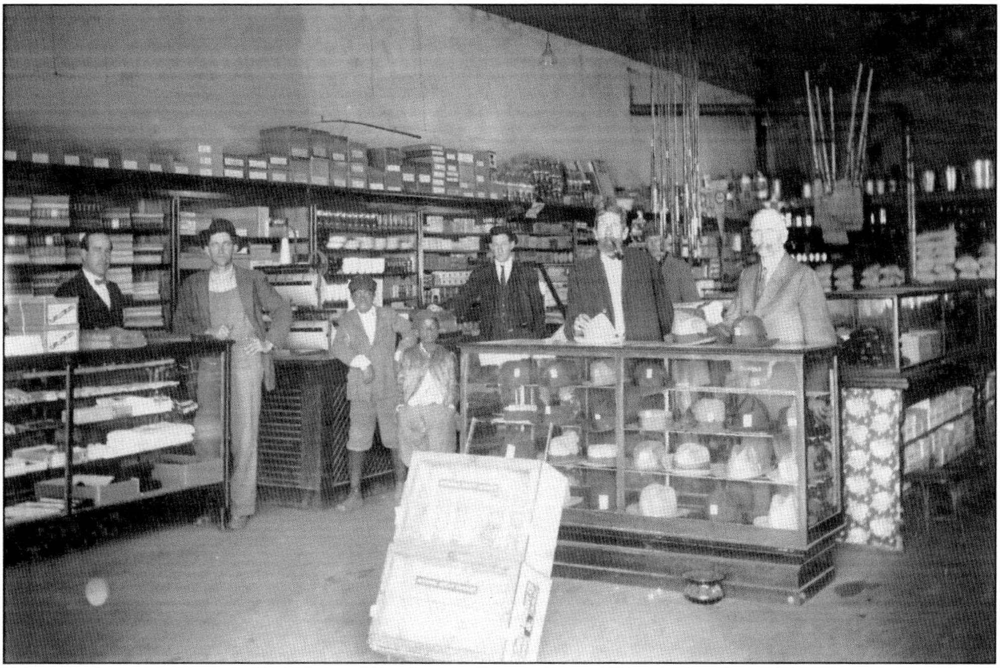

The Shelton Shoe Store was located on what was known as the east side. In this c. 1910 photograph, Gaston Shelton, the proprietor, is at far left. His father, Robert Winston Shelton, is on the far right. The other individuals are unidentified. (Courtesy of Edgar W. Spencer.)

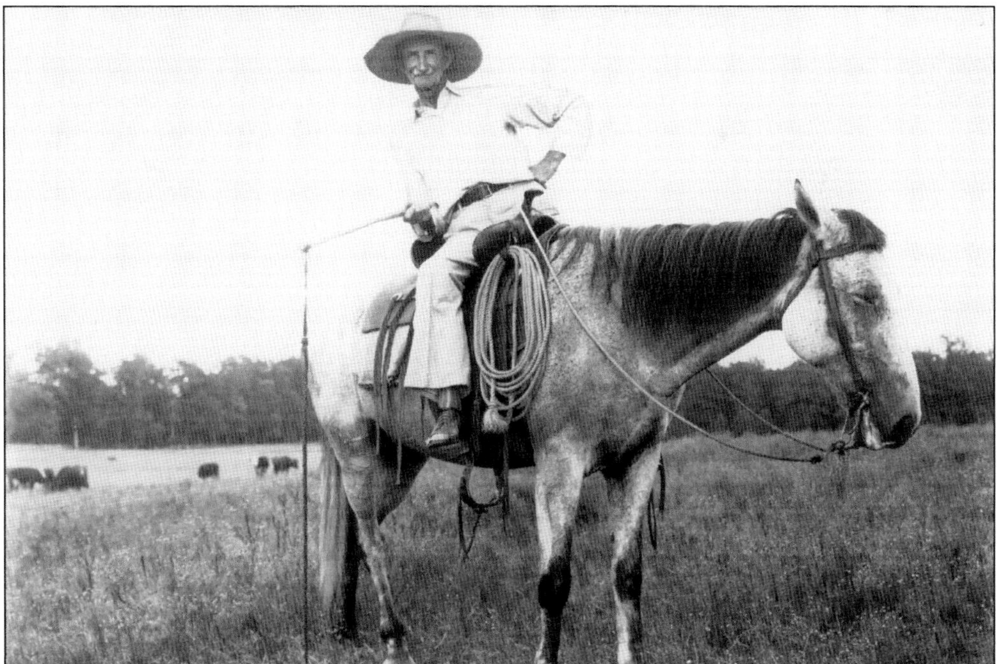

Edgar Spencer (1859–1942) was engaged in the mercantile business in Monticello until his store and all its goods were destroyed in a fire, at which time he retired to his family farm in Lacey, Arkansas. (Courtesy of Edgar W. Spencer.)

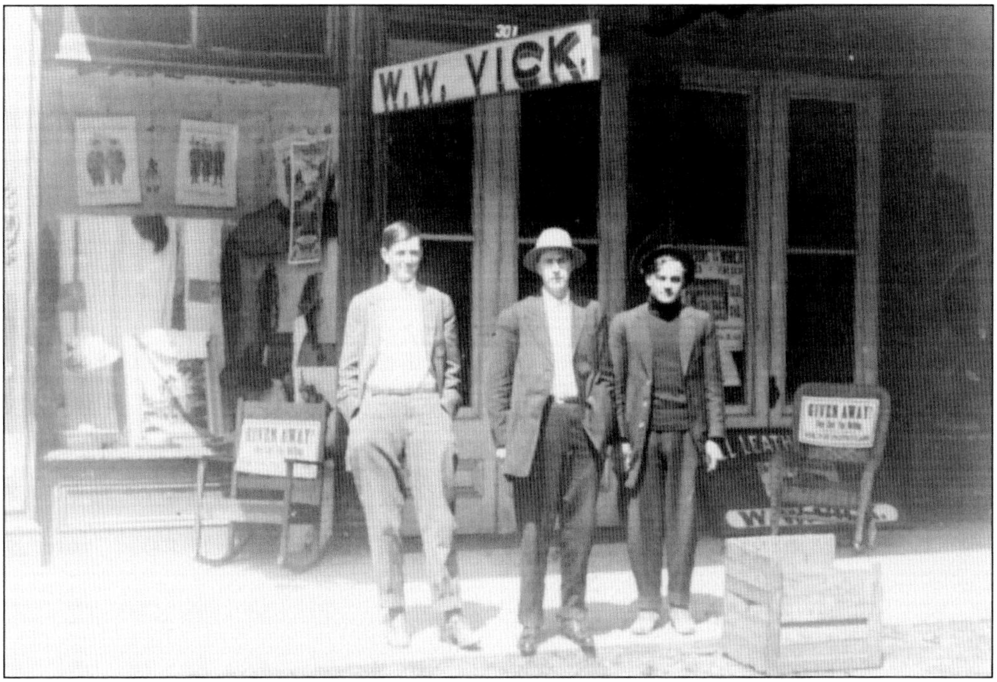

The W.W. Vick store was on East Gaines Avenue. Pictured in this October 1914 photograph are, from left to right, Rodney C. Stewart, W.W. Vick, and Jack Funderburg. The interior of the store is featured on the cover of this book. (Courtesy of Drew County Historical Society.)

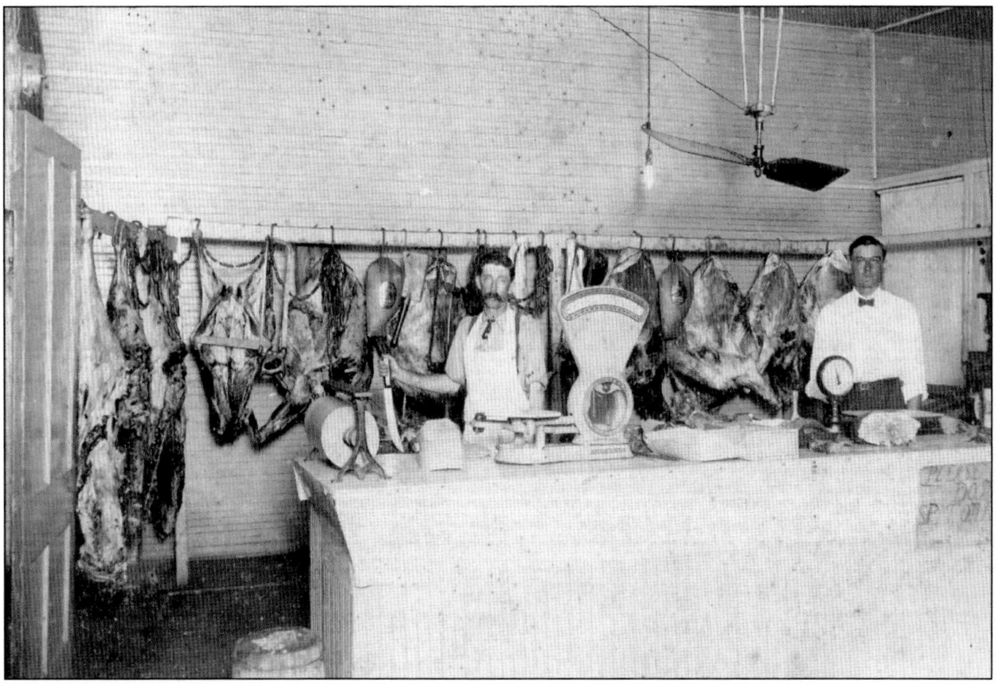

John Binns (left) and Gavin Ratteree are pictured here in 1915 in their meat market on South Main Street. As was typical at the time, the meat for sale hangs from the walls. (Courtesy of Drew County Historical Society.)

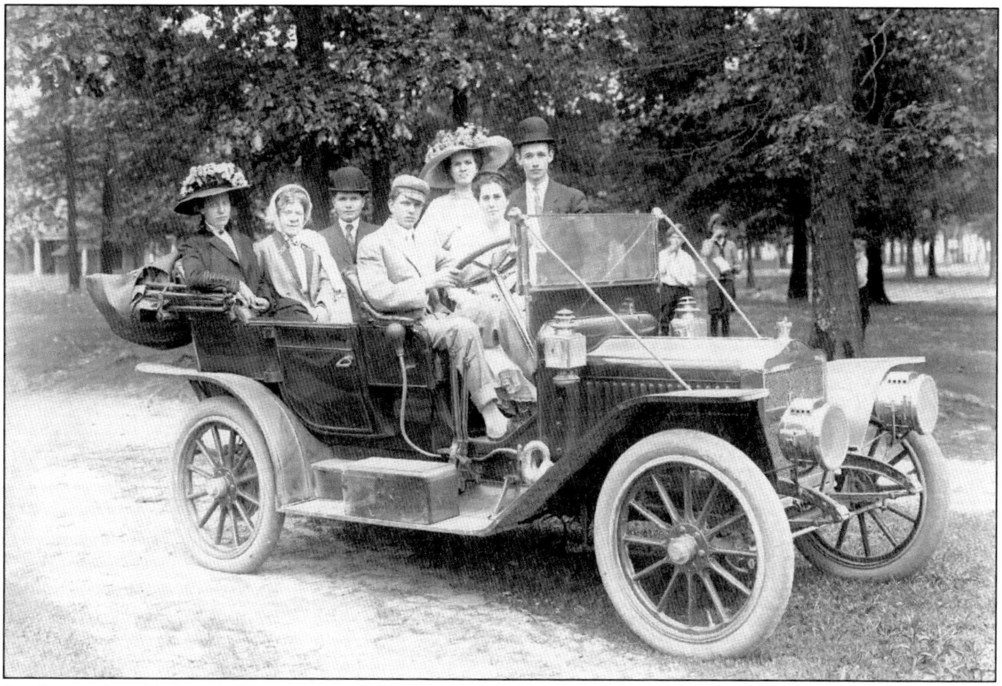

In the early 1900s, while most Monticellonians still used horses for transportation and could not afford the recently invented automobile, a few of the well-to-do proudly drove motor cars about town as a symbol of wealth. Here, a group of local residents pose with one of the new contraptions around 1905. (Courtesy of Drew County Historical Society.)

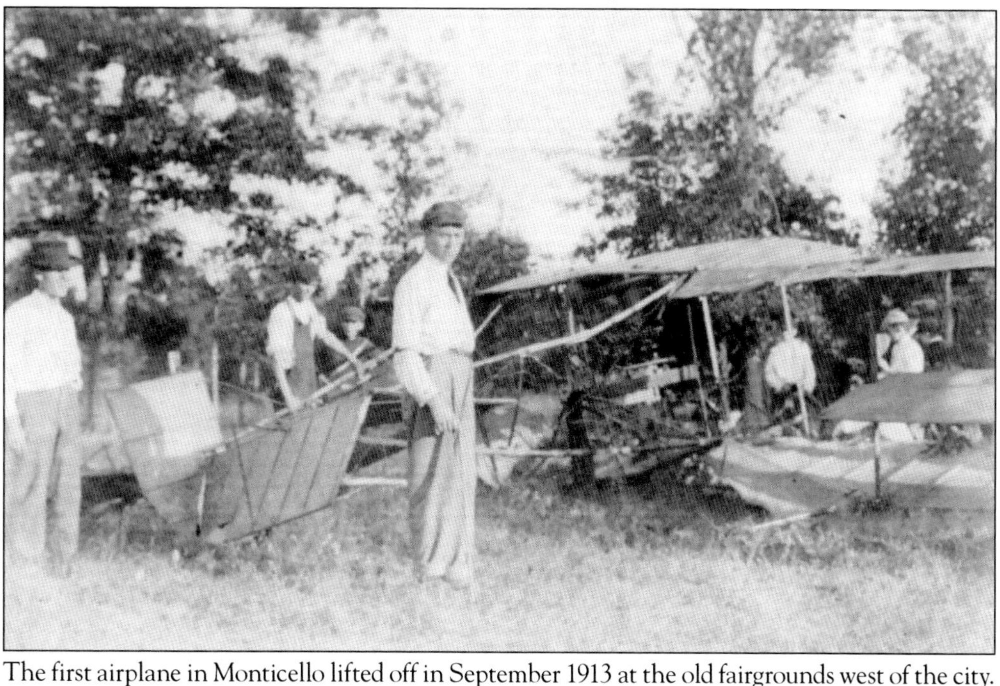

The first airplane in Monticello lifted off in September 1913 at the old fairgrounds west of the city. The plane hit a tree and crashed. The pilot was uninjured, but the airplane was badly damaged. (Courtesy of Drew County Historical Society.)

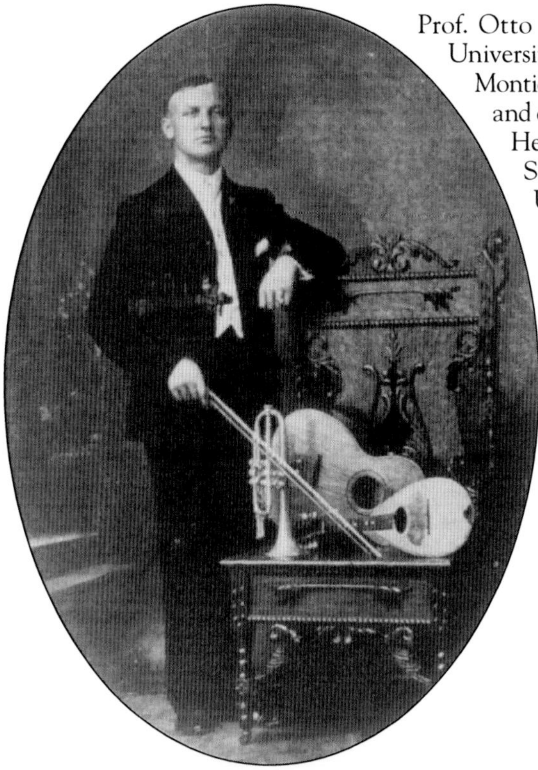

Prof. Otto Mahling, a faculty member at Hinemon University School on College Street, established the Monticello Band around 1905 for the entertainment and cultural enrichment of community residents. He later taught music at the Fourth District State Agricultural School. (Courtesy of UAM Library.)

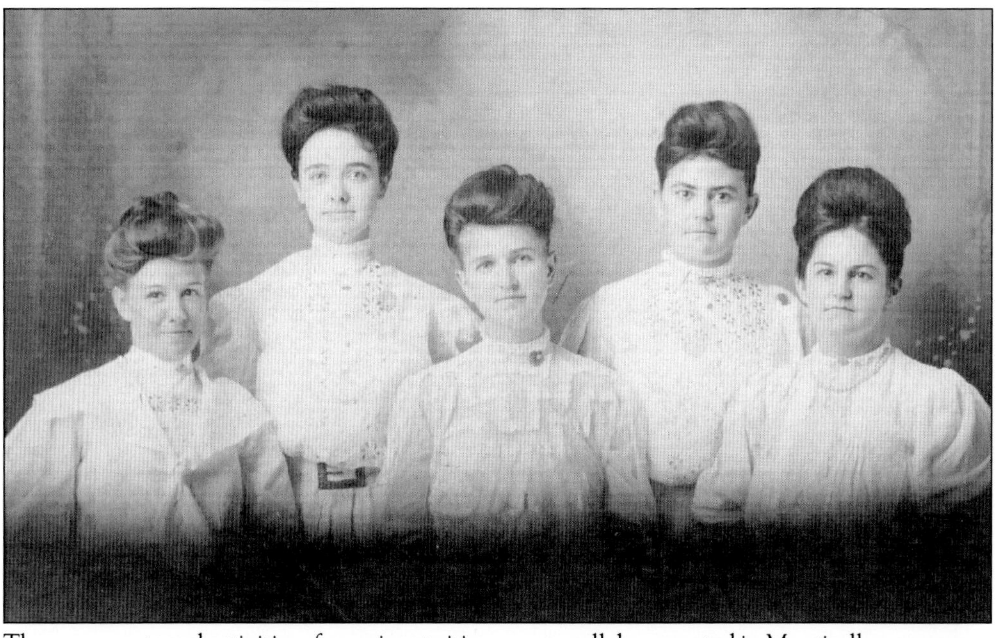

The movements and activities of prominent citizens were well documented in Monticello newspapers throughout the first half of the 20th century. Pictured here around 1905 are, from left to right, Ruth Wells, Ruby Hyatt Matthews, Mary Hart Stinson, Lizzie Cole, and Myrtle Wells Moffatt. Ladies such as these were frequently the subjects of social notes. (Courtesy of Drew County Historical Society.)

The prosperity of Monticello's golden age was largely driven by entrepreneur Joe Lee Allen (1863–1917), who rose to prominence from modest beginnings on a farm near Monticello. Allen's father died before Joe Lee's sixth birthday and his mother was left to run the family farm and raise Joe Lee and his two older siblings. (Courtesy of Drew County Historical Society.)

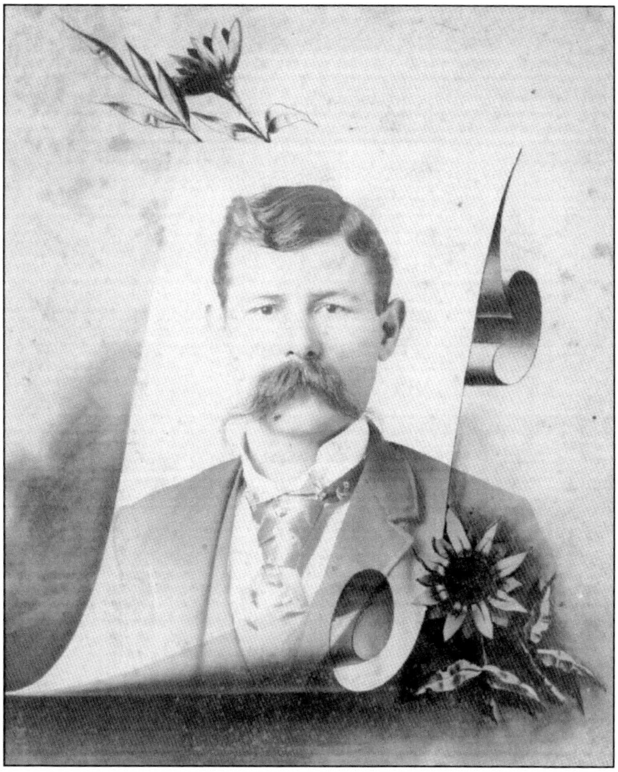

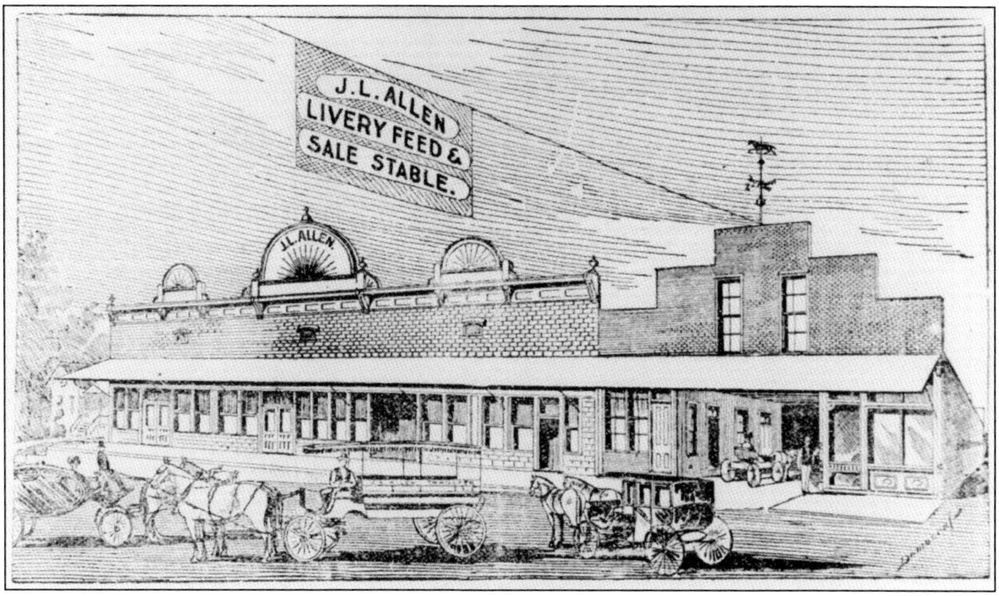

By the 1890s, Joe Lee Allen was operating a prosperous livery stable on East Gaines Avenue and traveling extensively to purchase quality horses from Missouri, Kentucky, Mississippi, Kansas, and Nebraska. He owned timberlands, several rental properties in town, a taxi service, a hotel, and a horse-drawn rental hearse. The advertisement pictured here is from 1908. A 1907 advertisement declared, "I have the swellest buggies, run-a-bouts and surries ever seen in this town. Come in and look at some fancy rigs." (Courtesy of UAM Library.)

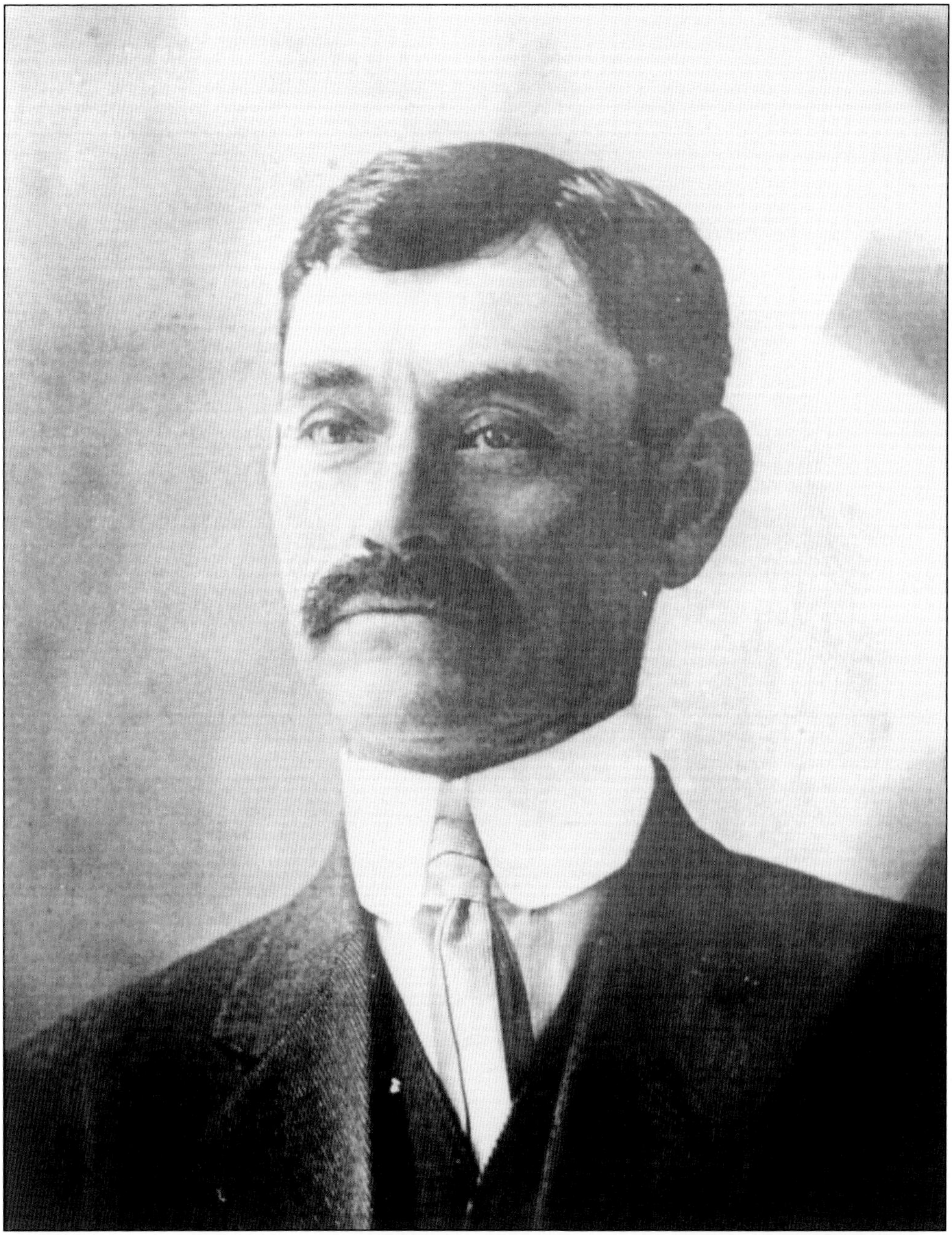

Joe Lee Allen was also a town alderman and was subsequently appointed county treasurer by acting governor X.O. Pindall in 1908. Allen was the first president of Commercial Loan and Trust Company and served as president of the Southeast Arkansas Fair Association. By the mid-1910s, he was an automobile dealer as well, selling Dorts and Buicks. While demonstrating an automobile to a prospective buyer in Collins, Arkansas, on October 23, 1917, he died suddenly of a heart attack. Upon news of his death, several carloads of friends left for Collins to bring his body back to his house. This photograph is from about 1916. (Courtesy of Drew County Historical Society.)

The inscription on the back of this photograph taken around 1915 says, "Mr. Joe Lee Allen on a cold day in Kansas. There to buy mules for his livery stable in Monticello, Ark." A colorful story passed down about Allen stated that he used to keep a bear chained up behind the Allen Hotel. One day, he got angry at the bear, shot it, and had a flamboyant coat made for himself. A certain fact is that he was a doting father. In 1912, as chief investor in a new community south of Monticello, he named the town after his middle daughter, Ladelle. (Courtesy of Drew County Historical Society.)

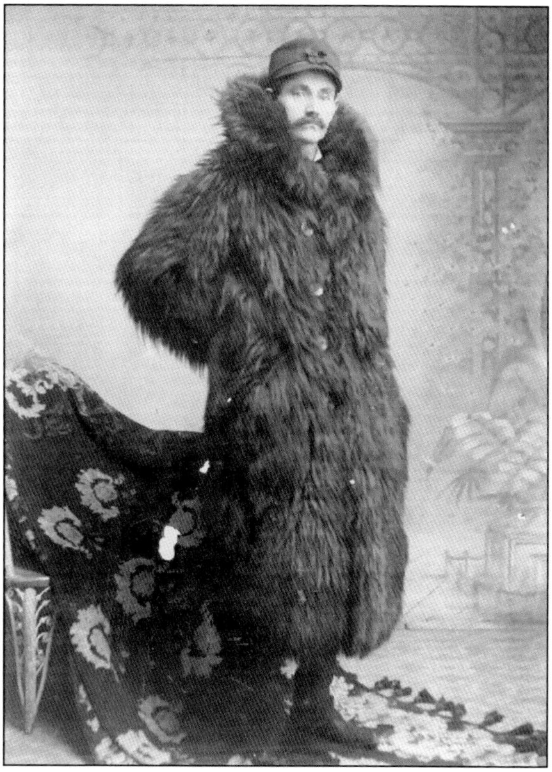

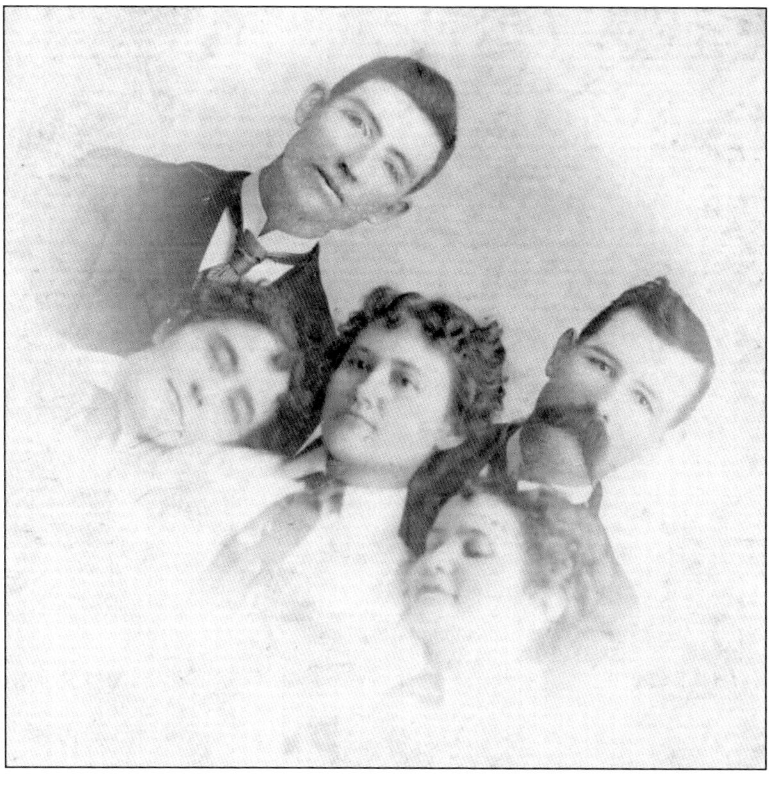

This photograph of Joe Lee Allen (right) is from about 1907. The young man on the left may have been Allen's nephew, P.A. Whiteaker, who lived in Monticello. The girls—Allen's daughters—are, from left to right, Ladelle, Lonnie, and Lewie. (Courtesy of Drew County Historical Society.)

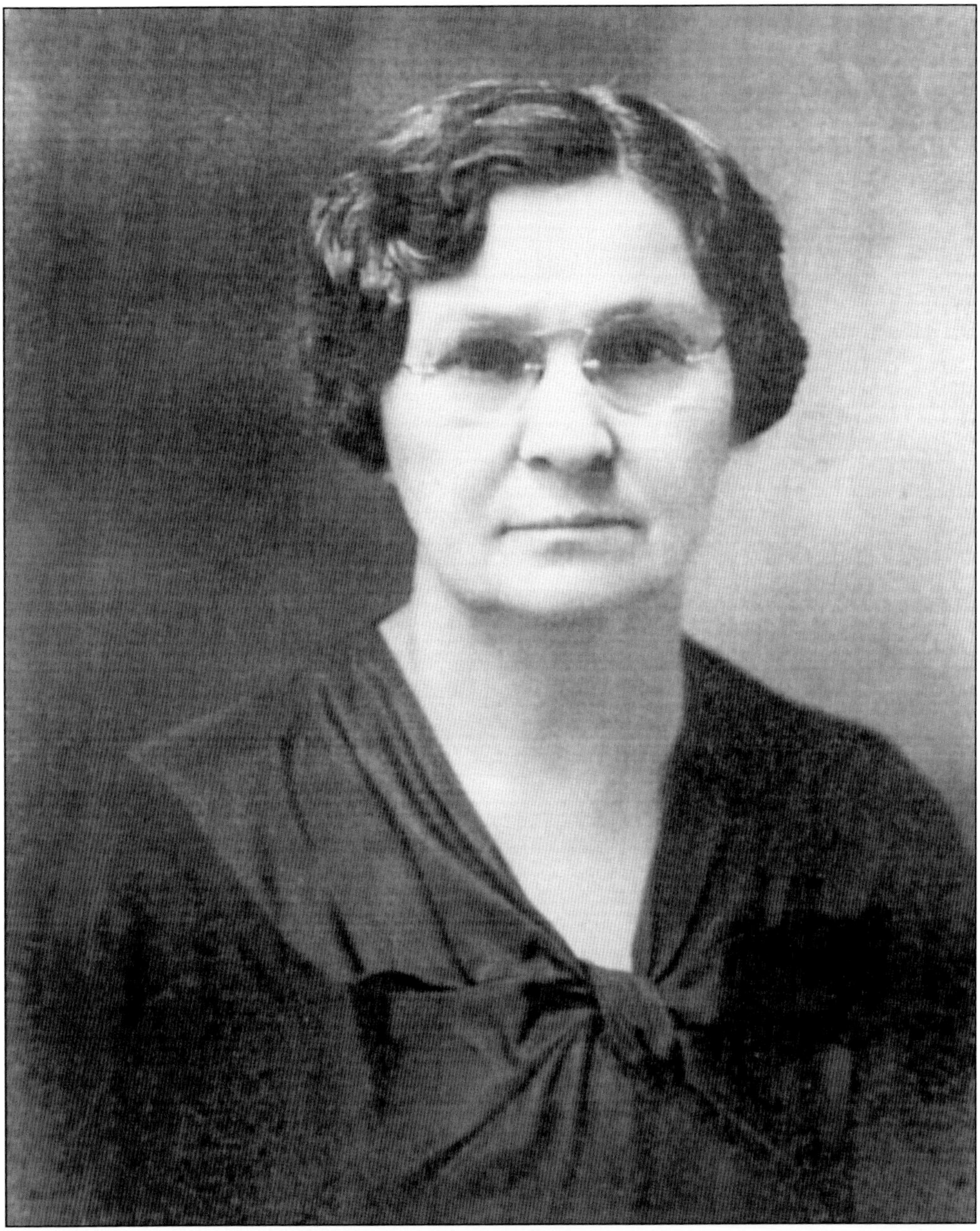

On October 1, 1890, Joe Lee Allen married Caddye McKennon (pictured here about 1930). Like Allen, McKennon lost her father at a young age—B.H. McKennon, a Confederate veteran from Memphis, was killed by a team of runaway horses before Caddye's fourth birthday. In addition to managing the family servants and rearing three daughters, Caddye won numerous blue ribbons for her baking and sewing at the Southeast Arkansas Fair. According to a history of the First Presbyterian Church, she was shrewd and frugal when it came to business, doubling the family fortune after Allen's death, primarily through investments in a motion picture theater operated by her son-in-law. Despite her wealth, she took in lodgers. She even charged her daughter Lonnie and Lonnie's husband, Karl Leidinger, $10 a month to live with her in the family mansion. (Courtesy of Drew County Historical Society.)

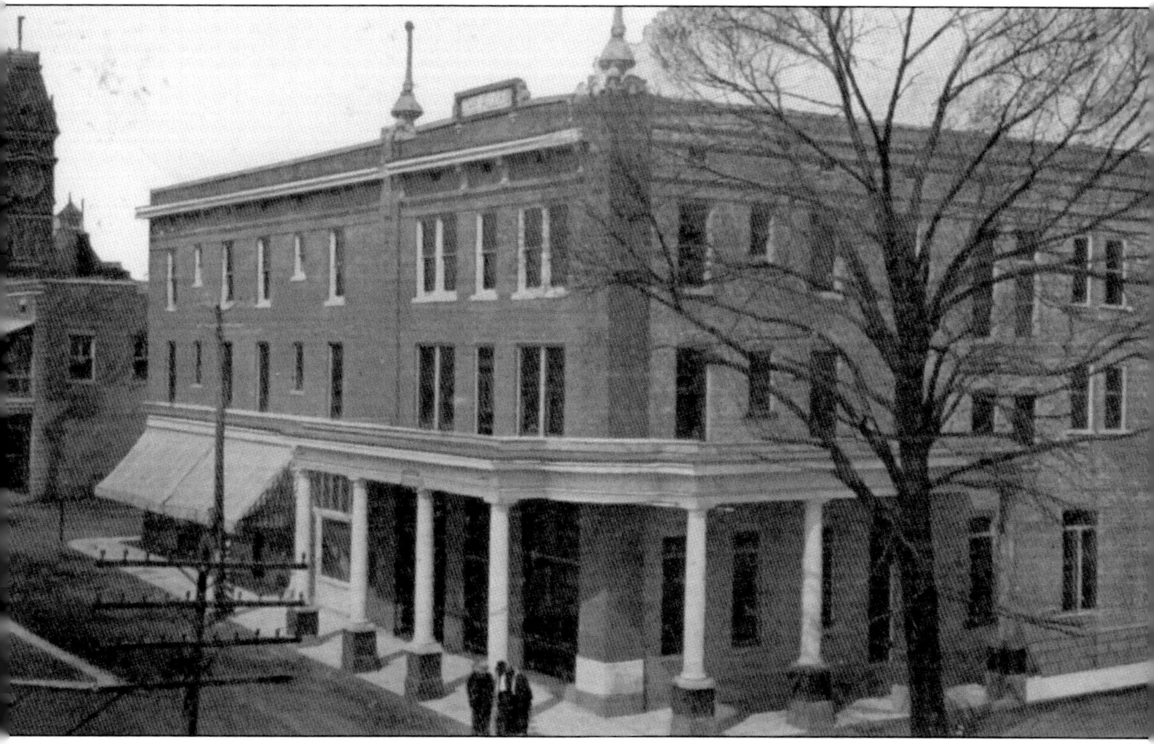

The three-story Allen Hotel, located near the train depot on East Gaines Street, opened in 1912 with 40 guest rooms and eight bathrooms, an amazing number of bathrooms at the time. Owners Joe Lee Allen and his wife, Caddye, frequently hosted grand parties at the hotel. After Joe Lee's death, Caddye sold the hotel but it retained the Allen name. In the early evening of December 15, 1943, the fire department was called to put out an electrical fire in the ceiling of the first floor. Satisfied that the fire was completely extinguished, the firefighters left. However, around 3:00 a.m. that night, the fire reignited and quickly raged out of control. The hotel was booked to capacity on that cold night, but all escaped the fire, although many did so wearing little more than their nightclothes. (Courtesy of UAM Library.)

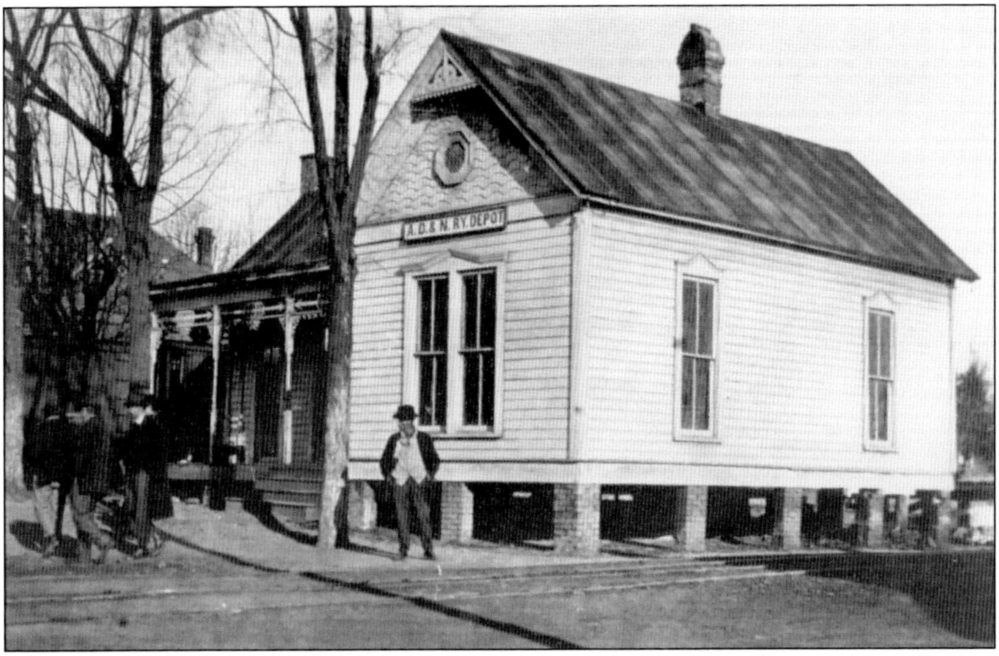

This picture shows the Ashley, Drew & Northern Railway depot around 1919, at a time when it bustled with the activity of travelers and the shipment of goods in and out of Monticello. (Courtesy of UAM Library.)

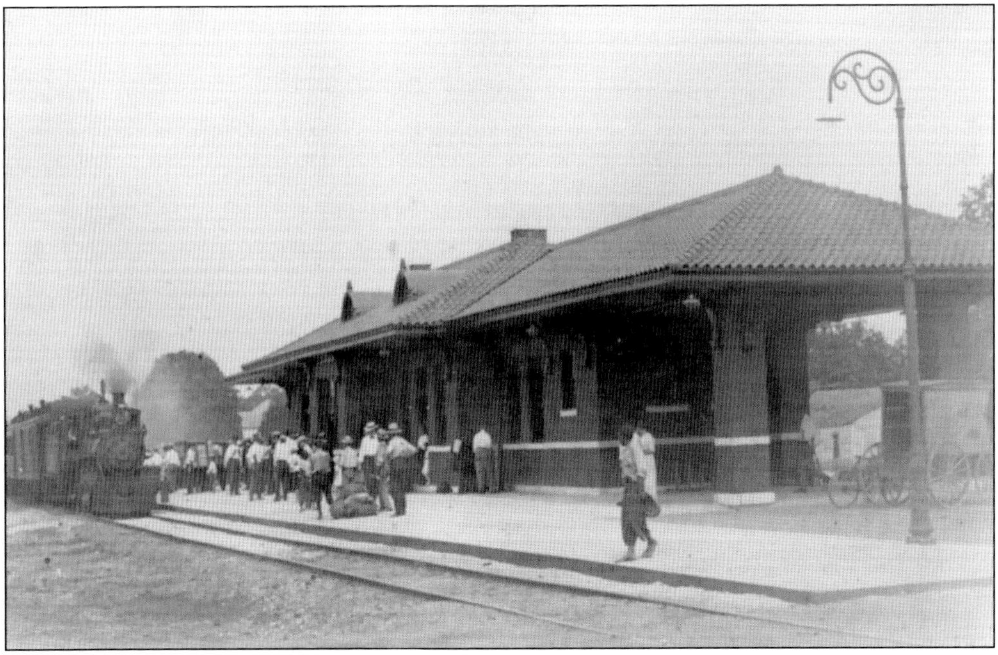

The Missouri Pacific passenger depot was built in 1912 and operated until passenger service was discontinued in 1935. Passenger trains provided relatively safe and easy travel for Monticello residents prior to the dominance of travel by car, bus, and airplane. This building was torn down in the early 1960s. (Courtesy of Drew County Historical Society.)

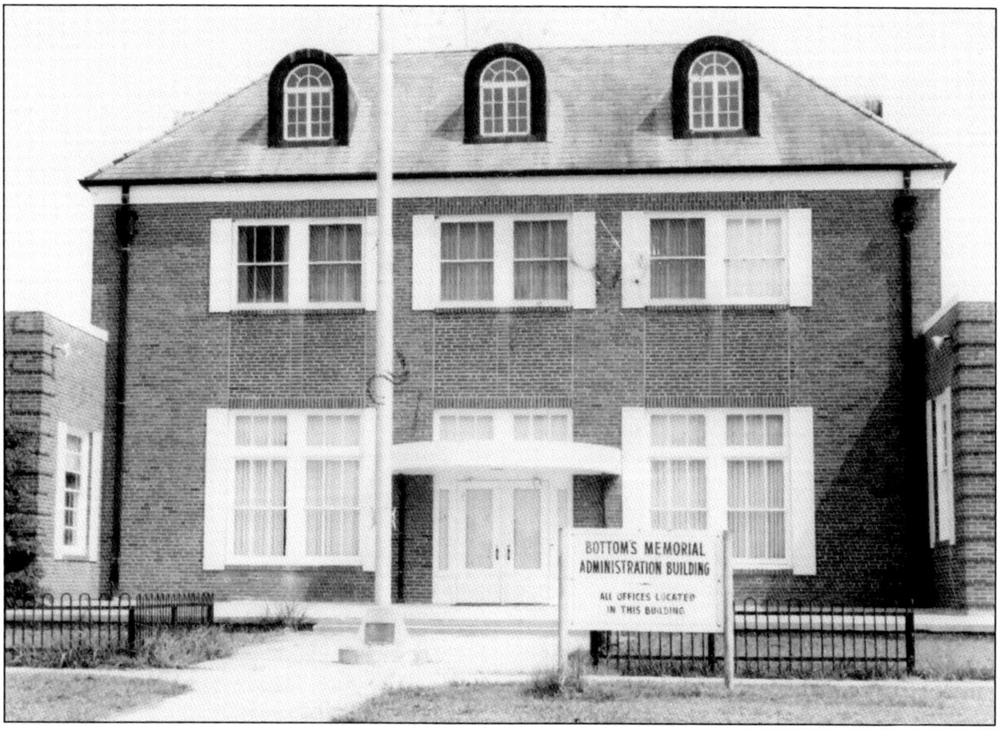

In 1887, Hannah Hyatt began caring for orphans in her home in Monticello. In 1894, she donated her house and 80 acres to the State Baptist Convention, thereby initiating the establishment of the Arkansas Baptist Home for Children. Pictured here is the administration building. (Courtesy of Drew County Historical Society.)

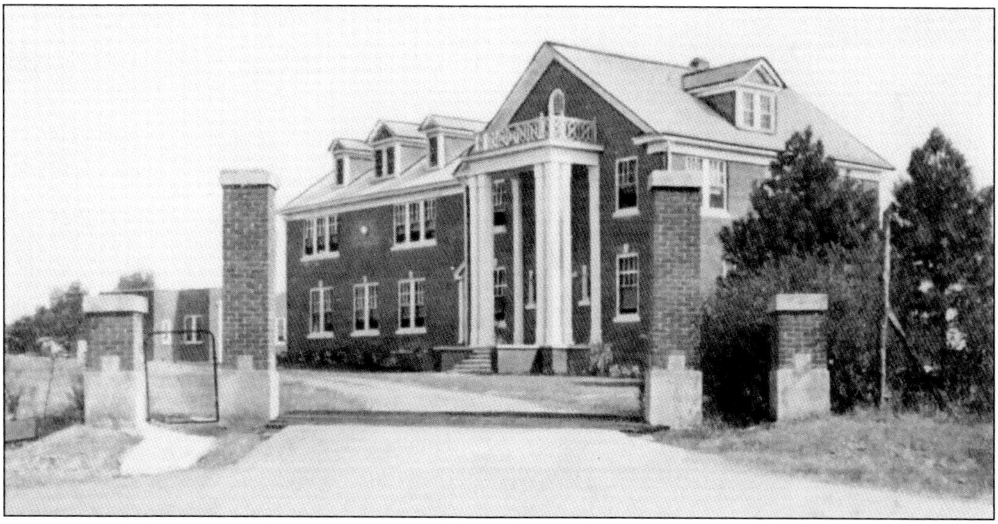

A local, Presbyterian-supported nursery, first established in 1910 for children whose mothers worked at the Monticello Cotton Mill, expanded its mission when twin girls were abandoned at the train station. Because there was no proof that the girls were true orphans, they were not eligible for state orphanages, and the nursery therefore took in the girls. In 1924, the nursery officially became the Vera Lloyd Presbyterian Home for Children. (Courtesy of Drew County Historical Society.)

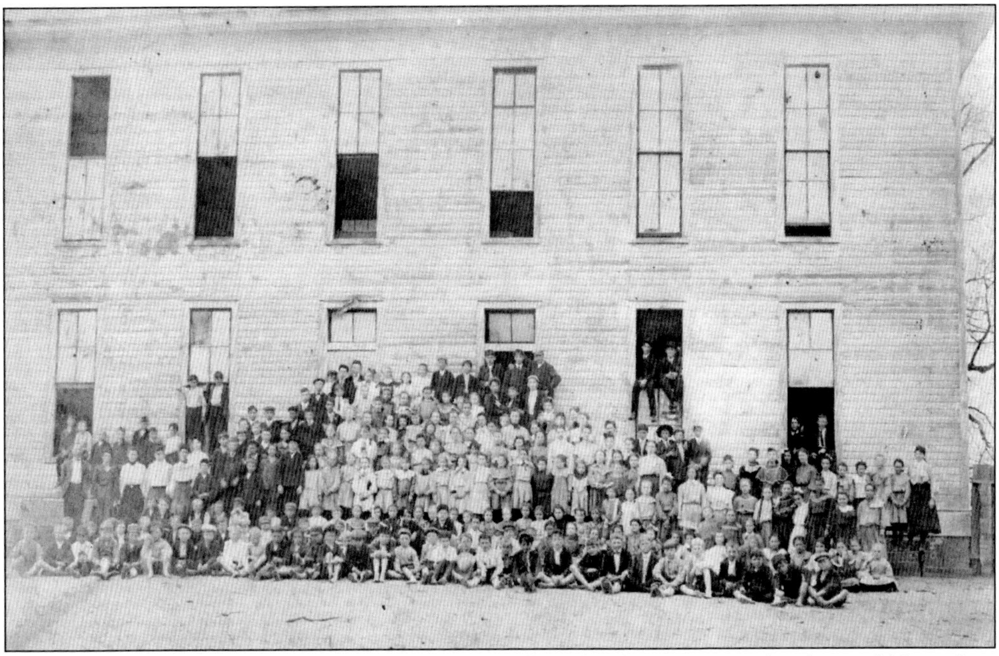

Education has always been important in Monticello. The first private school, a girls' boarding academy, opened in 1857. The Monticello Public School was established in 1876 for a three-month session. In 1883, it offered a nine-month school year. Pictured here is the Monticello Public School in 1905. (Courtesy of Edgar W. Spencer.)

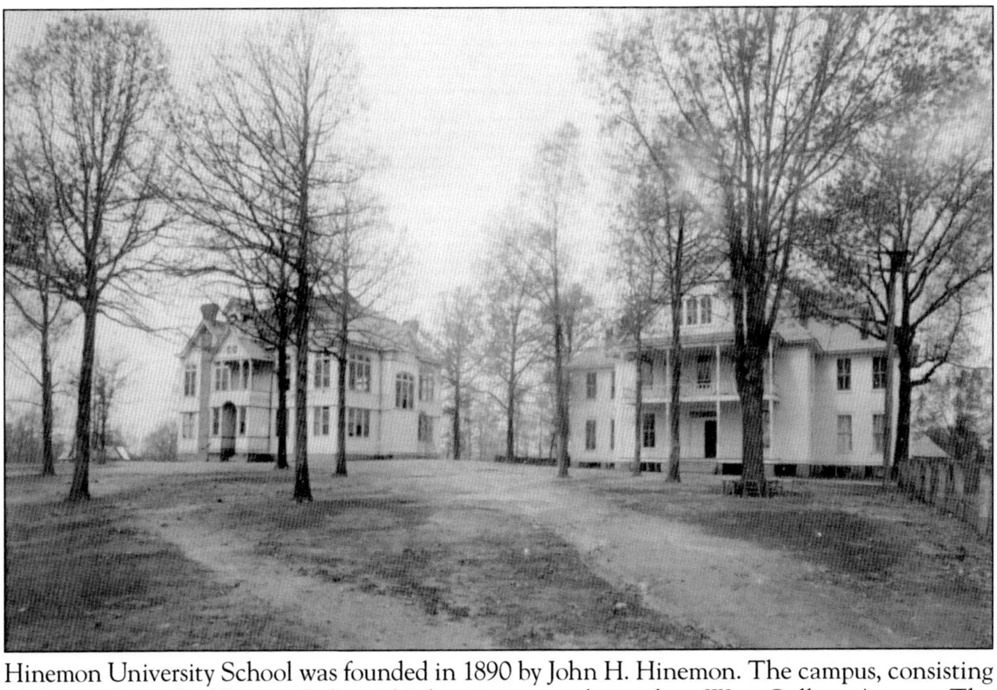

Hinemon University School was founded in 1890 by John H. Hinemon. The campus, consisting of the academic building and the girls' dormitory, was located on West College Avenue. The buildings burned down in 1915 and the campus subsequently became the site of Monticello High School. (Courtesy of Drew County Historical Society.)

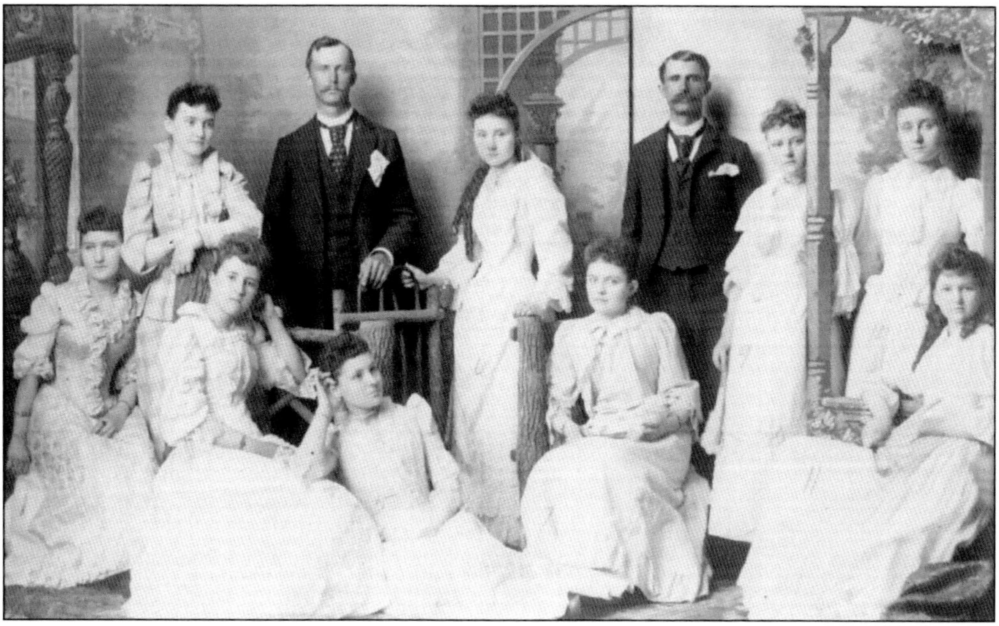

The top photograph shows a group of Hinemon University teachers and students gathered in 1891. The young ladies pictured are, from left to right, Virgil Cavaness, May McKenney, Coley Bell, Maggie Blaine, Sallie Green, Tommie Tool, Marie Bell, Maggie Lee Harris, and Gussie McKenney. The gentlemen are school founder John H. Hinemon (left) and a Mr. Erwin. The other image, also from 1891, shows a scene from a play performed by Hinemon University students. The students are, from left to right, Velma Wood, Virgil Cavaness, Maggie Blaine, Blanch Hall, Ethel Hyatt (reclining), LaDelle Welsh, Zola McIntyre, and Lizzie Claire Hyatt. (Both, courtesy of Drew County Historical Society.)

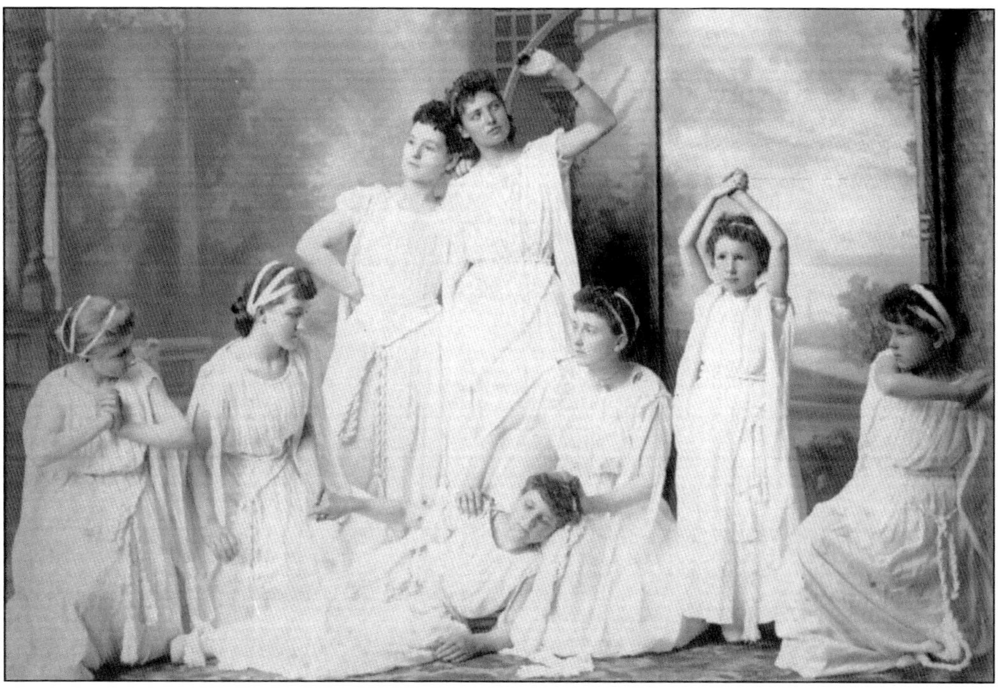

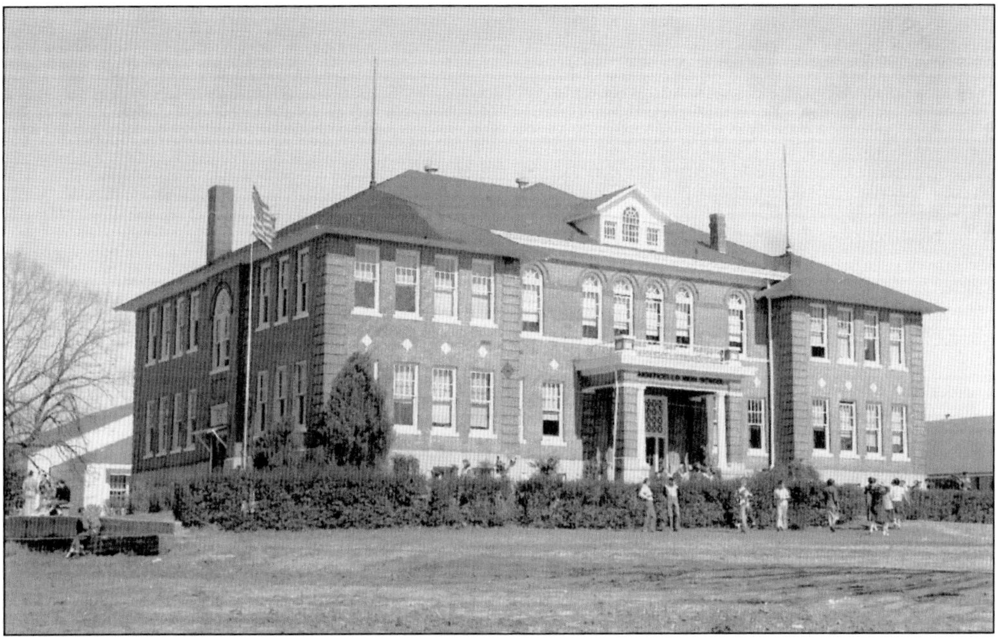

The 1915 Monticello High School building was constructed on West College and North Hyatt Streets at the former site of Hinemon University, which had been destroyed by fire. It was torn down in 1989. (Courtesy of Dorothy McWhorter.)

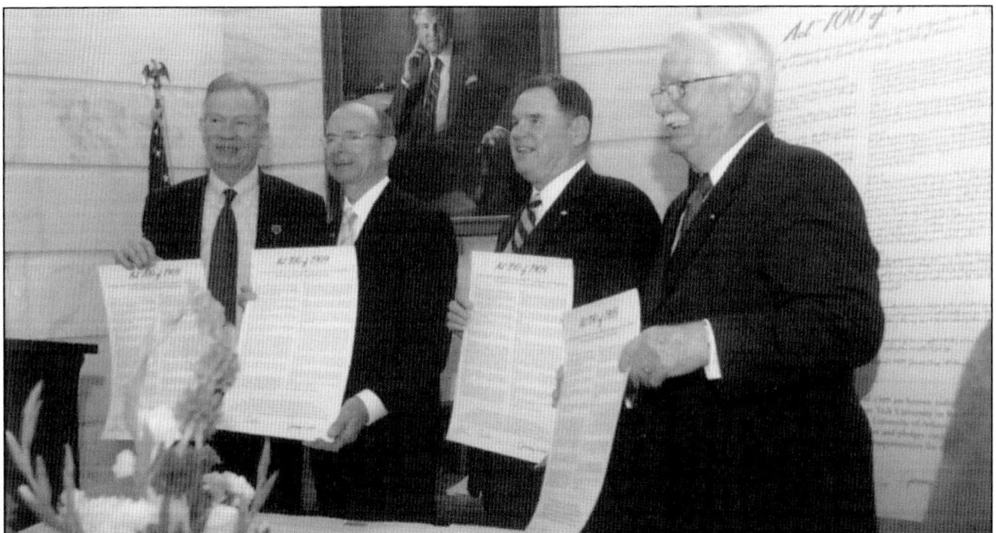

The University of Arkansas at Monticello (UAM) is one of four Arkansas universities created by Act 100 of the 1909 Acts of Arkansas, which authorized the establishment of four district agricultural schools. The four schools became UAM, Southern Arkansas, Arkansas Tech, and Arkansas State. This 2009 photograph shows a reenactment of the signing of Act 100. Pictured from left to right are Robert Potts, David Rankin, Robert Brown, and UAM chancellor Jack Lassiter. (Courtesy of UAM Media Services.)

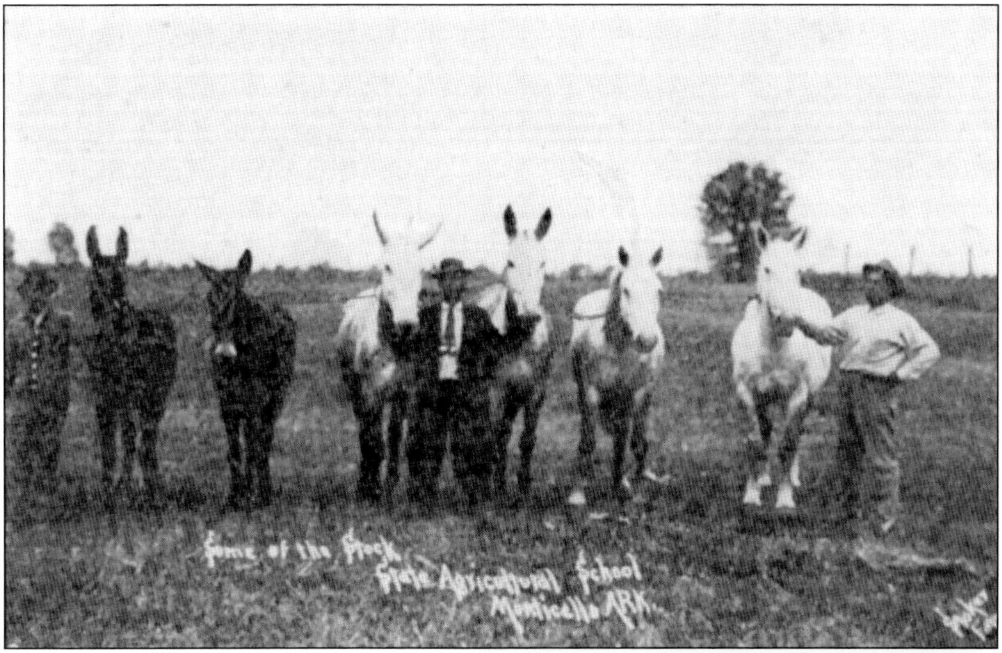

This 1913 image of some of the livestock at the Fourth District State Agricultural School (now UAM) illustrates the school's early mission to teach the young people of southeast Arkansas about agriculture and farm management. (Courtesy of UAM Library.)

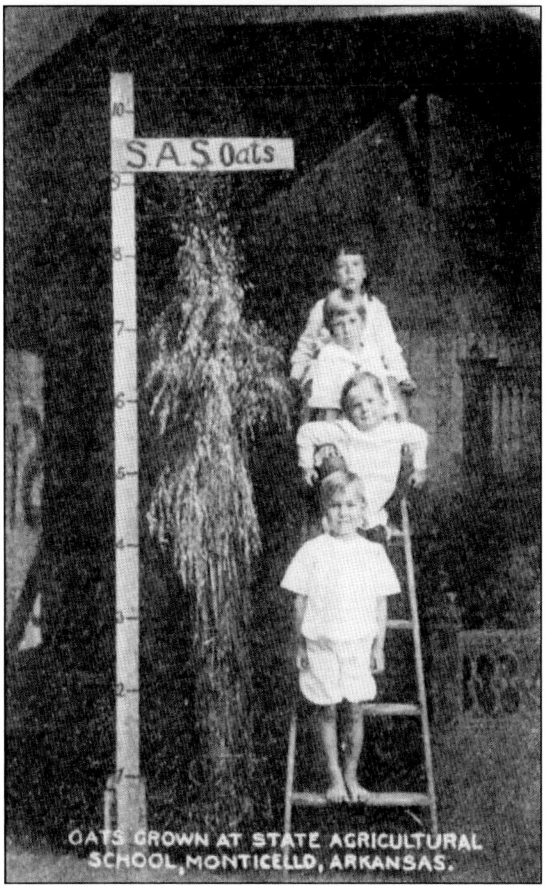

Around 1911, dynamite was used to clear stumps from fields on the campus of the State Agricultural School in Monticello and the cleared acreage was used for growing crops, like oats. The children on the stepladder help to provide a scale against which to measure the oats. (Courtesy of UAM Library.)

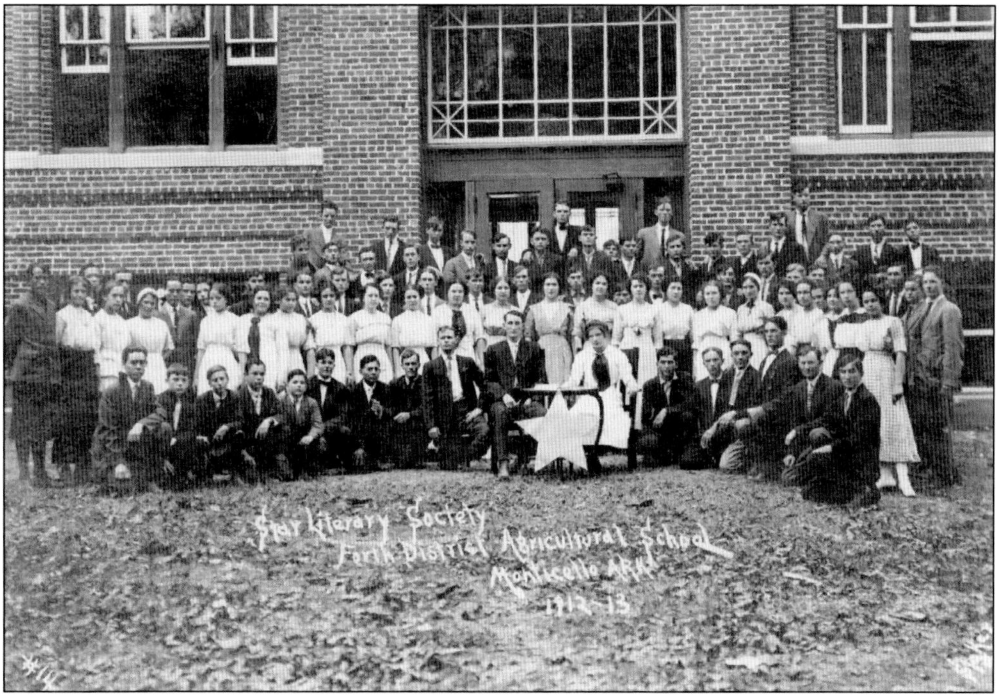

The Fourth District State Agricultural School was concerned not just with the science and practicality of farming but also aimed to provide a well-rounded education. The Star Literary Society promoted students' understanding and appreciation of classic works of poetry, drama, and prose. This photograph was taken during the 1912–1913 school year. (Courtesy of UAM Library.)

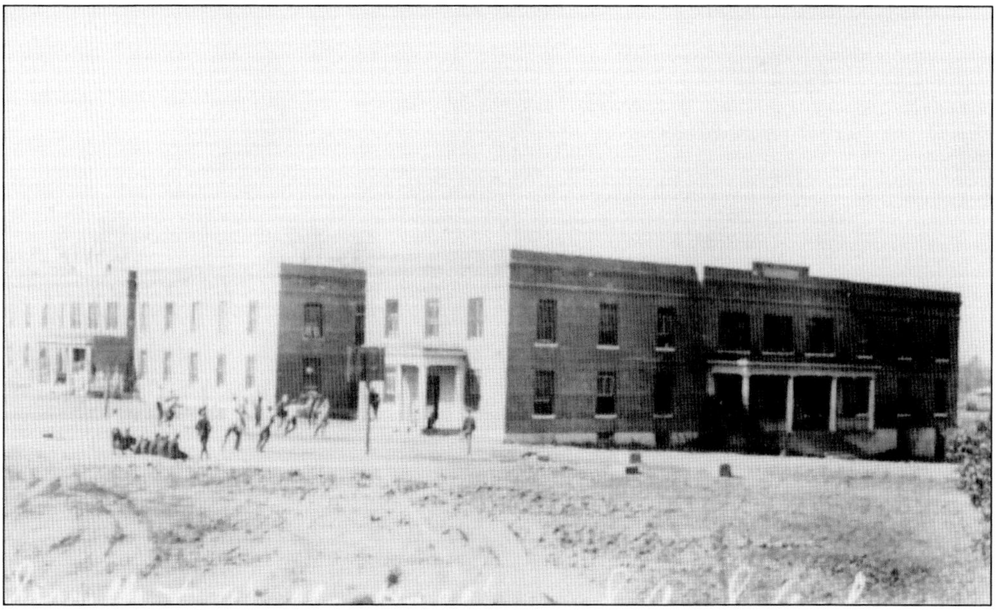

Boys play basketball outside of Sorrells Hall and Wells Hall on the campus of the State Agricultural School around 1912. Both buildings still stand on the UAM campus; they were renovated in 2008. (Courtesy of UAM Library.)

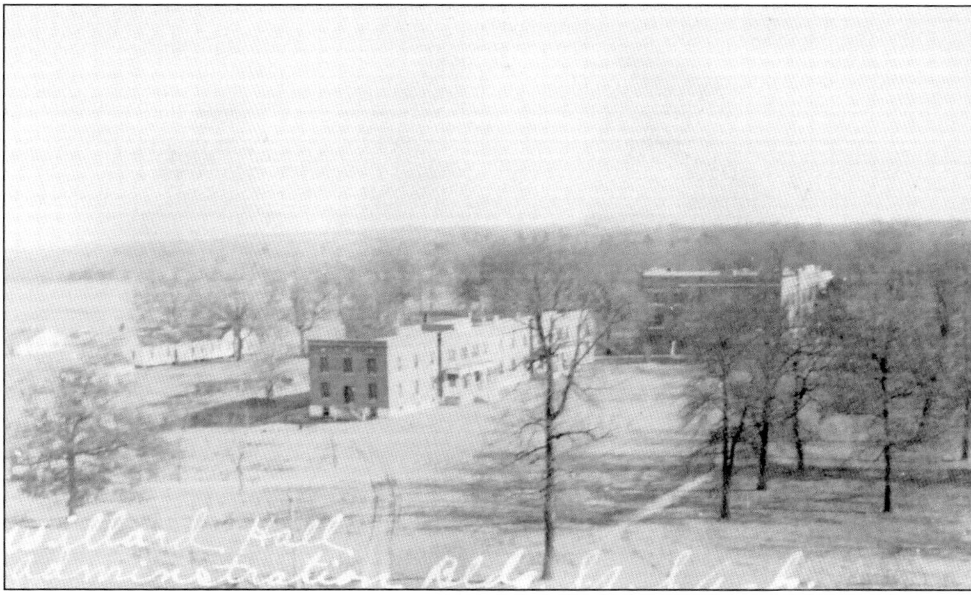

This 1914 image shows Willard Hall, on the State Agricultural School campus, when it was a dormitory. In 2011, Willard Hall provides classroom and office space for UAM's School of Education. (Courtesy of UAM Library.)

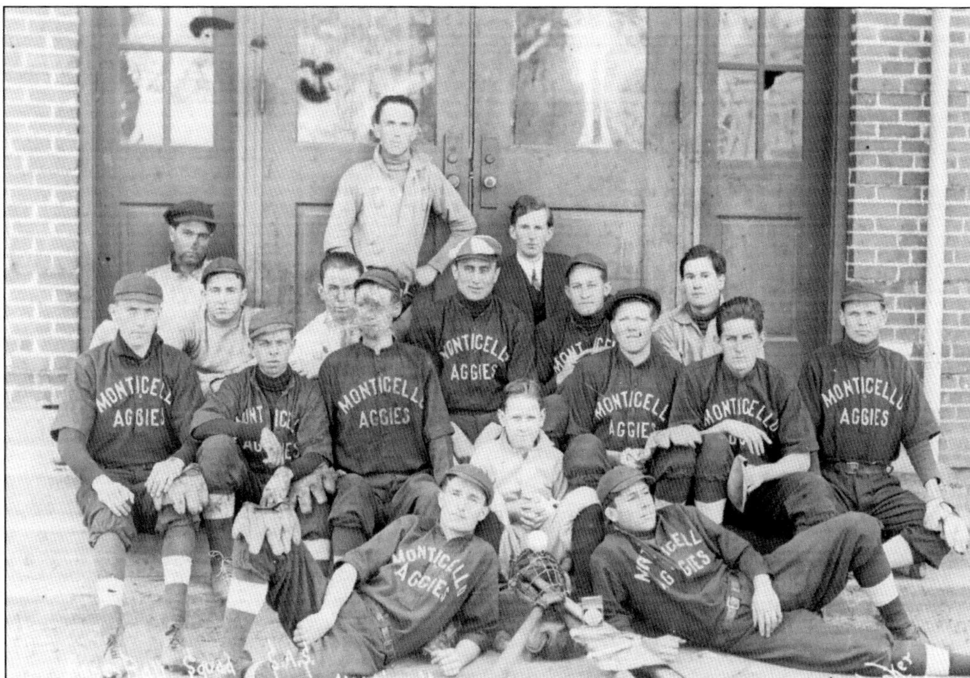

By 1914, baseball was America's most popular sport. In addition to schools, lumber companies in towns like Blissville (later known as Jerome) and Crossett fielded their own baseball teams. Rivalries were intense and betting was common. Pictured here is the 1914 team from Monticello's State Agricultural School. (Courtesy of UAM Library.)

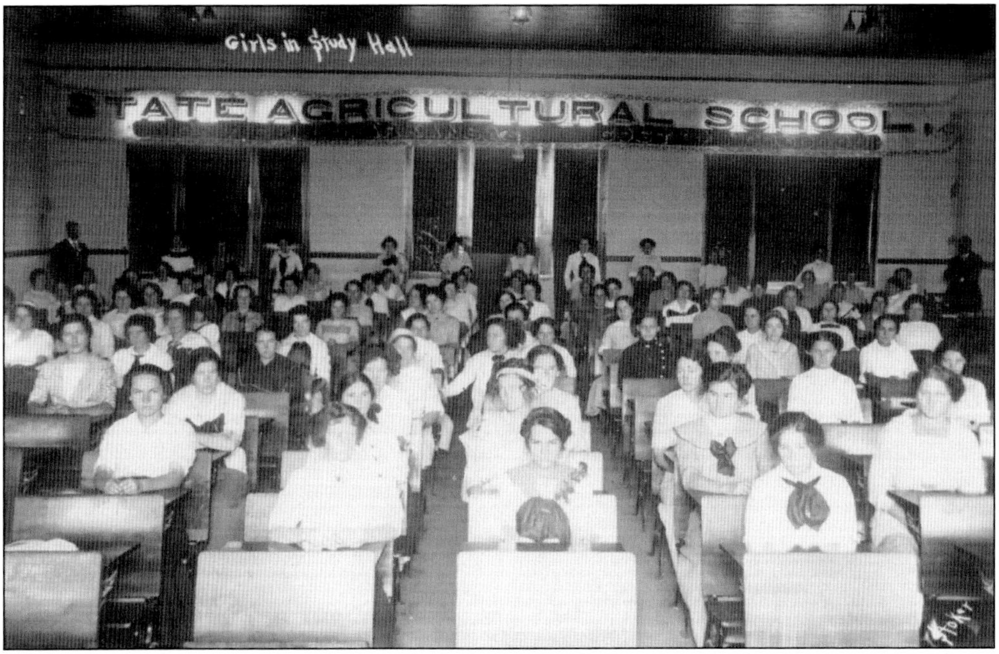

This photograph, taken in 1910 or 1911 during the school's first or second year in existence, shows female students at the Fourth District State Agricultural School in study hall. These serious-looking young ladies would primarily learn how to cook, sew, and generally become exemplary homemakers. (Courtesy of UAM Library.)

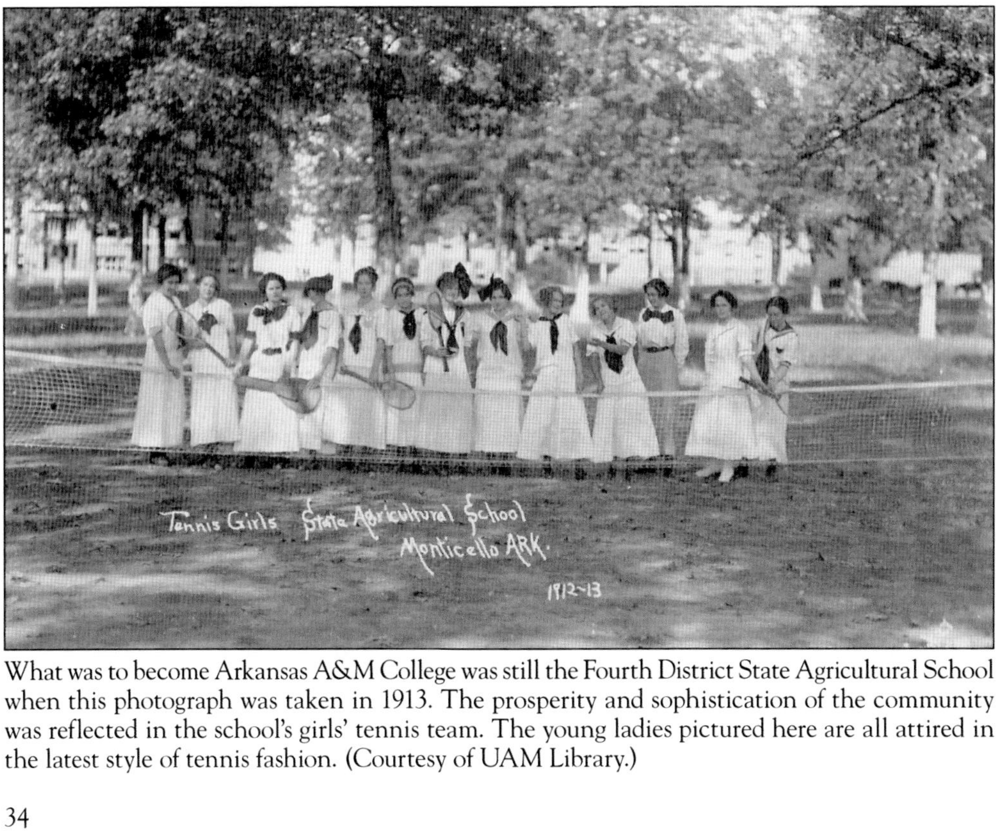

What was to become Arkansas A&M College was still the Fourth District State Agricultural School when this photograph was taken in 1913. The prosperity and sophistication of the community was reflected in the school's girls' tennis team. The young ladies pictured here are all attired in the latest style of tennis fashion. (Courtesy of UAM Library.)

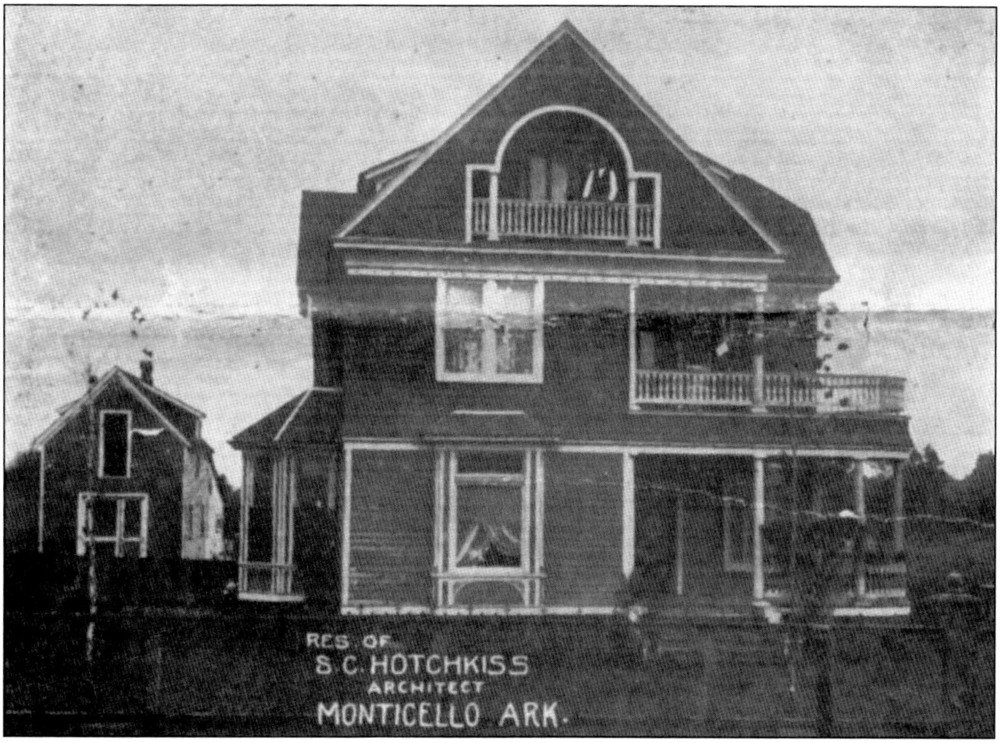

Chicago-trained architect Sylvester Hotchkiss (1842–1909), shown standing on the third-story porch in this photograph from 1907, built his Monticello home in 1902 as a showcase for his architectural skills. Each room is a different shape and has different styles of moldings and windows. Hotchkiss moved south for his health in the closing years of the 19th century and is the only Union veteran of the Civil War who is buried in Oakland Cemetery. (Courtesy of Drew County Historical Society.)

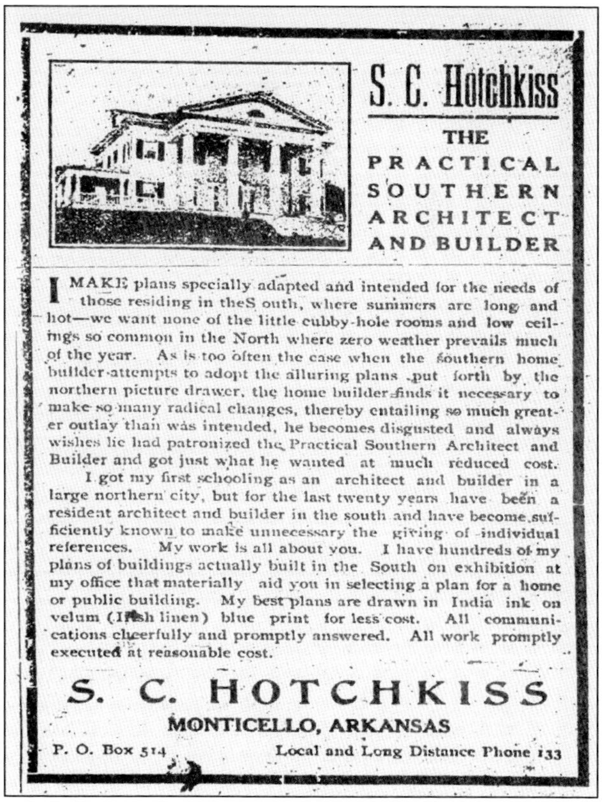

S. C. Hotchkiss

THE PRACTICAL SOUTHERN ARCHITECT AND BUILDER

I MAKE plans specially adapted and intended for the needs of those residing in the South, where summers are long and hot—we want none of the little cubby-hole rooms and low ceilings so common in the North where zero weather prevails much of the year. As is too often the case when the southern home builder attempts to adopt the alluring plans put forth by the northern picture drawer, the home builder finds it necessary to make so many radical changes, thereby entailing so much greater outlay than was intended, he becomes disgusted and always wishes he had patronized the Practical Southern Architect and Builder and got just what he wanted at much reduced cost.

I got my first schooling as an architect and builder in a large northern city, but for the last twenty years have been a resident architect and builder in the south and have become sufficiently known to make unnecessary the giving of individual references. My work is all about you. I have hundreds of my plans of buildings actually built in the South on exhibition at my office that materially aid you in selecting a plan for a home or public building. My best plans are drawn in India ink on velum (Irish linen) blue print for less cost. All communications cheerfully and promptly answered. All work promptly executed at reasonable cost.

S. C. HOTCHKISS

MONTICELLO, ARKANSAS

P. O. Box 514 Local and Long Distance Phone 133

Hotchkiss's claim in this 1907 newspaper advertisement of being "The Southern Architect," despite his roots in New York and Chicago, was possibly based on his designs that enhanced air circulation and made the hot Southern summers more bearable for the occupants of his buildings. (Courtesy of Drew County Historical Society.)

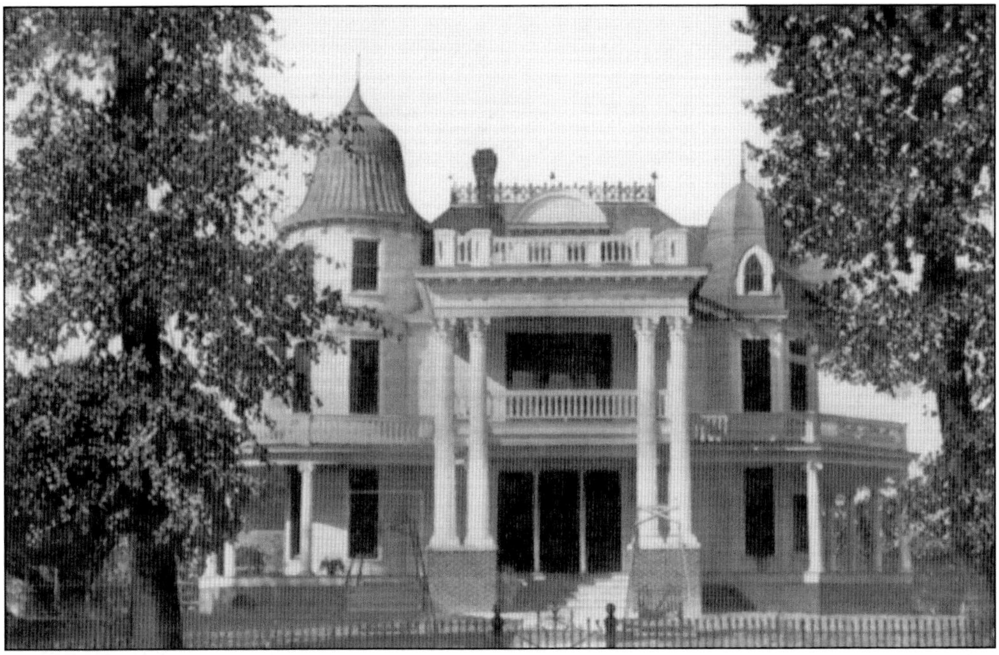

Designed by Sylvester Hotchkiss with a blend of Gothic, neoclassical, and Queen Anne styles, the Allen House was built in 1905–1906 on the site of the original Allen family home, which was moved across the street. The builder was Josiah Barkley White. The new house was not only Joe Lee Allen's gift to his wife, Caddye, and their three daughters, but also a monument to his success and status in the community. (Courtesy of Mark Spencer.)

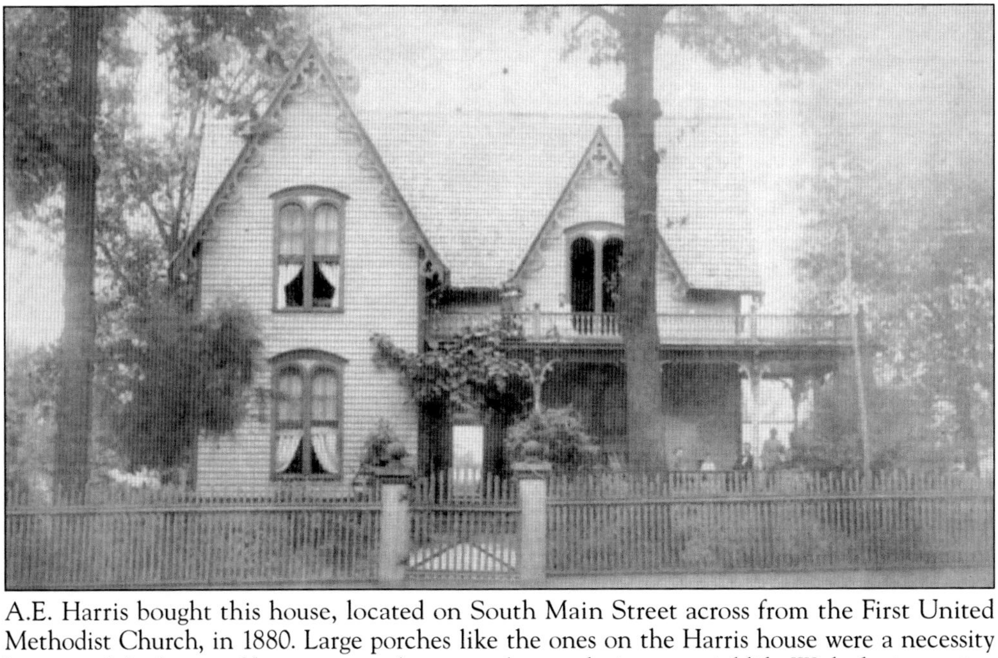

A.E. Harris bought this house, located on South Main Street across from the First United Methodist Church, in 1880. Large porches like the ones on the Harris house were a necessity because of the long and hot summers, but were also conducive to social life. With the invention of air conditioning, porches began to disappear from houses by the mid-20th century. (Courtesy of Drew County Historical Society.)

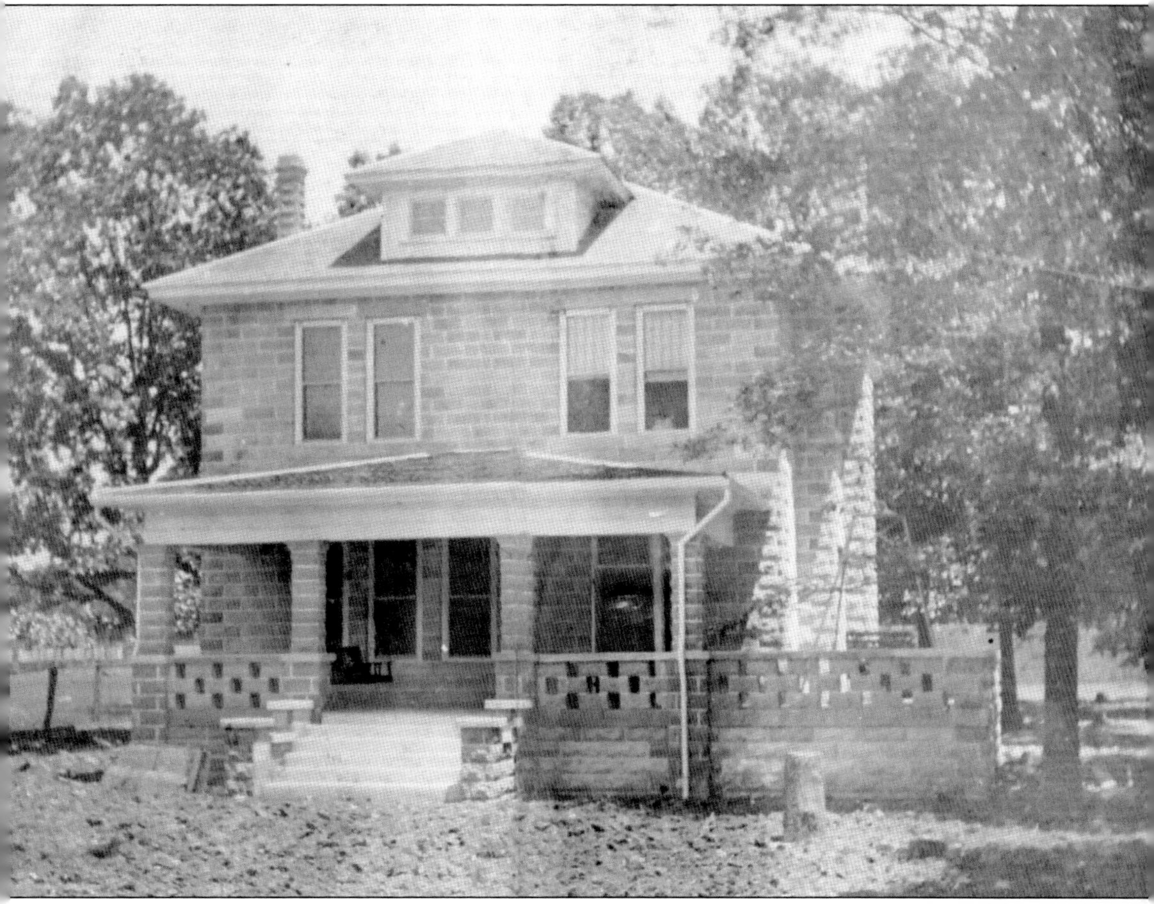

This type of dwelling was known as a "Sears House" because it could actually be purchased from a Sears Roebuck catalogue in the early years of the 20th century. At least two such houses still stand in Monticello in 2011, and both are on North Main Street. In 1906, the Arthur Lee Wells family began construction on the house pictured here. The house kit ordered from Sears Roebuck was delivered to Monticello by rail and then transported from the depot to the building site by horse-drawn wagon. The cost of the kit, which did not include the exterior concrete blocks, was $895. Additionally, the Wells family purchased a block-making machine from Sears for $39.95. The machine made two blocks at a time and was subsequently used in the construction of other buildings, including the Mittie Wells house on the corner of Oakland Avenue and North Main Street, the Christian Science Church at the corner of Wood Avenue and North Main, and the Cavaness House, which now serves as the Drew County Museum. The Wells family moved into their Sears house in 1909 and lived there until 1926. This photograph was taken between 1912 and 1915. (Courtesy of Betty Evans.)

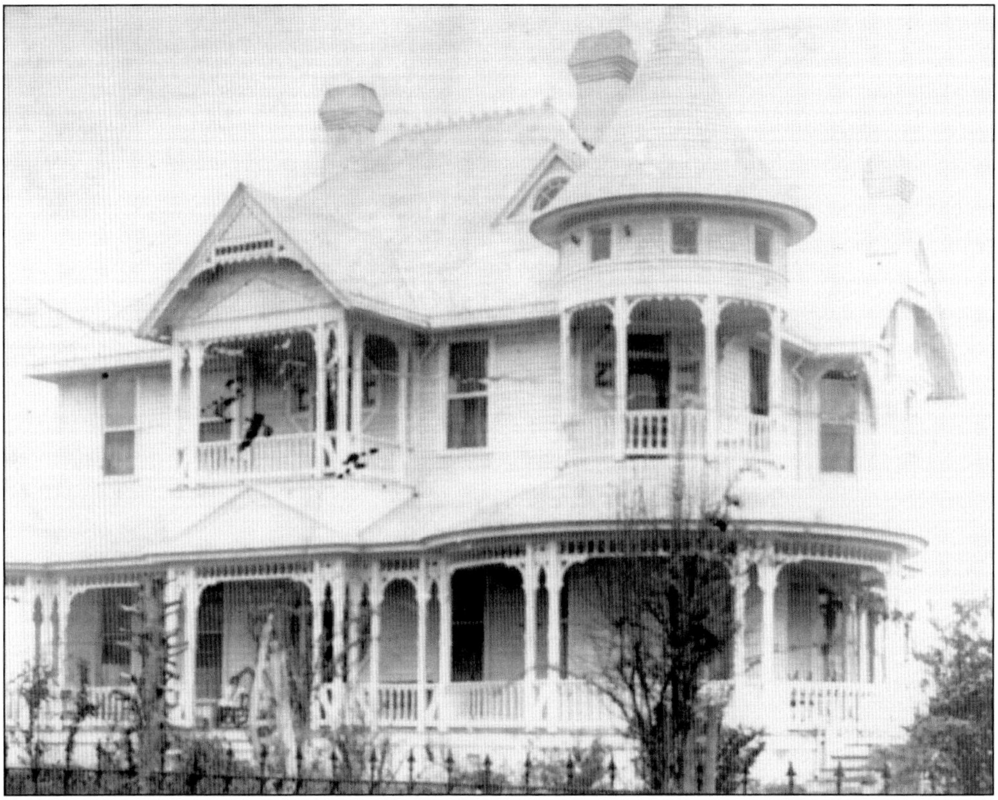

The Charles Monroe Boyd home on Boyd Street was an exquisite example of Queen Anne–style architecture with its lacy gingerbread details, multiple gables, and round turrets. (Courtesy of Drew County Historical Society.)

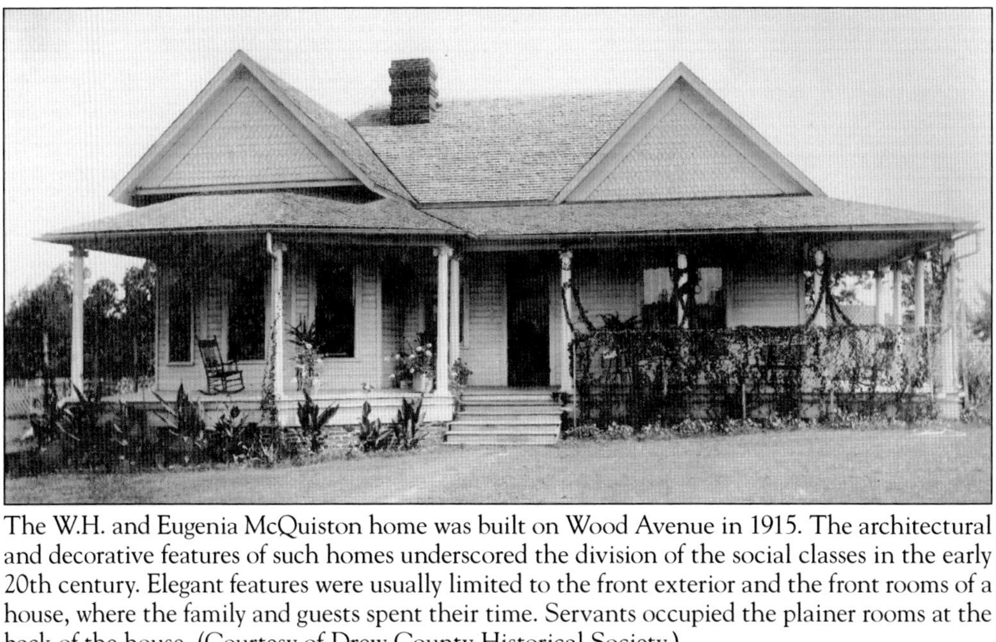

The W.H. and Eugenia McQuiston home was built on Wood Avenue in 1915. The architectural and decorative features of such homes underscored the division of the social classes in the early 20th century. Elegant features were usually limited to the front exterior and the front rooms of a house, where the family and guests spent their time. Servants occupied the plainer rooms at the back of the house. (Courtesy of Drew County Historical Society.)

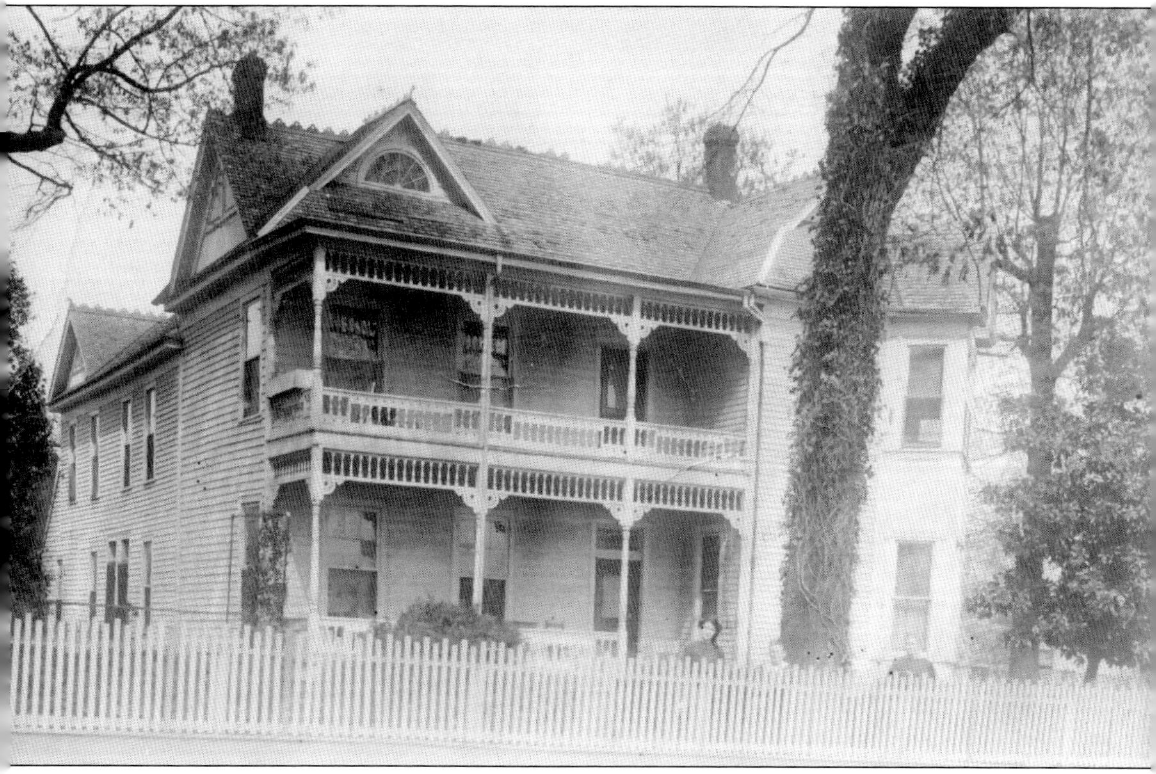

Robert Winston Shelton and his wife, Linnie Burks Shelton, lived in this house on South Main Street in the last decades of the 19th century and the early decades of the 20th century. Robert died in 1927. The house originally had only three rooms and no bathrooms. Additions eventually gave it a total of 20 rooms. Part of the house was built of yellow heart pine, which repels termites. When the house was more than 100 years old, it was dismantled and its lumber was used in new constructions; its architectural details, such as the nine-foot doors, were purchased by antique dealers. Robert was a co-owner of Shelton & Wells Livery and Vehicle and was later a district manager for the Singer Sewing Company. He was the son of pioneer residents who moved to Drew County prior to the Civil War and owned a large portion of the land that the town of Monticello was built on. (Courtesy of Edgar W. Spencer.)

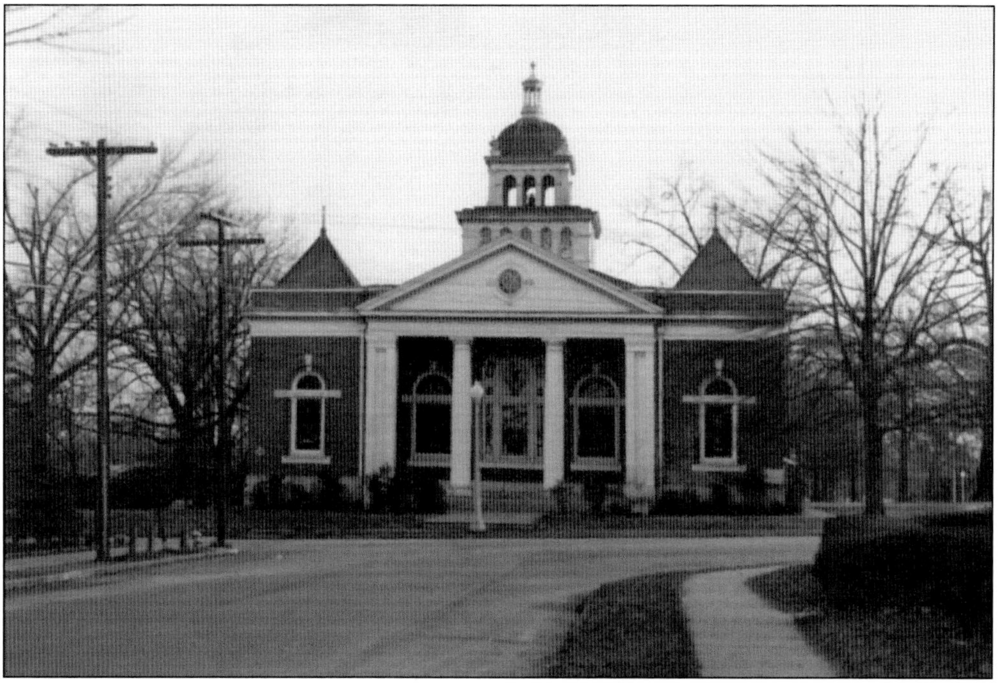

One of the most architecturally impressive constructions of the early 20th century was the First United Methodist Church on South Main Street. This photograph was taken in the 1950s. (Courtesy of Edgar W. Spencer.)

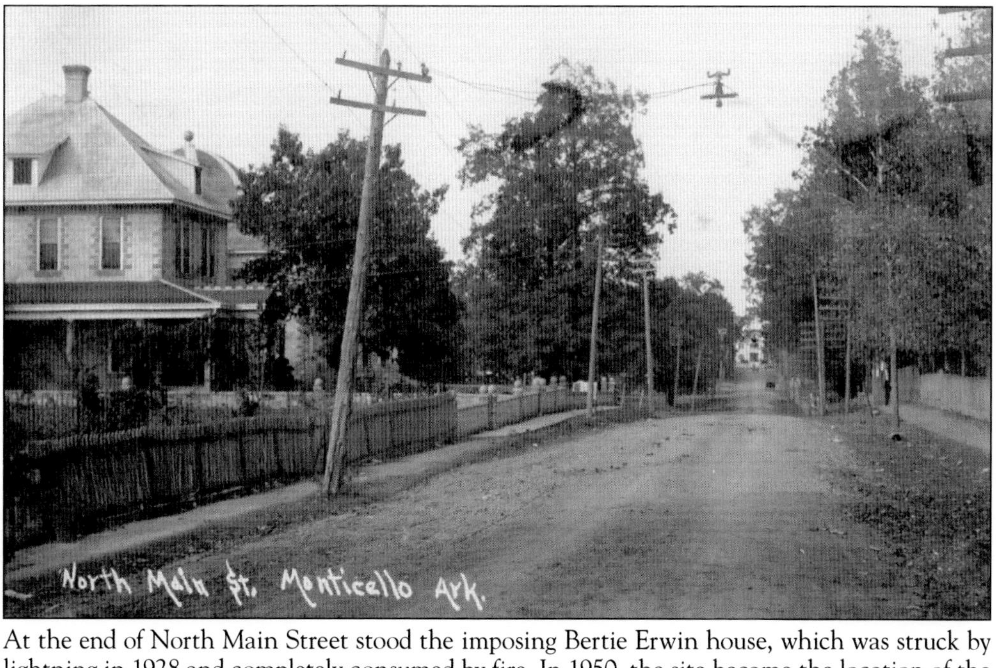

At the end of North Main Street stood the imposing Bertie Erwin house, which was struck by lightning in 1928 and completely consumed by fire. In 1950, the site became the location of the Drew County hospital. In 2011, the site is the proposed location for a new county library. (Courtesy of Drew County Historical Society.)

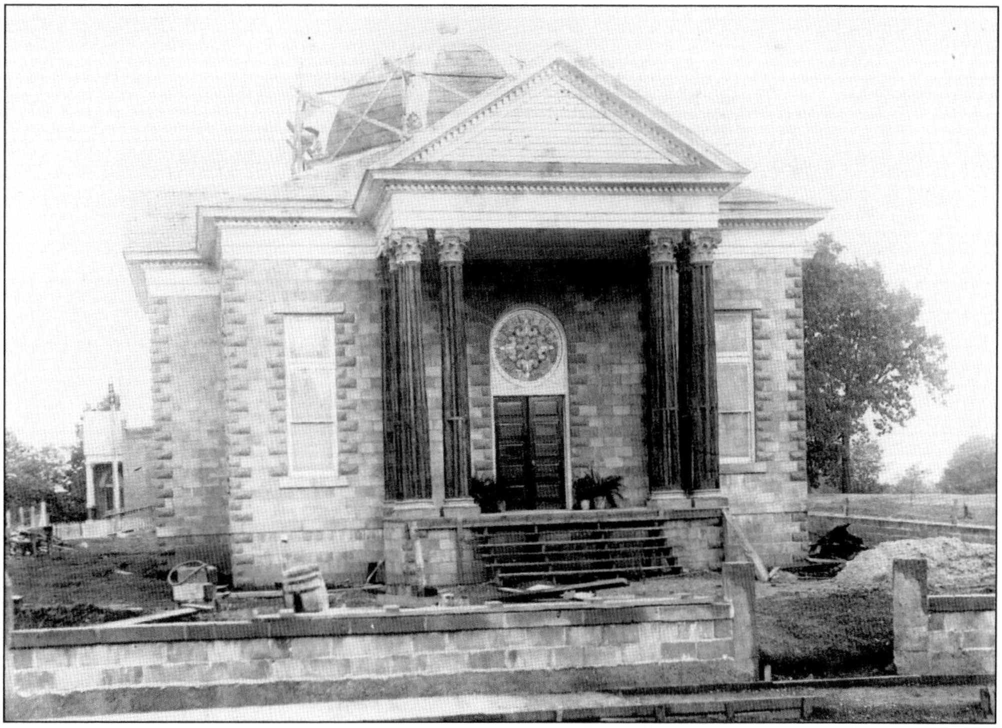

The Christian Science Church, one of the last buildings designed by Sylvester Hotchkiss, was under construction at the time of Hotchkiss's death in 1909. It still stands and is located on North Main Street. (Courtesy of UAM Library.)

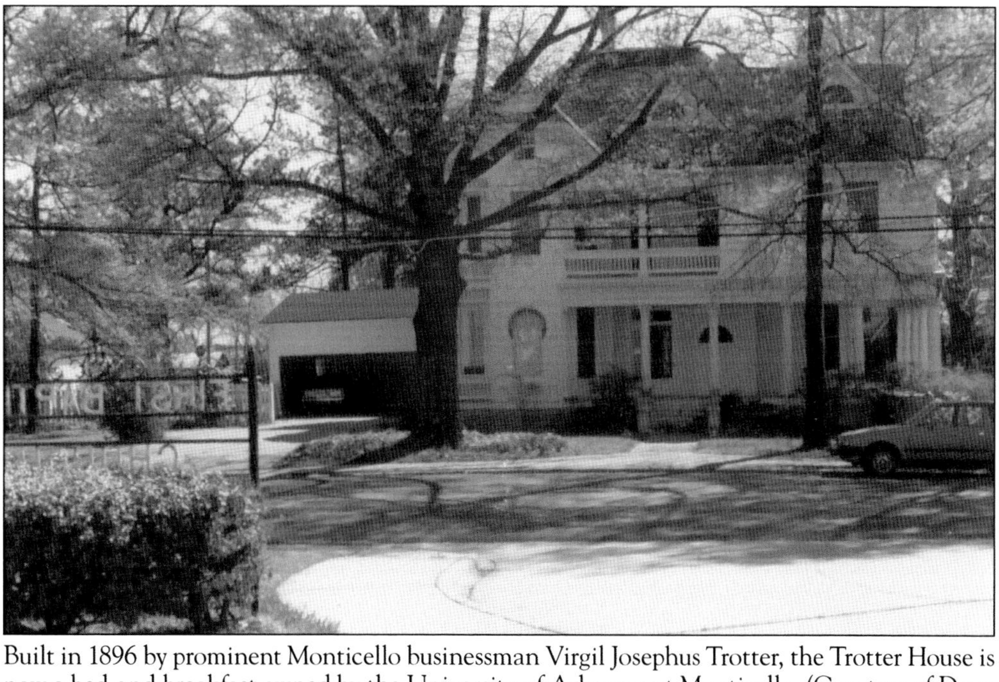

Built in 1896 by prominent Monticello businessman Virgil Josephus Trotter, the Trotter House is now a bed-and-breakfast owned by the University of Arkansas at Monticello. (Courtesy of Drew County Historical Society.)

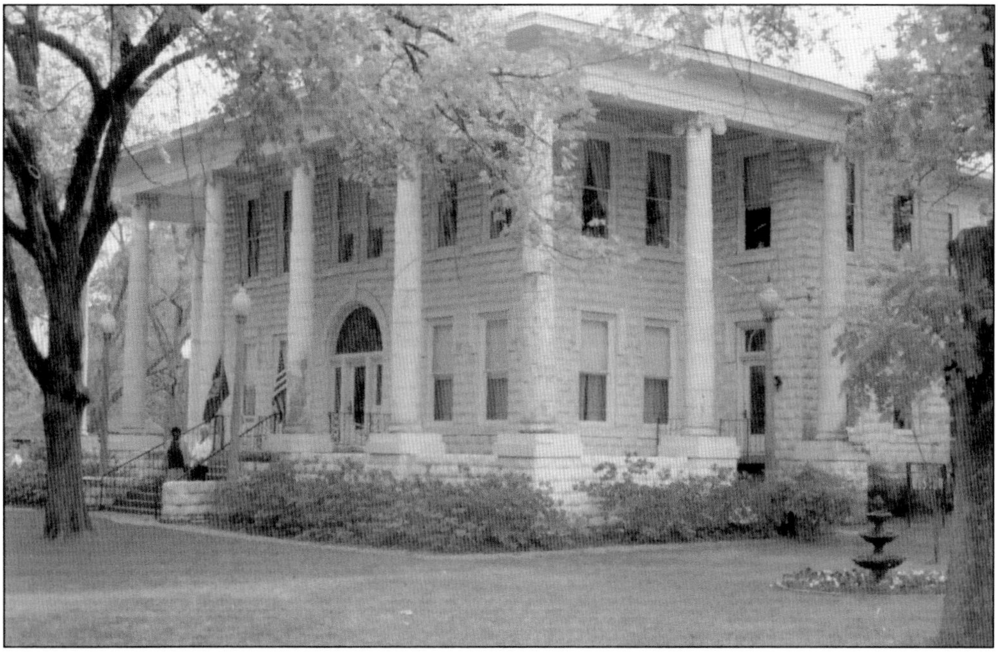

Constructed by Garvin Cavaness incrementally from 1906 to 1916, this imposing and elegant structure on South Main Street now serves as the Drew County Historical Museum. (Courtesy of Drew County Historical Society.)

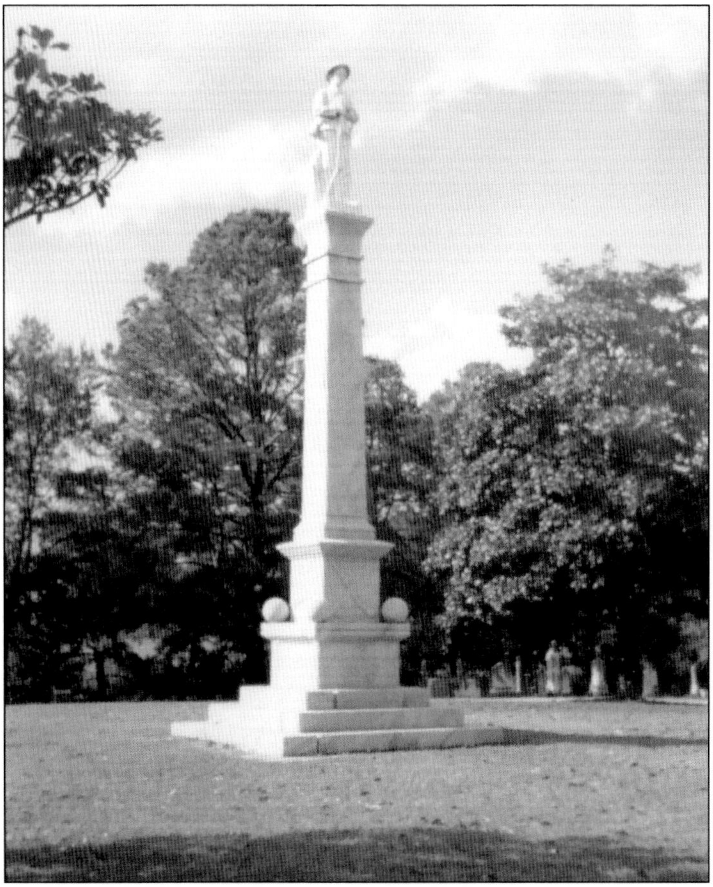

The United Daughters of the Confederacy erected this Confederate monument in front of the "French castle" courthouse in 1914. After the demolition of the courthouse in 1932, the monument was moved to Oakland Cemetery, in part because automobiles kept running into it on the square. (Courtesy of UAM Library.)

Two

THE ROARING TWENTIES

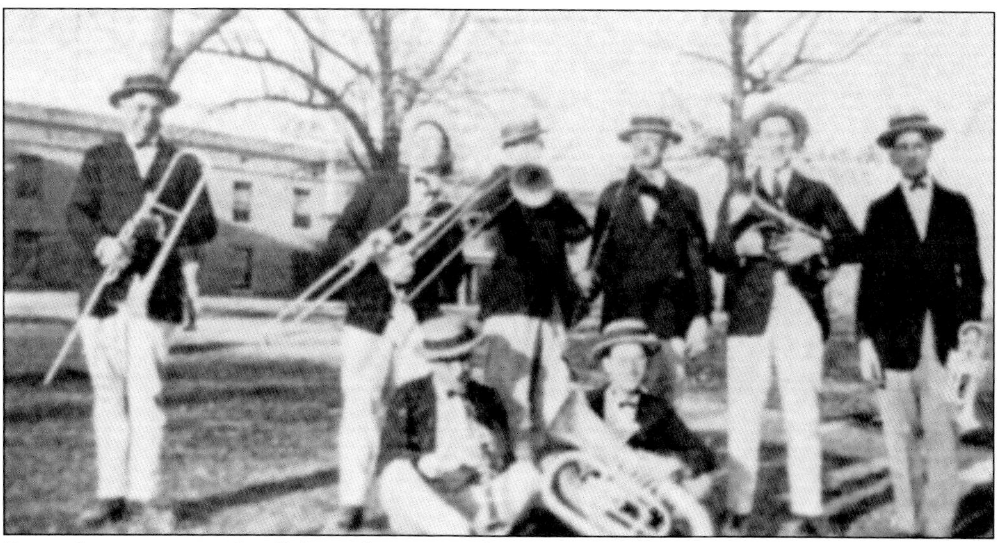

Being dapper, neat, and well dressed was critical to a young man's social success. This photograph, taken in 1925, captures some of the ebullience of the Jazz Age—a term ascribed to the time by F. Scott Fitzgerald, author of the quintessential Jazz Age novel, *The Great Gatsby*. (Courtesy of UAM Library.)

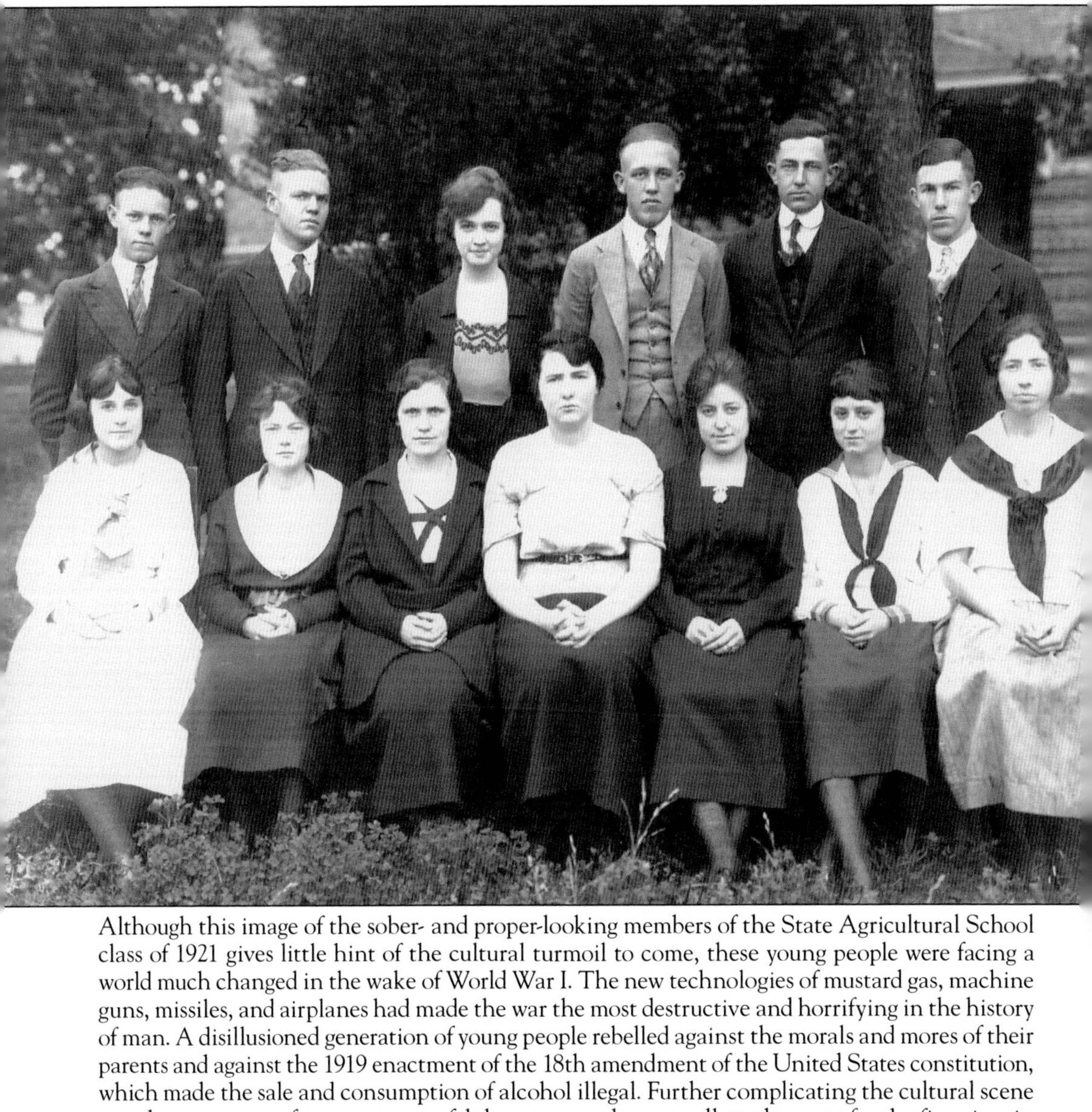

Although this image of the sober- and proper-looking members of the State Agricultural School class of 1921 gives little hint of the cultural turmoil to come, these young people were facing a world much changed in the wake of World War I. The new technologies of mustard gas, machine guns, missiles, and airplanes had made the war the most destructive and horrifying in the history of man. A disillusioned generation of young people rebelled against the morals and mores of their parents and against the 1919 enactment of the 18th amendment of the United States constitution, which made the sale and consumption of alcohol illegal. Further complicating the cultural scene was the new sense of empowerment felt by women, who were allowed to vote for the first time in 1920. The women's styles that arrived by the mid-1920s—short hair and short skirts—reflected women's desires to assert their equality to men and to express a new and open female sexuality. Fueled by bootleg whiskey, jazz, the freedom provided by automobiles, and an artificially inflated stock market, the youth of the 1920s pursued good times with little concern for the values of their elders. Writer Gertrude Stein has been credited with dubbing them the "Lost Generation." (Courtesy of UAM Library.)

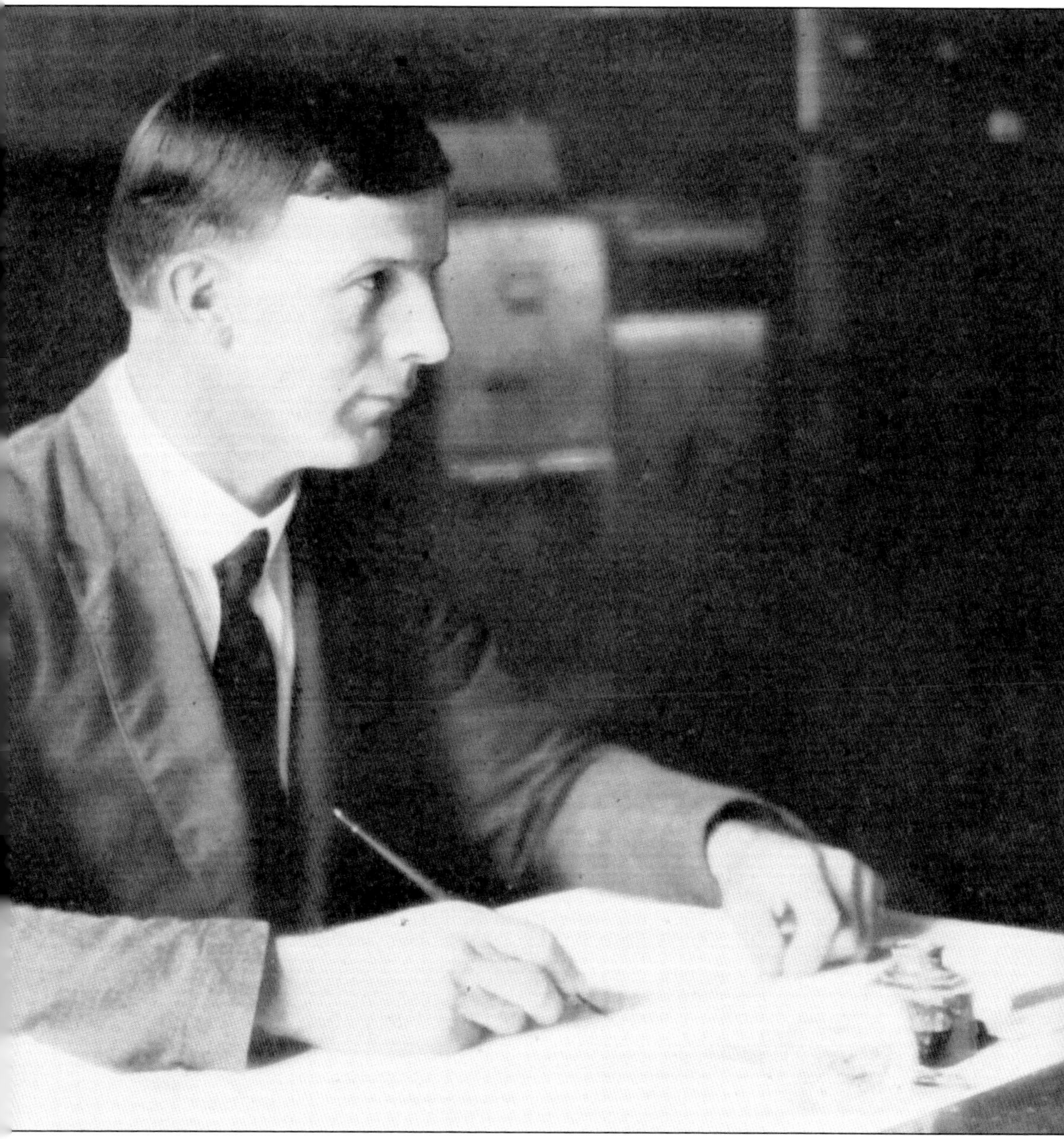

Frank Horsfall, a product of the Victorian Age and a daunting force opposed to the social changes of the 1920s, was the first principal of the Fourth District State Agricultural School and subsequently the first president of the Fourth District Agricultural and Mechanical College. Horsfall imposed tight restrictions on the social lives of students throughout the Roaring Twenties—or at least he tried to. Dances were banned during his 25 years as head of the school, and he required male and female students to remain on opposite sides of an invisible line through campus. However, as the institution made the transition from an agricultural school that students entered at the sixth-grade level to a two-year, and then four-year, college, students began to demand more student activities, programs, and personal freedom. Horsfall remained obstinate until pressures forced him to resign in 1935. (Courtesy of UAM Library.)

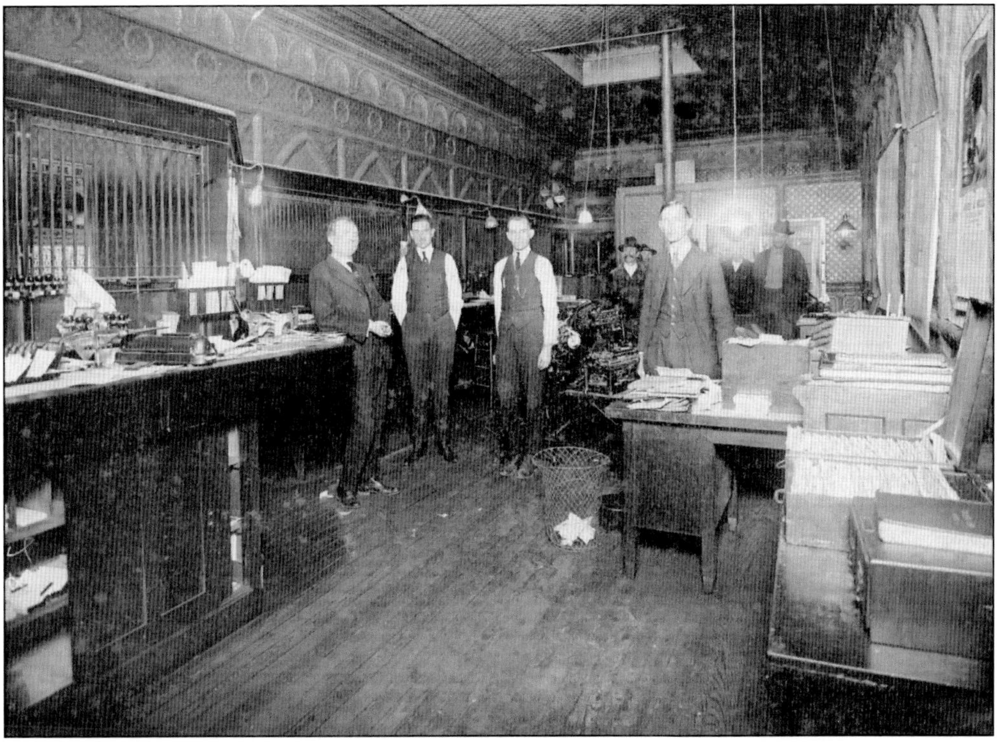

The Drew County Bank and Trust Company is pictured here in the early 1920s. Despite the dour look of the men in this photograph, business was good—until October 1929, when the stock market crashed. (Courtesy of Edgar W. Spencer.)

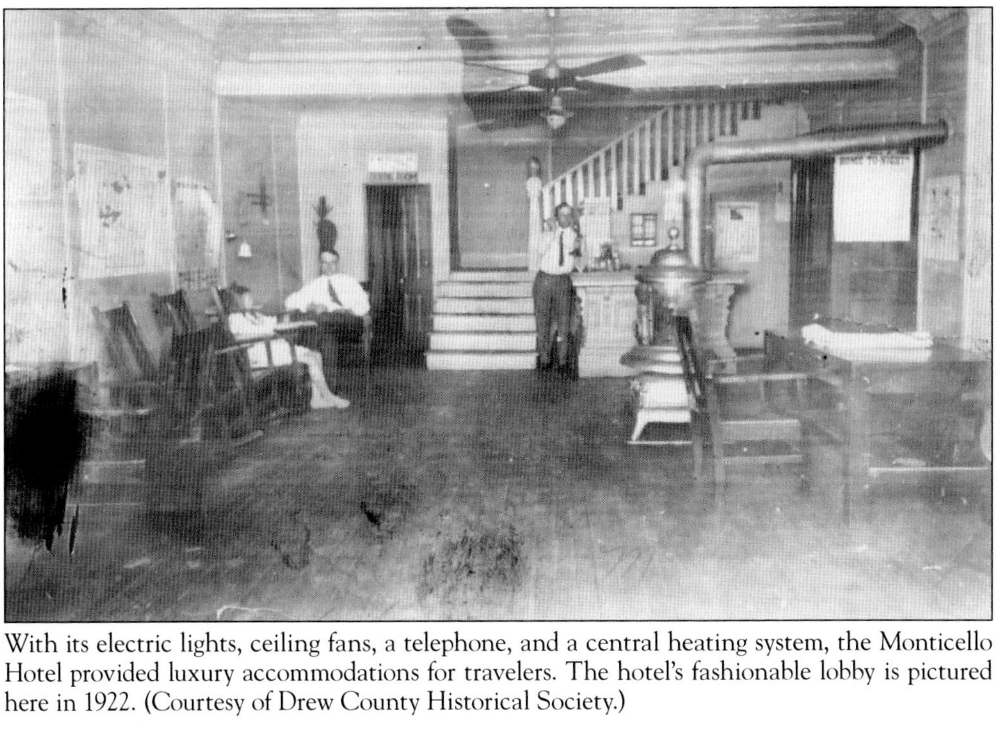

With its electric lights, ceiling fans, a telephone, and a central heating system, the Monticello Hotel provided luxury accommodations for travelers. The hotel's fashionable lobby is pictured here in 1922. (Courtesy of Drew County Historical Society.)

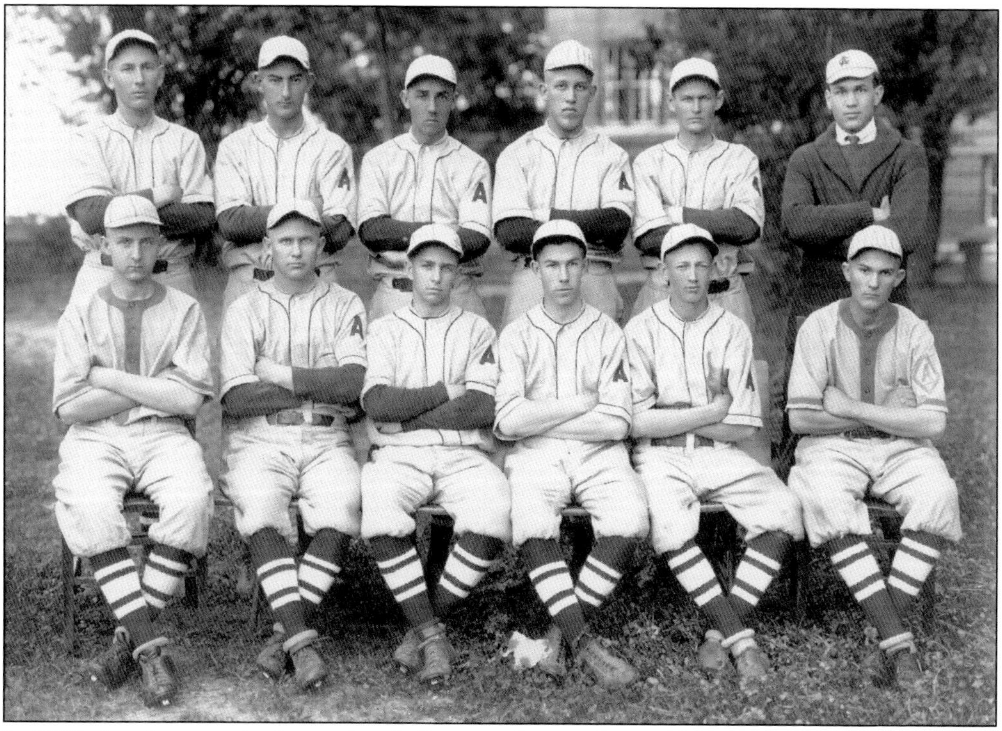

In 1920, the closest major-league baseball teams that residents of Monticello could root for were the St. Louis Cardinals, of the National League, and the St. Louis Browns, of the American League. Locally, students at the Fourth District State Agricultural School rooted for their Aggies. (Courtesy of UAM Library.)

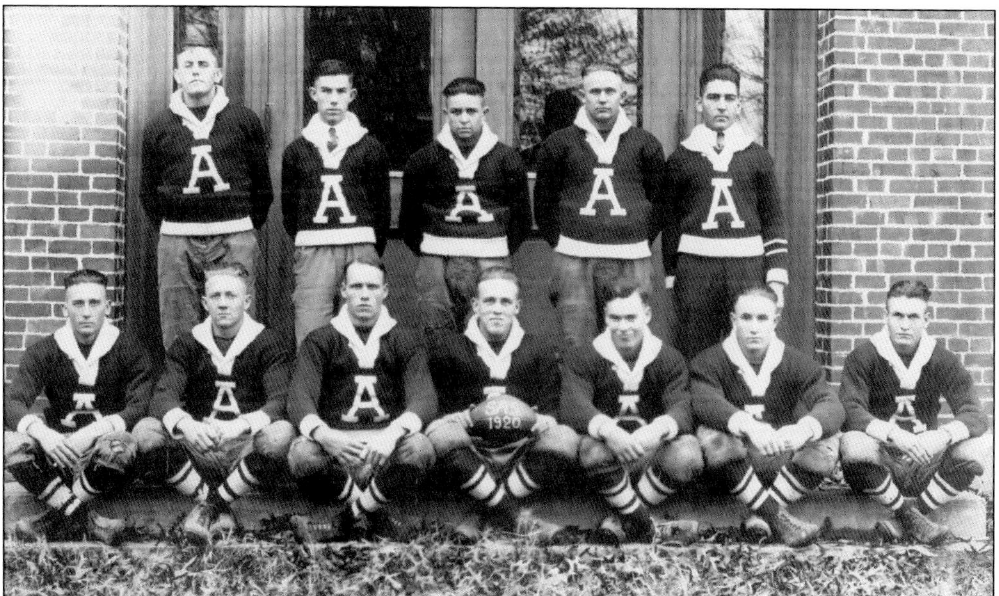

Football was played on the campus of the Fourth District State Agricultural School as early as 1911. Pictured here is the 1920 SAS team. The "A" on the team members' jerseys stood for "Aggies." (Courtesy of UAM Library.)

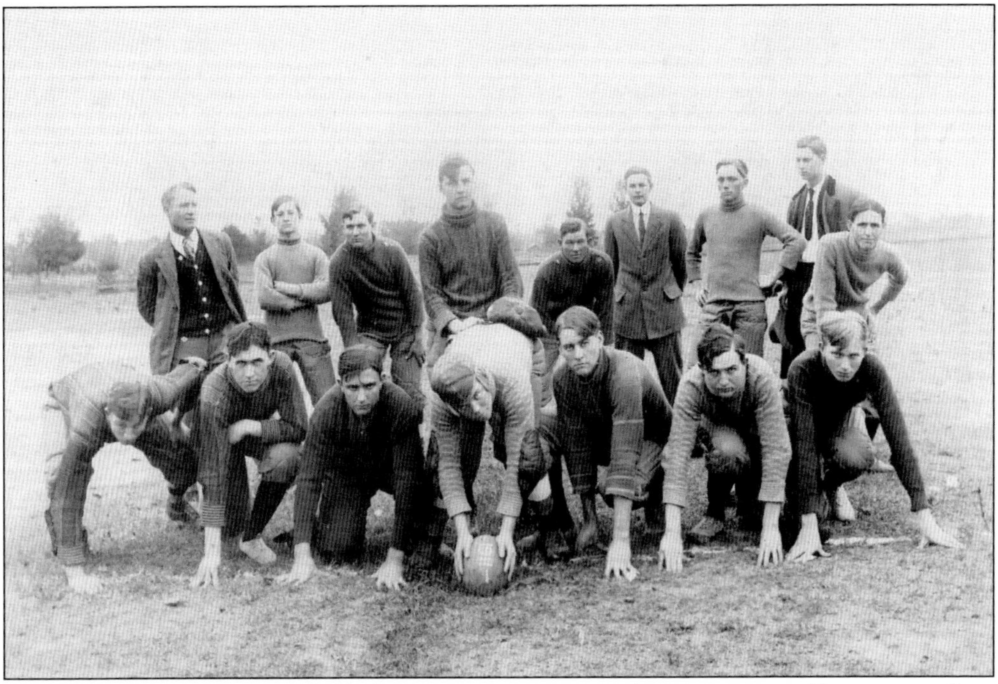

In the early 20th century, football players wore a minimum of protective gear. Plastic was still an invention of the future, so helmets were made of leather and provided no face protection. Shown here are the fighting Aggies of the State Agricultural School. (Courtesy of UAM Library.)

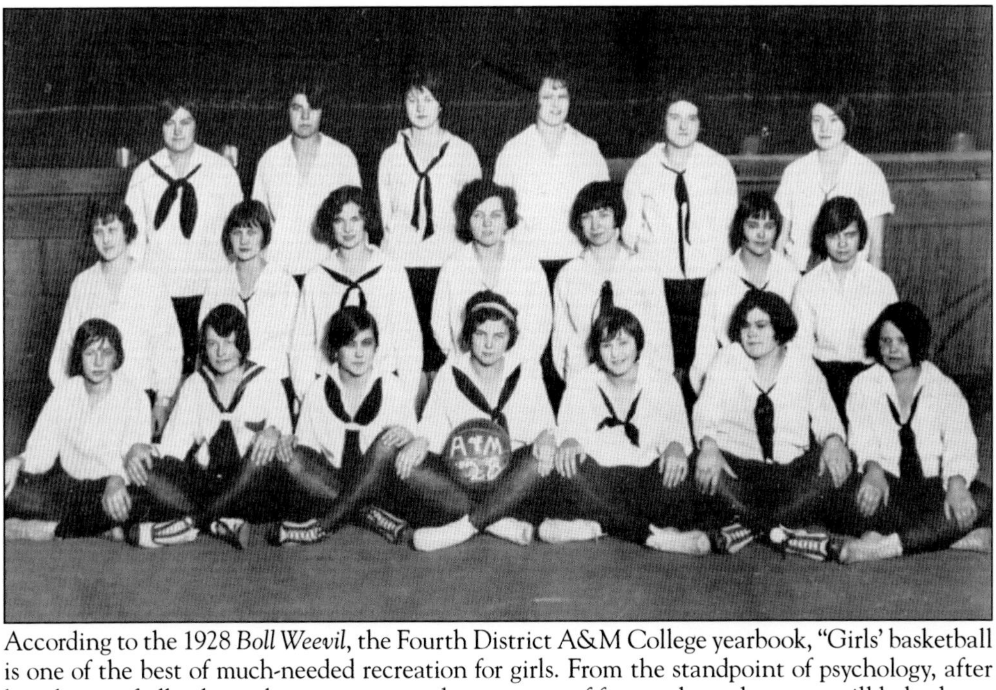

According to the 1928 *Boll Weevil*, the Fourth District A&M College yearbook, "Girls' basketball is one of the best of much-needed recreation for girls. From the standpoint of psychology, after long hours of idle physical movements, an hour or two of fast work on the court will help throw off all accumulated poisons. Basketball also is a clean game, which offers no chance of a player's becoming enraged, but tends to perpetual friendship." (Courtesy of UAM Library.)

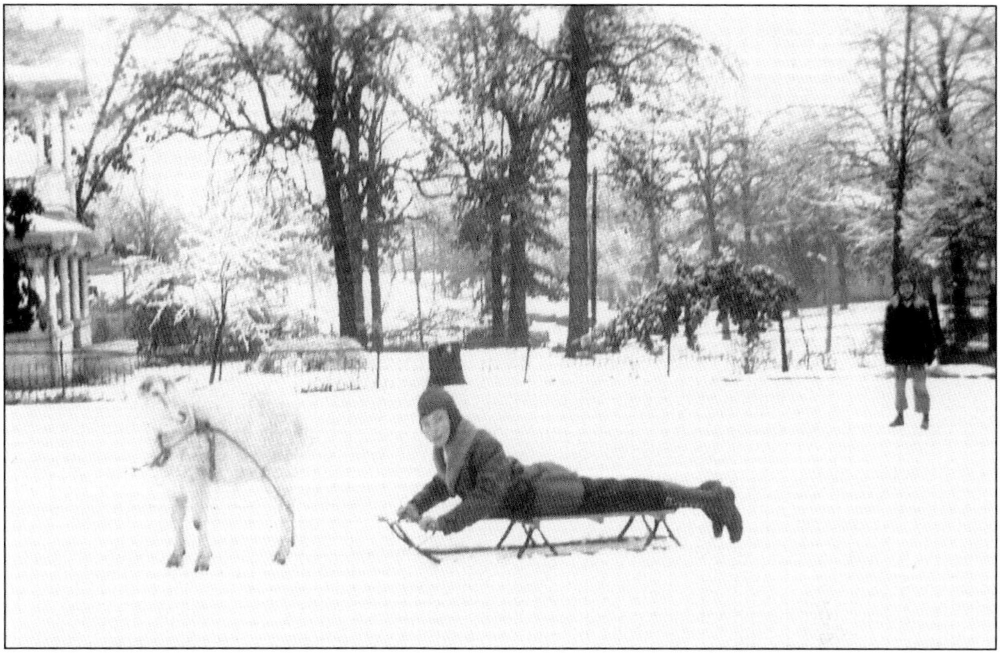

E. Allen "Duke" Bonner, the grandson of Joe Lee and Caddye Allen, enjoys a rare snowfall about 1925. A child of the fun-loving 1920s, he wrote a humorous column for the local college's newspaper, *The Southeasterner*, before transferring to Baylor University, where he was a member of the notorious organization of jokesters called the Nose Brotherhood. (Courtesy of Mark Spencer.)

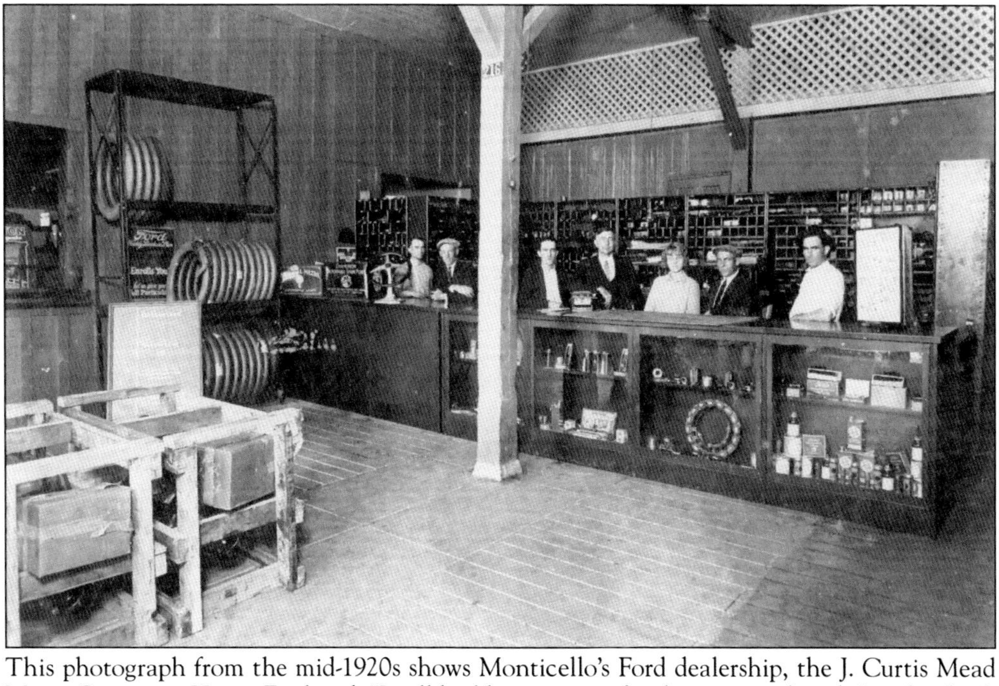

This photograph from the mid-1920s shows Monticello's Ford dealership, the J. Curtis Mead Motor Company. Henry Ford said, "I will build a motorcar for the great multitude," and indeed, the Model T, which was manufactured from 1909 to 1927, helped transform America. (Courtesy of Drew County Historical Society.)

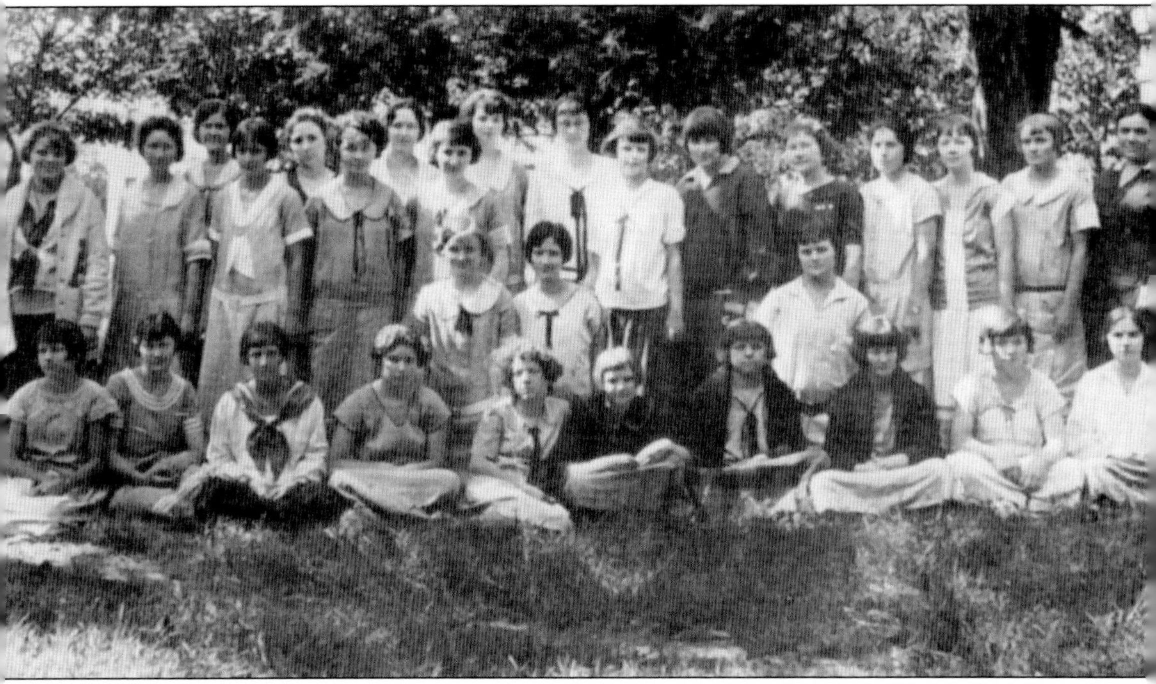

In 1925, the Fourth District State Agricultural School was renamed the Fourth District Agricultural and Mechanical College and published its first yearbook. Called *The Boll Weevil*, the yearbook's first page made the following declaration: "Boll-Weevil! Boll-Weevil! Boll-Weevil! We're little but we're loud. Don't laugh too soon. Wait. Lend your ears. Listen. Say, what you got against the boll-weevil anyhow? . . . We shall emulate his good tendencies, and leave off the bad." Pictured here is the yearbook photograph of the Women's Glee Club of 1925, with a caption reading, "Music is the greatest factor in our appreciation of life. The world is drab; a bird sings, and, lo, the light appears. Our friends have forsaken us; there is gloom everywhere. Wafted on the breeze, reaching our ears faintly, comes a melody. It takes our soul. Instantly, a radiance overspreads our environment." (Courtesy of UAM Library.)

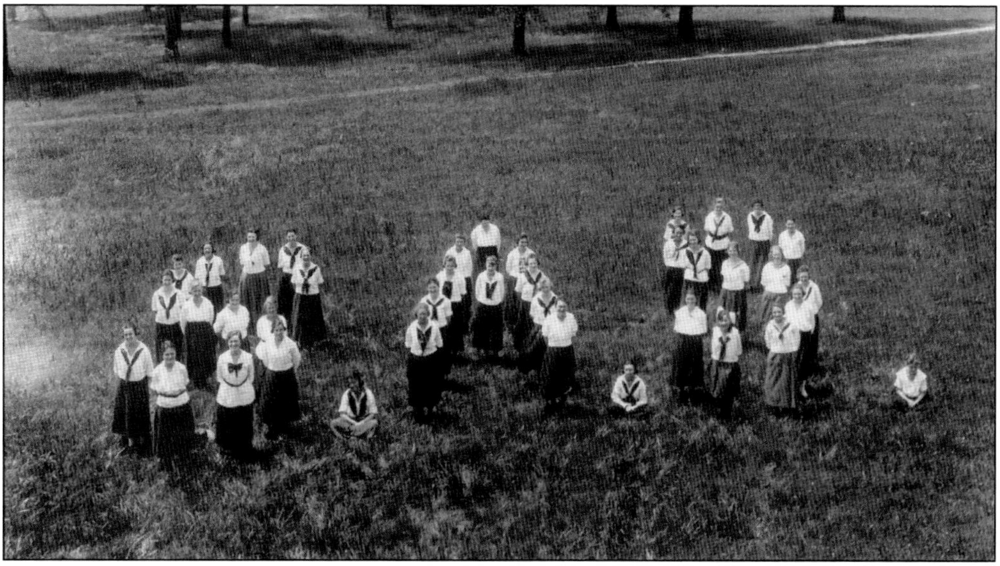

On May 19, 1920, the girls of the Fourth District State Agricultural School demonstrated their school spirit by forming the letters "S.A.S." for this picture. (Courtesy of UAM Library.)

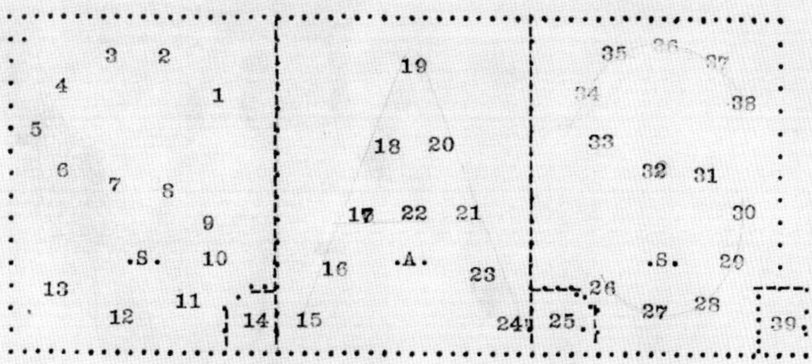

May 19. 1920.
Girls at the 4th. State Agricultural School,
Monticello, Drew County, Arkansas. Standing in the
form of the letters S.A.S.

Name	County.		
1. Smith, Maude, Lincoln.		21. Arrington, Lurline, D	
2. Sullivan, Mary, Drew.		22. Haley, Annie Laurie, D	
3. Hulsey, Mary, Union.		23. Sawyer, Essie,	
4. Starling, Josephine, Drew.		24. Turnage, Viola,	
5. Riley, Bertha, Ashley.		25. Boren, Mary, Lincoln.	
6. Hulsey, Winnie, Union.		26. Stegall, Versa Lee, Un	
7. Crick, Norma, Drew.		27. Smith, Myra, Drew.	
8. Whiting, Edna, Arkansas.		28. Maxwell, Ruth, Drew.	
9. Stubblefield, Angeline, Dw.		29. Boston, L. Mae, Drew.	
10. Rogers, Gladys, Chicot.		30. Gardner, Helen, Ashlg	
11. Parker, Jewell, Jefferson.		31. Aycock, Rosa, Desha.	
12. Overton, Sue Bell,		32. Willet, Mary, Union.	
13. Bledsoe, Iva, Ashley.		33. Rogers, Odelle,	
14. Jackson, Thelma, Drew.		34. Jones, Verlee, Drew.	
15. Crook, Maurice, Drew.		35. Stewart, Nannie,	
16. Stegall, Annie Lois, Union.		36. Rich, Susie, Woodruf.	
17. Sullivan, Myrtis, Ashley.		37. Anderson, Mabelle, Dr	
18. Willis, Grace. Drew.		38. Brown, Era.	
19. Jones, Sallie, Lonoke.		39. Wisdom, Nina, Arkansa	
20. Groce, Modelle, Drew.			

The back of the previous image provides the names of the students who posed for the S.A.S. photograph. Each number corresponds to the person's position in the formation. (Courtesy of UAM Library.)

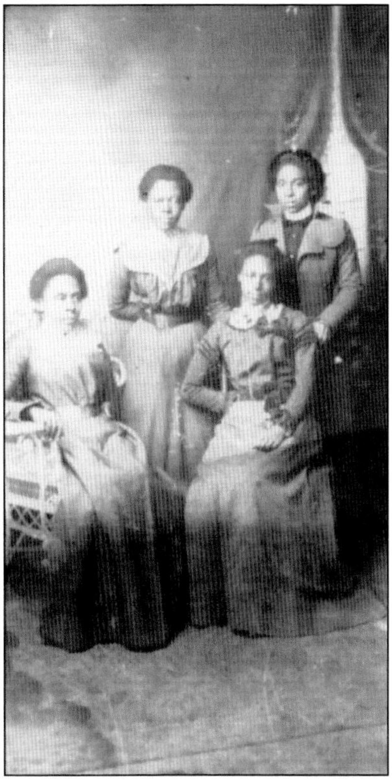

Pictured here are teachers from the Monticello Academy, a parochial school for African American children. The Monticello Academy was established in a one-room cabin in 1890. Presbyterian missionary Mary Emilie Holmes and Rev. Charles Mebane of the Second Presbyterian Church (now Holmes Chapel) worked together to gather funds for a new building. The building was completed in 1891 and moved to a location north of town in 1909. The school closed on June 1, 1933. (Courtesy of Drew County Historical Society.)

A large crowd gathers for a sale at Ray A. Sparks' Fair Store sometime between 1926 and 1928. Sparks was an innovative and creative merchandiser in the spirit of the flamboyant 1920s, opening his store at midnight on at least one occasion and selling a set of silverware to the first 10 customers for pennies. At another sale, Sparks held a drawing for a free bedroom suite. While bootleg alcohol and a repudiation of Victorian stodginess fueled Americans' pursuit of a good time, a bullish stock market and general optimism about the economy—not to mention the greater availability and affordability of new technologies such as automobiles, refrigerators, and radios—fueled consumerism. (Courtesy of Drew County Historical Society.)

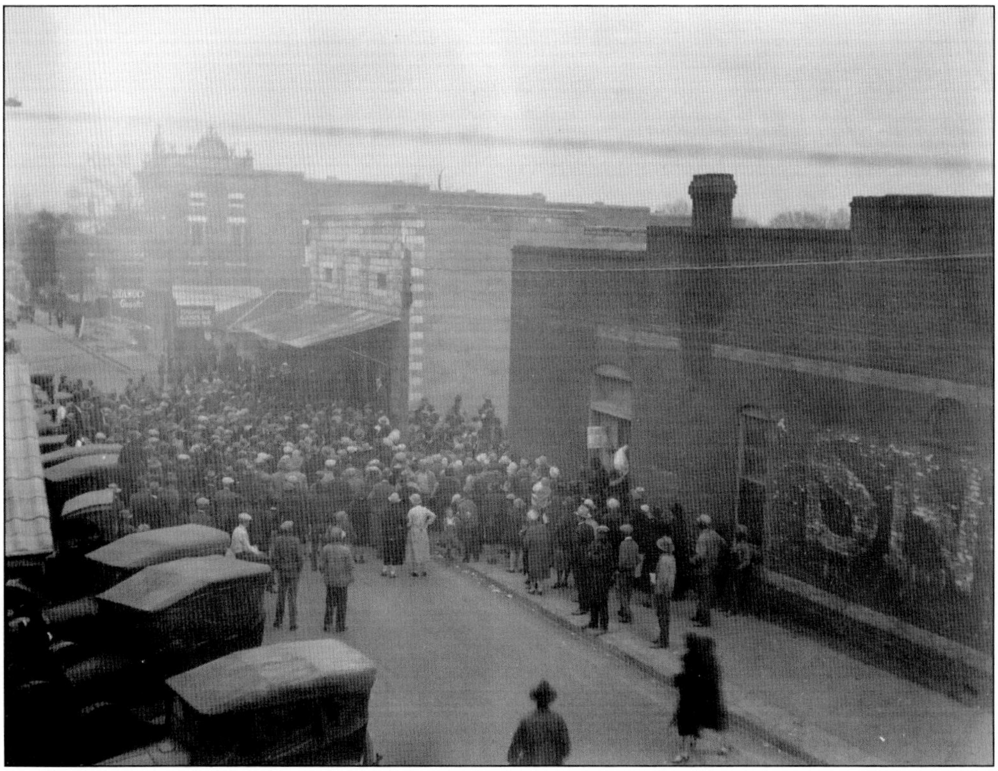

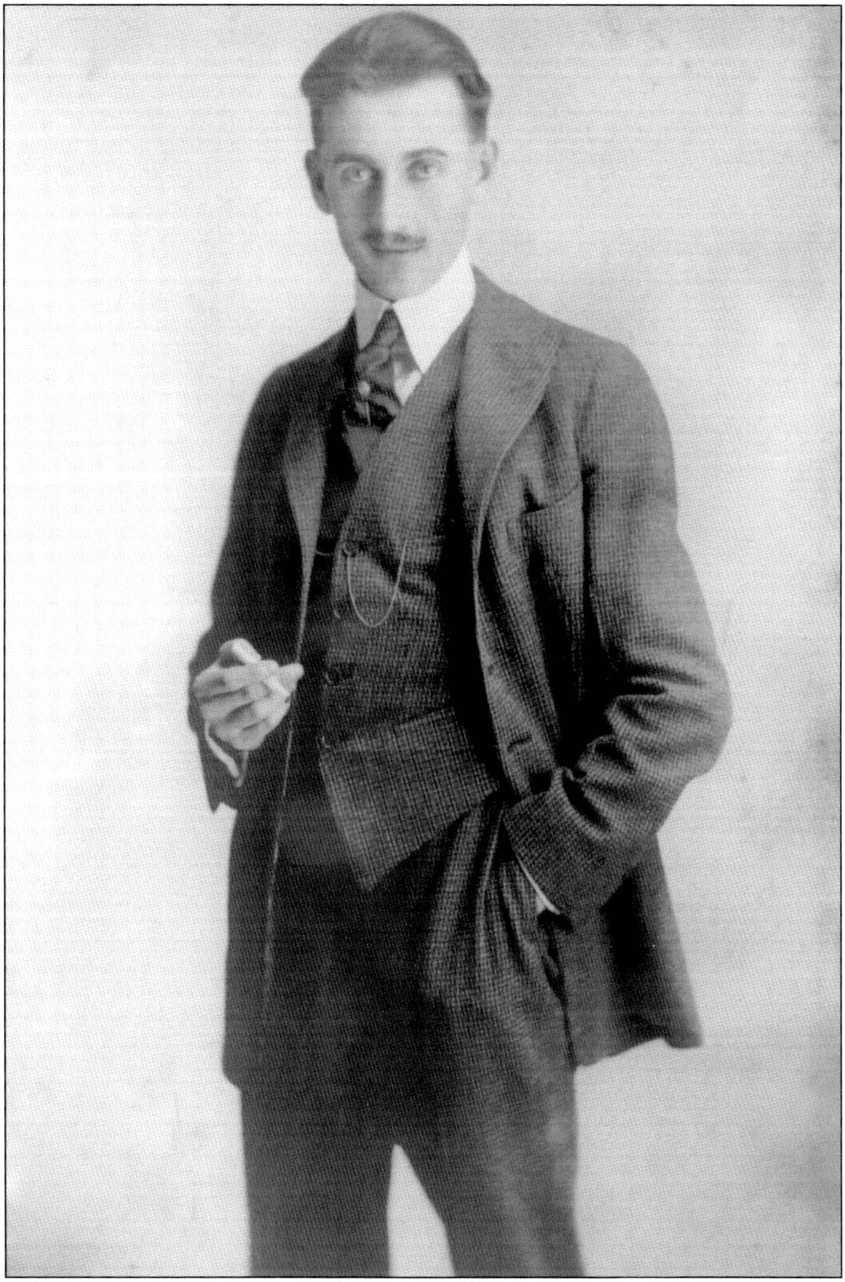

A graduate of the law school at the University of Arkansas at Fayetteville, William Edgar Spencer was a member of the state legislature at the age of 22 and a county and probate judge at 26. Not entirely fulfilled by a law career, he was in tune with the exciting young generation of literary arts of the 1920s, including the novels of F. Scott Fitzgerald, Ernest Hemingway, and William Faulkner and the poetry of writers like T.S. Eliot, Robert Frost, and William Carlos Williams. Concerned that people would not take him seriously as a judge if they knew he wrote poetry, he published poems under the pseudonym Henri Faust. In the late 1920s, he was the winner of the Yale Series of Younger Poets, a national poetry competition for poets under 30. In 1929, Yale University Press published his book *Half Light and Overture*. (Courtesy of Edgar W. Spencer.)

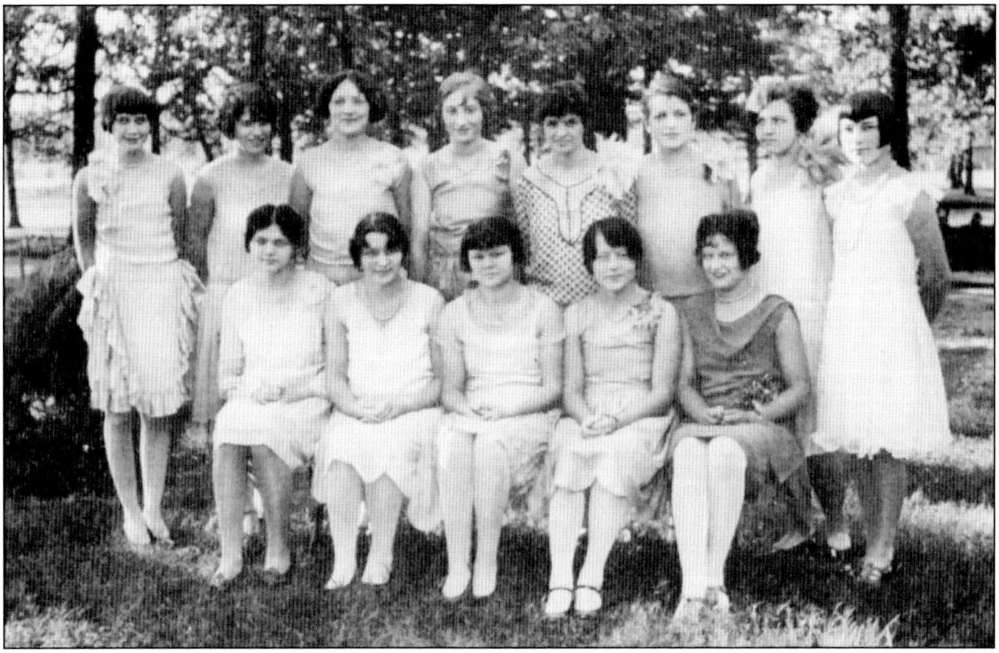

By 1928, when this photograph was taken, women's post-Victorian attitudes were clearly reflected in the styles of the day. Gone were the long tresses that marked a "lady," the high collars, corsets, long sleeves, and long skirts. Dipping necklines, bare arms, bare shins, and bobbed hair reflected a new freedom and a focus on fun, as demonstrated in this photograph of the Arkansas A&M Girls Glee Club. (Courtesy of UAM Library.)

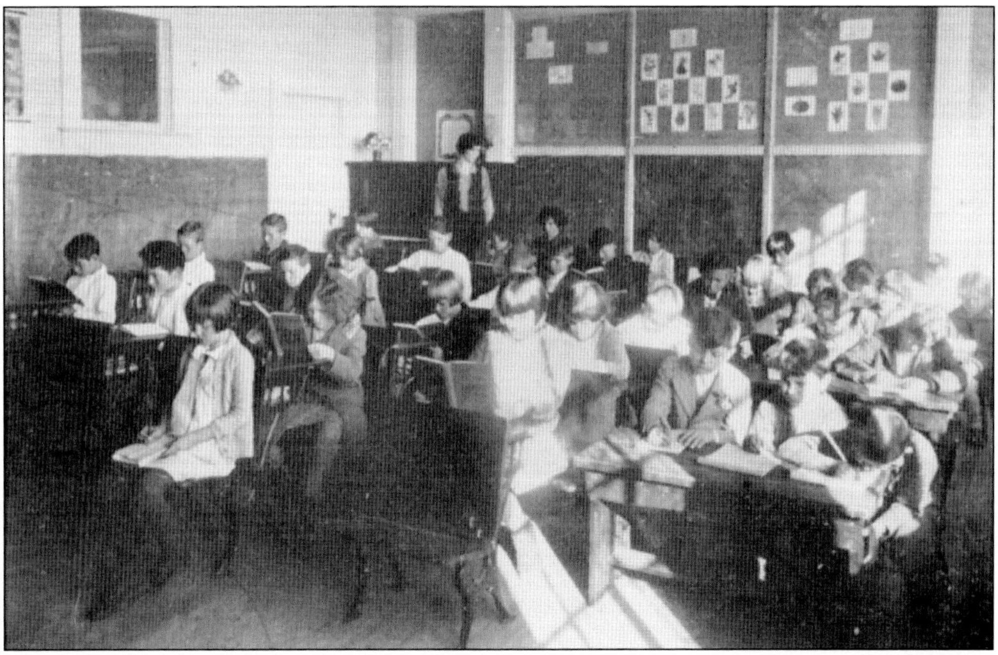

Children from around Drew County were bused to the training school on the campus of Arkansas A&M College. This photograph of pupils at work in the classroom was taken in 1928. (Courtesy of UAM Library.)

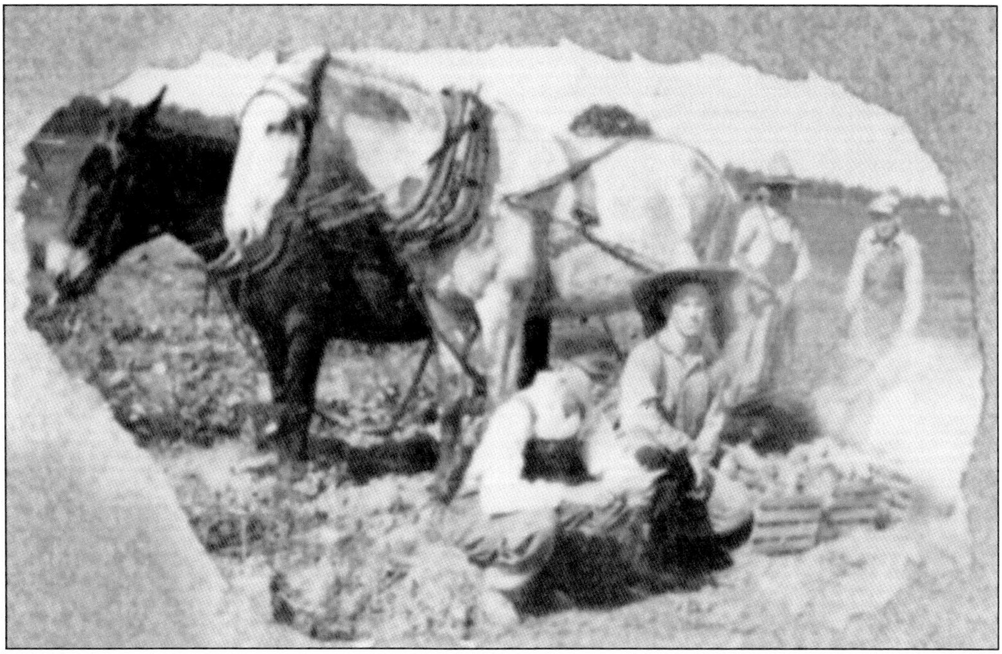

Despite the technological advances of the early 20th century, this 1928 photograph is a reminder that many people, especially those residing in rural areas, still lived much as they had in the 19th century—without automobiles, electricity, plumbing, or telephones. (Courtesy of UAM Library.)

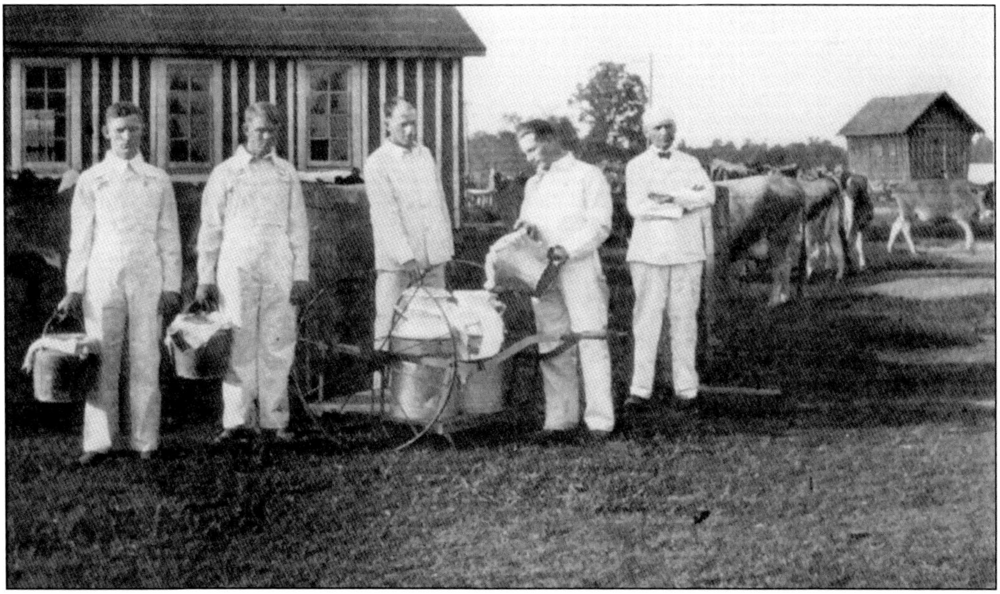

In this 1925 photograph, students learn how to be dairy farmers. According to the 1925 *Boll Weevil* yearbook, the Animal Husbandry Department was "well equipped with everything necessary for the teaching of the different branches of the subject." (Courtesy of UAM Library.)

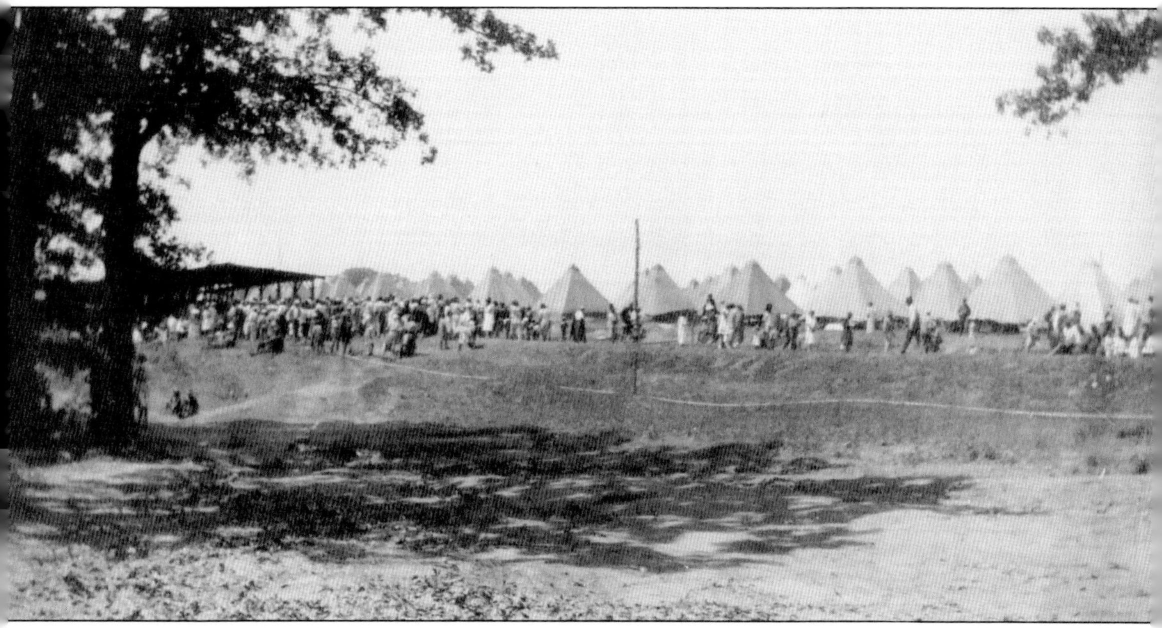

This tent city for African American refugees of the Great Mississippi River Flood of 1927 was located at the fairgrounds just west of Monticello. While America was enjoying the peak of Roaring Twenties prosperity, in the spring of 1927, the Mississippi River flooded 6,600 square miles of Arkansas and affected the lives of 350,000 Arkansans. Almost 100 people died in the state. Other states along the river were affected, but none was as devastated by the disaster as Arkansas. US Secretary of Commerce Herbert Hoover called the flood "America's greatest peacetime disaster," but there was no federal response under Republican president Calvin Coolidge. Not one dollar of federal money went directly toward the relief of victims. The segregated tent cities could not adequately accommodate the refugees, and since much of Arkansas remained under water until September, disease rapidly spread over the weeks and months. Relief efforts were hampered, in part, by the insistence of some plantation owners that they control the distribution of aid provided by agencies like the Red Cross. (Courtesy of Drew County Historical Society.)

Three

DEPRESSION AND A NEW DEAL

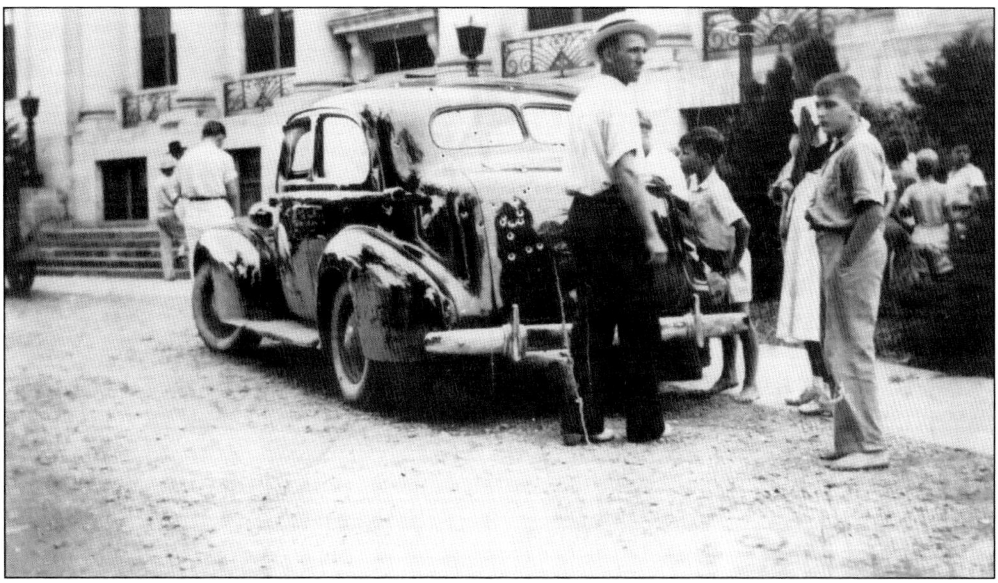

As Americans lost life savings in bank failures and had homes foreclosed on by the surviving banks, many frustrated and angry citizens romanticized outlaws like Bonnie and Clyde and Baby Face Nelson. This bullet-riddled 1936 Pontiac belonged to a fugitive who hid out for several weeks in Seven Devils Bottom. When Monticello sheriff W.C. Cruce attempted to arrest the man, a shoot-out ensued and the outlaw was killed. (Courtesy of Drew County Historical Society.)

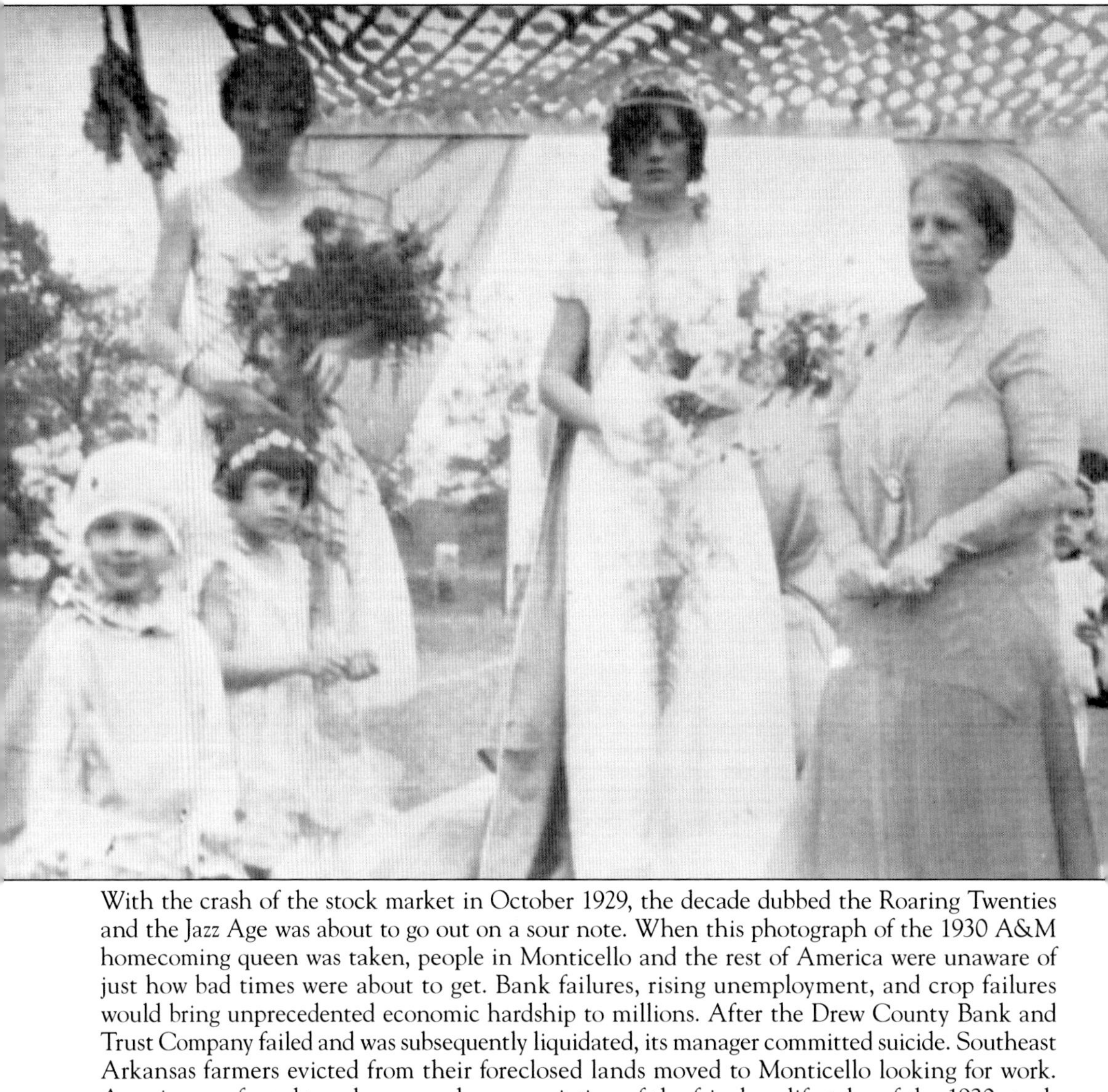

With the crash of the stock market in October 1929, the decade dubbed the Roaring Twenties and the Jazz Age was about to go out on a sour note. When this photograph of the 1930 A&M homecoming queen was taken, people in Monticello and the rest of America were unaware of just how bad times were about to get. Bank failures, rising unemployment, and crop failures would bring unprecedented economic hardship to millions. After the Drew County Bank and Trust Company failed and was subsequently liquidated, its manager committed suicide. Southeast Arkansas farmers evicted from their foreclosed lands moved to Monticello looking for work. America was forced to sober up and a renunciation of the frivolous lifestyles of the 1920s took hold. In women's fashions, necklines became more modest and hemlines dropped to the floor. Monticellonians looked to homecoming queens and Hollywood for reminders of life's potential for glamour and a brief escape from the hardships. (Courtesy of UAM Library.)

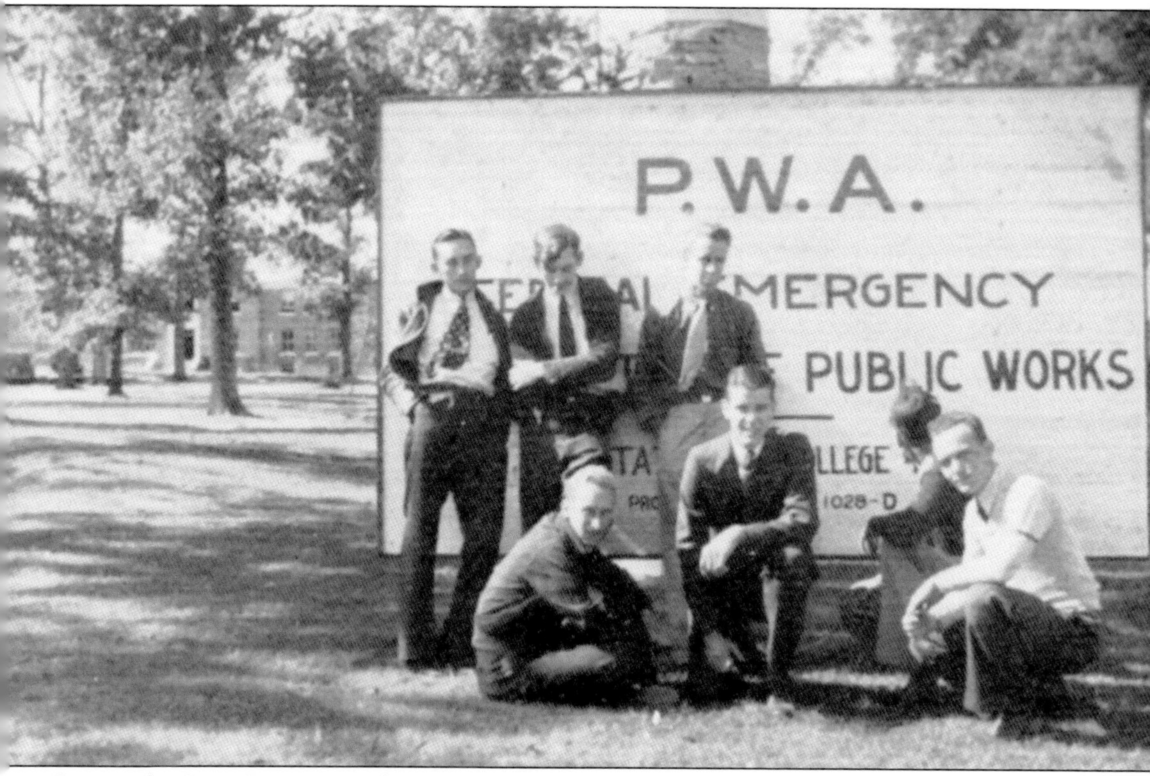

During the Great Depression, the national unemployment rate exceeded 25 percent. As part of Pres. Franklin Delano Roosevelt's New Deal, the National Industrial Recovery Act created the Public Works Administration (PWA) in June 1933 to enhance the country's infrastructure and to decrease unemployment. As only one of a number of New Deal programs, the PWA generally concentrated on the construction of large-scale projects such as bridges and dams. Successful in lowering unemployment, it also created local infrastructure that generated pride in communities across America. Spending arrived in two waves, the first from 1933 to 1935 and the second in 1938, when this photograph was taken. The PWA closed down in 1939. (Courtesy of UAM Library.)

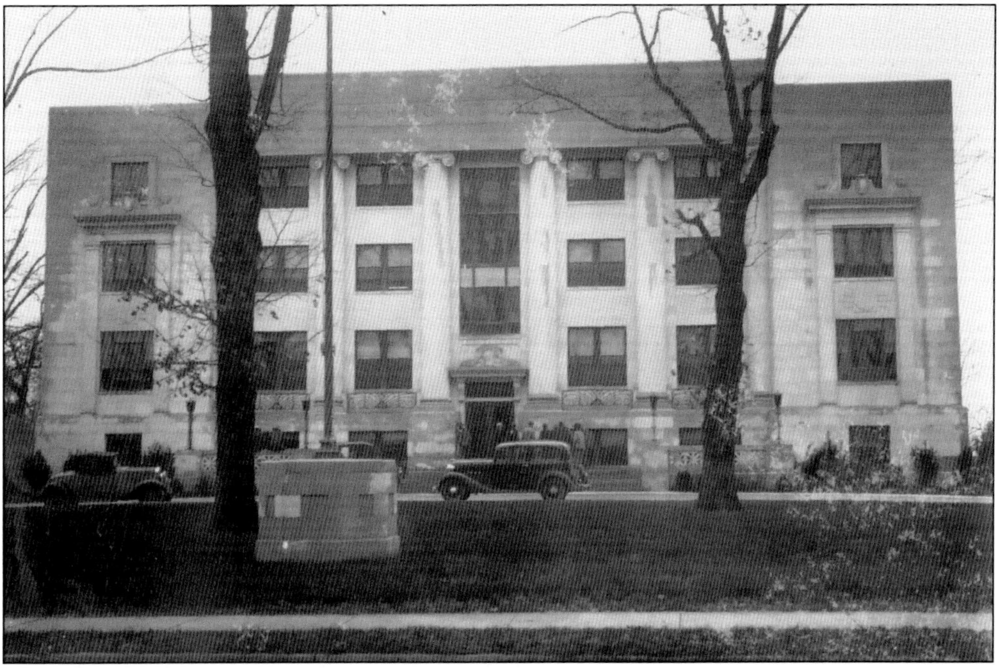

The Drew County Courthouse on South Main Street, completed in 1932, had greater square footage than the 60-year-old "French castle" courthouse on the town square. This new courthouse also provided safer and more modern accommodations. Its design displays the popular Art Deco architectural style of the period. (Courtesy of Drew County Historical Society.)

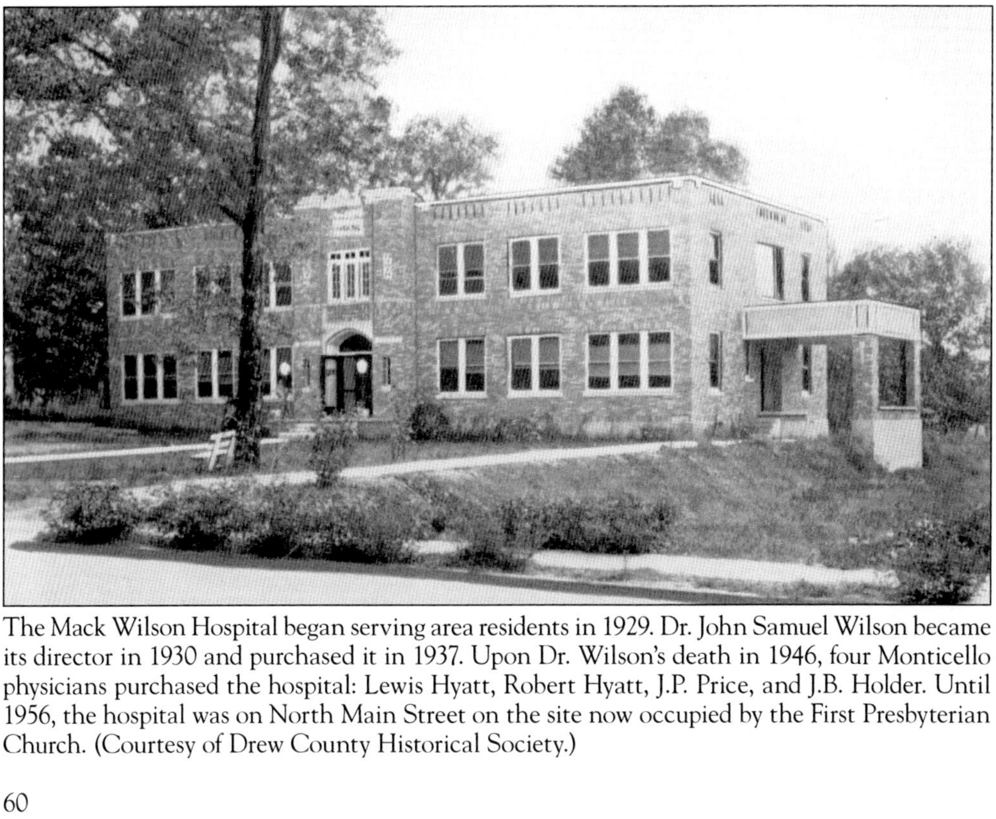

The Mack Wilson Hospital began serving area residents in 1929. Dr. John Samuel Wilson became its director in 1930 and purchased it in 1937. Upon Dr. Wilson's death in 1946, four Monticello physicians purchased the hospital: Lewis Hyatt, Robert Hyatt, J.P. Price, and J.B. Holder. Until 1956, the hospital was on North Main Street on the site now occupied by the First Presbyterian Church. (Courtesy of Drew County Historical Society.)

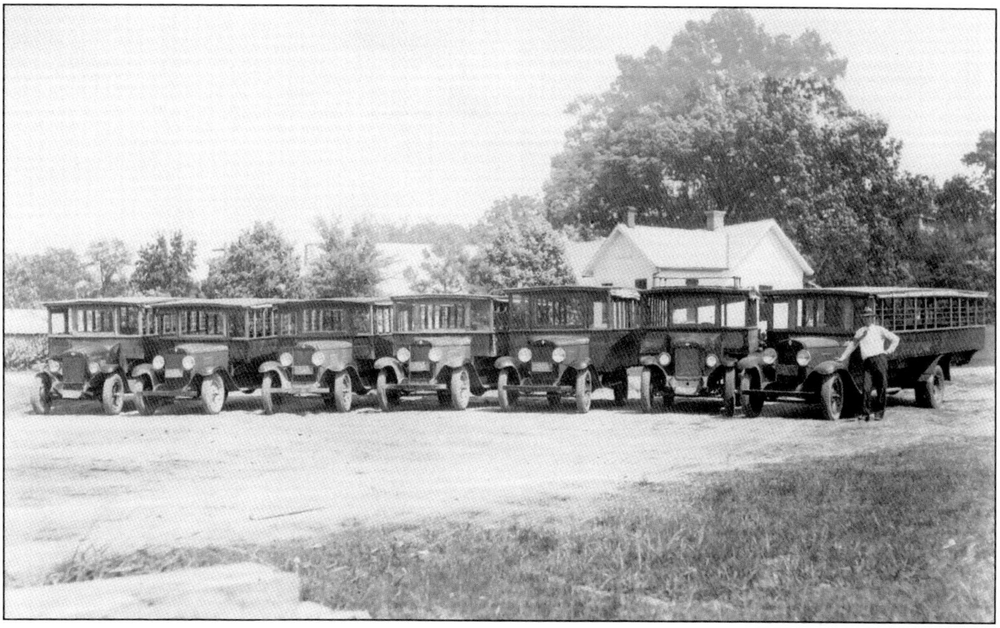

In 1932, the Fourth District A&M College purchased a fleet of Model A Chevrolets without bodies from Union Motor Company. Personnel on campus built and installed the bus bodies on the chassis. The buses were used to transport athletic teams and musical groups, and perhaps to bring county children to the elementary training school on campus. (Courtesy of Drew County Historical Society.)

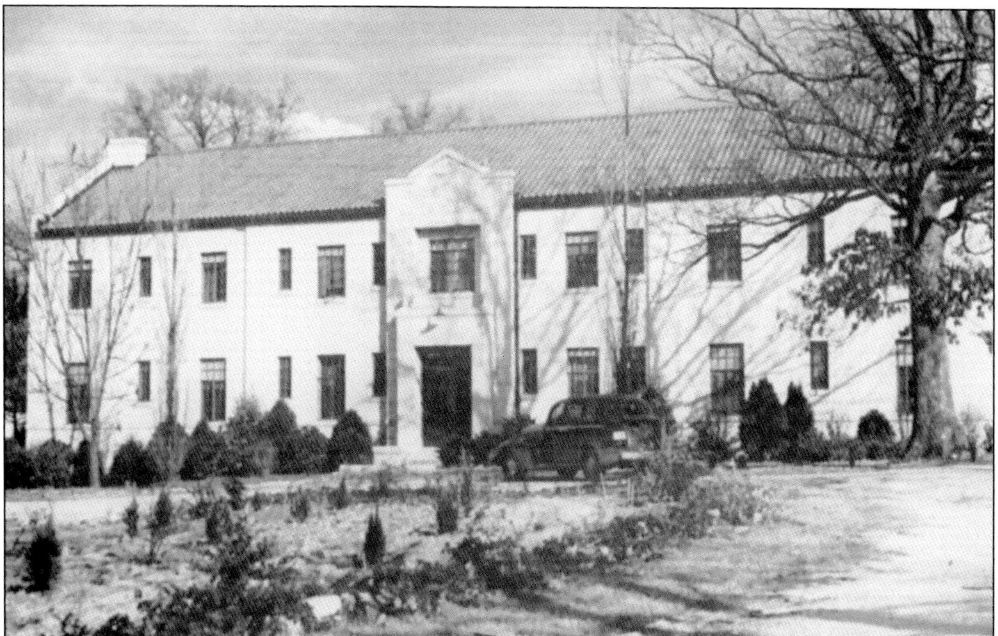

During its time on campus, Gates Hall served as the college library building as well as a dormitory for students and apartments for faculty and staff. Constructed of Batesville marble in 1933, Gates Hall was built by students under the supervision of Alaga H. Boyd. This photograph was taken in 1941. Gates Hall was razed in 1997. (Courtesy of UAM Library.)

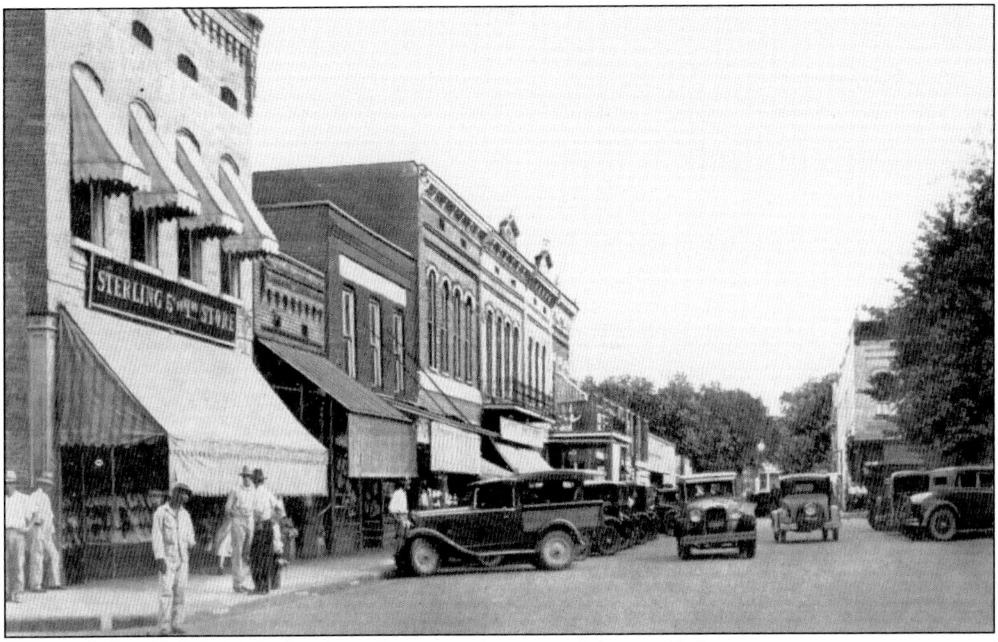

This image of a busy South Main Street underscores Monticello's importance as a center of commerce and government. As people in smaller towns and on farms in southeast Arkansas sought job opportunities in the midst of the Great Depression, many moved to Monticello. In fact, while the population of Drew County held steady between 1930 and 1940, the population of Monticello increased by nearly 20 percent. (Courtesy of Drew County Historical Society.)

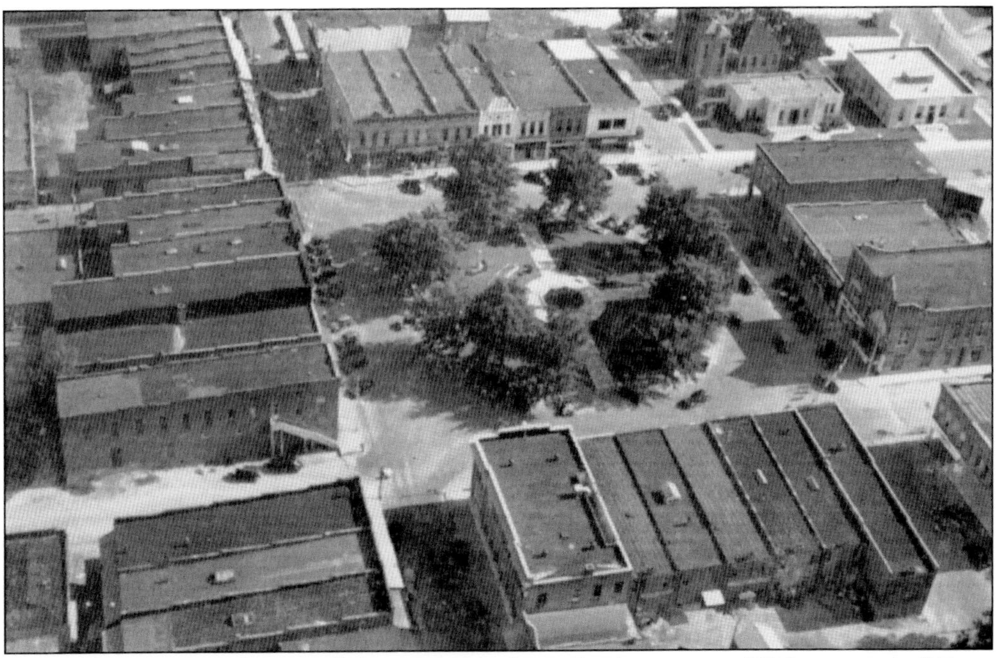

This 1940 aerial view of Monticello's town square shows the dominance of 19th-century buildings, with the exception of the mid-1930s Art Deco city hall and post office in the upper right corner. (Courtesy of UAM Library.)

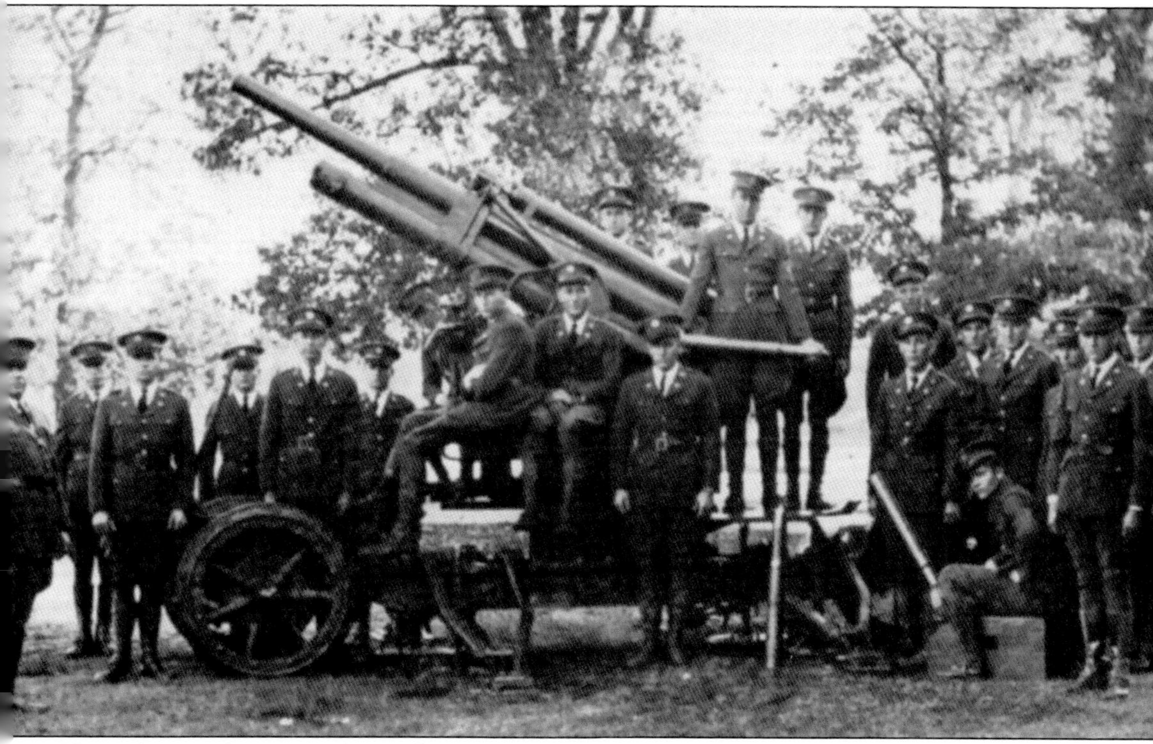

Shown here is the National Guard's 1st Gun Section of Battery B of the 206th Coast Artillery in 1936. Battery B was organized on the State Agricultural School campus in 1923, and the National Guard Armory building was completed in July 1926. The battery assisted with rescue efforts during the Great Mississippi Flood of 1927. In 1936, most Americans were determined to be isolationist and neutral in the context of world affairs; they remained so right up to the attack on Pearl Harbor in 1941. While Americans wanted to focus on the continuing economic challenges of their local communities and the nation as a whole in 1936, Japan was already buying up America's scrap iron to be used in the construction of warplanes and warships, and Hitler was building his army and the autobahn in Germany in preparation for the invasions of Austria, France, and Poland. (Courtesy of UAM Library.)

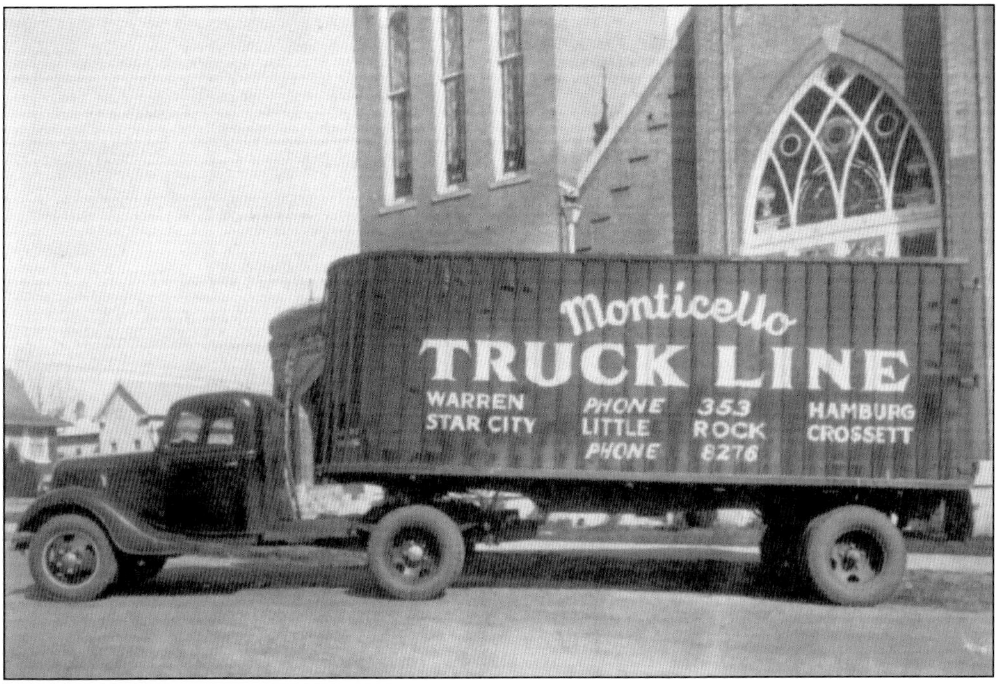

This photograph, from a 1937 advertisement for Monticello Truck Line, was accompanied by text that states: "Catering to and serving south Arkansas and northeast Louisiana with a rapid modern reliable economical truck line." The truck line serviced an area from "Little Rock to Monroe." (Courtesy of UAM Library.)

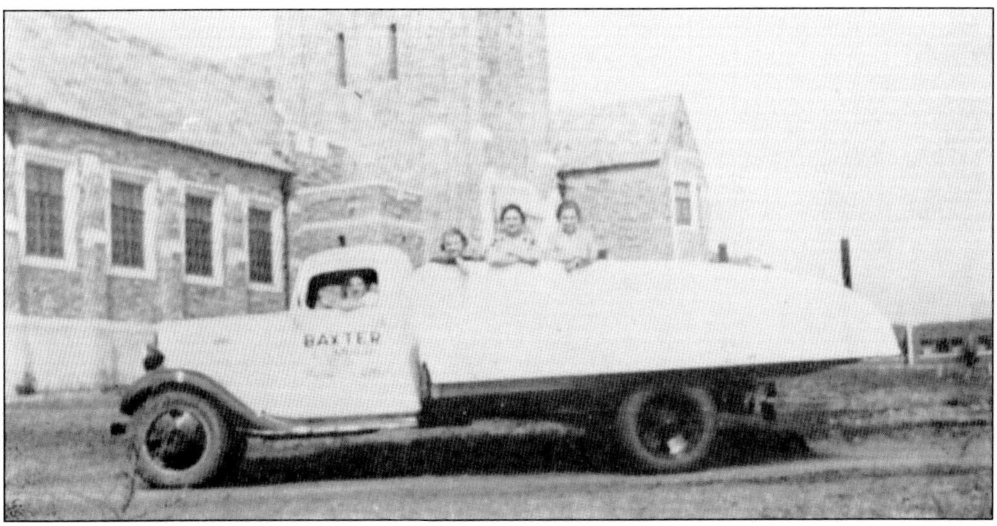

Another interesting advertising juxtaposition from 1937 shows a truck from the Baxter Lumber Company in front of the Fine Arts building on the A&M campus. Also intriguing is the use of female models. Is this business that deals in lumber, paint, roofing shingles, and hardware attempting to strike a note of irony? (Courtesy of UAM Library.)

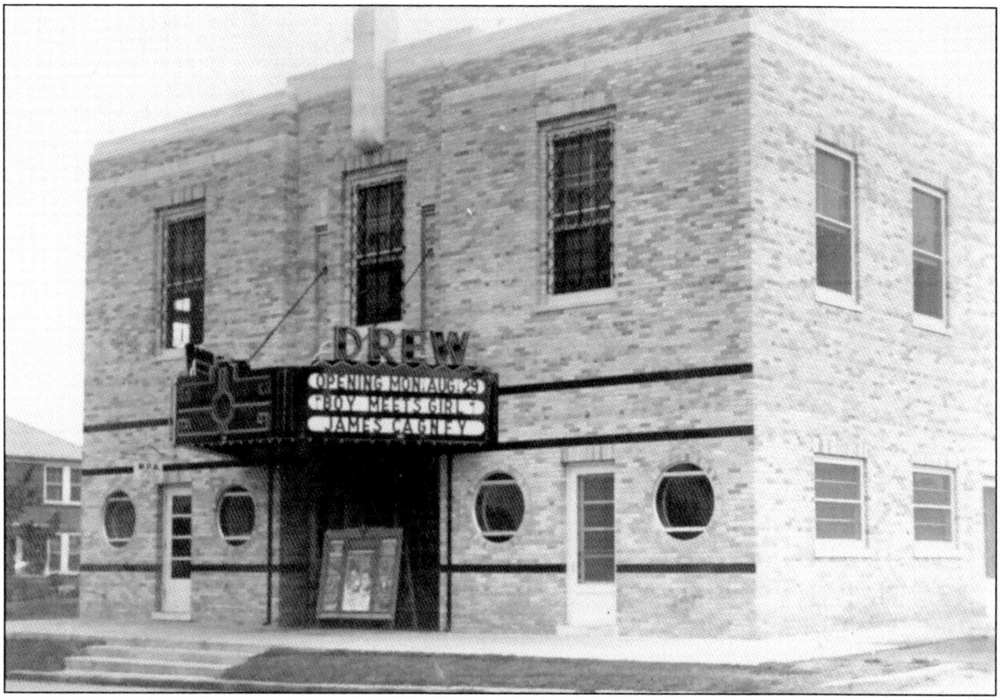

The reality of the Great Depression was only occasionally portrayed in Hollywood movies of the 1930s, an avoidance of the real world that was fine with most moviegoers, who sought escape from everyday life. *Boy Meets Girl*, the movie advertised here on the marquee of the Drew Theater on West Gaines Avenue, was originally a Broadway farce. The 1938 movie version starred James Cagney and Marie Wilson, with a brief appearance by Ronald Reagan. (Courtesy of Drew County Historical Society.)

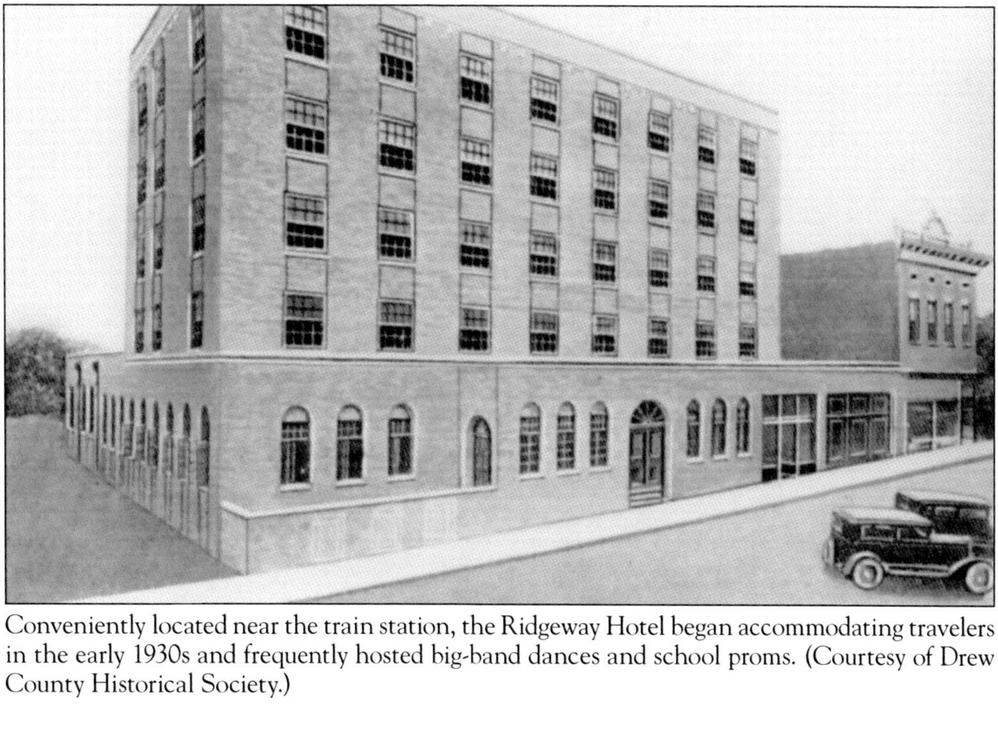

Conveniently located near the train station, the Ridgeway Hotel began accommodating travelers in the early 1930s and frequently hosted big-band dances and school proms. (Courtesy of Drew County Historical Society.)

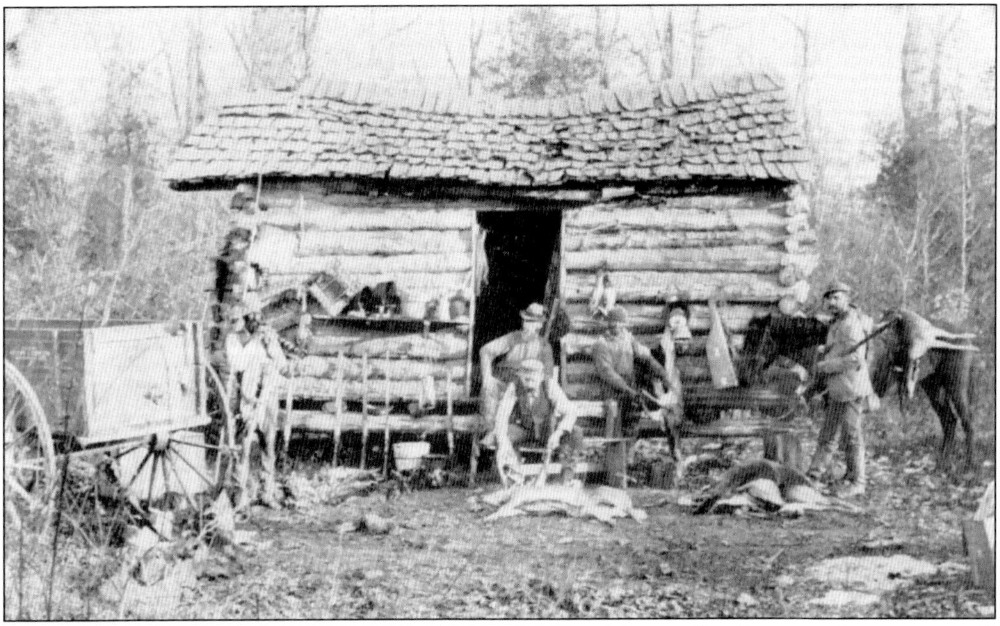

This 19th-century scene shows an early deer camp near Monticello. Big game hunting is still popular in the 21st century. In 2011, the whitetail deer population of Arkansas was an estimated one million animals. (Courtesy of Edgar W. Spencer.)

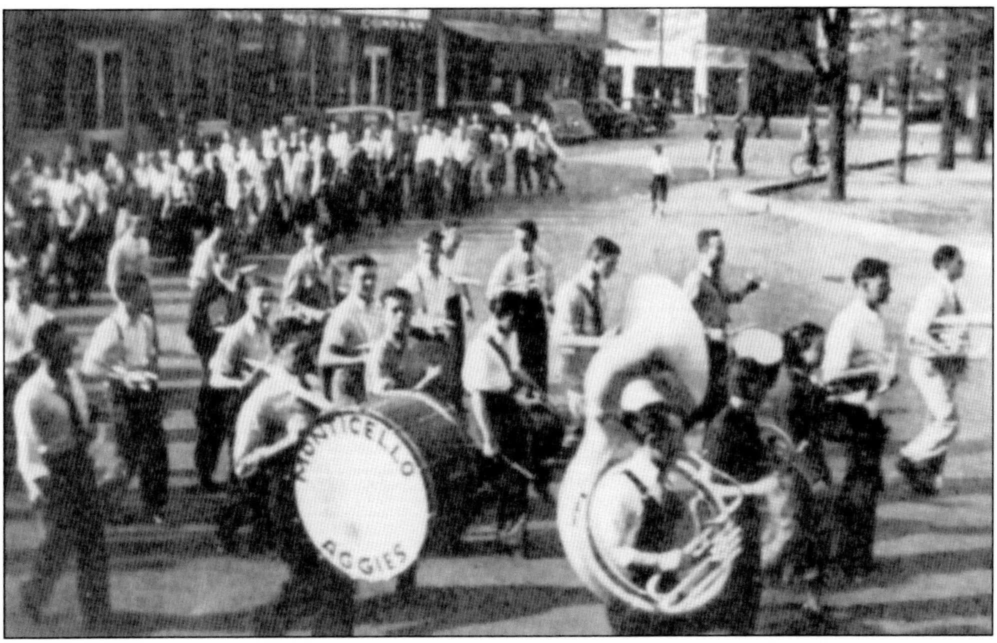

Trying to keep traditions alive and spirits high, the Arkansas A&M College band marches around the square in 1936. (Courtesy of UAM Library.)

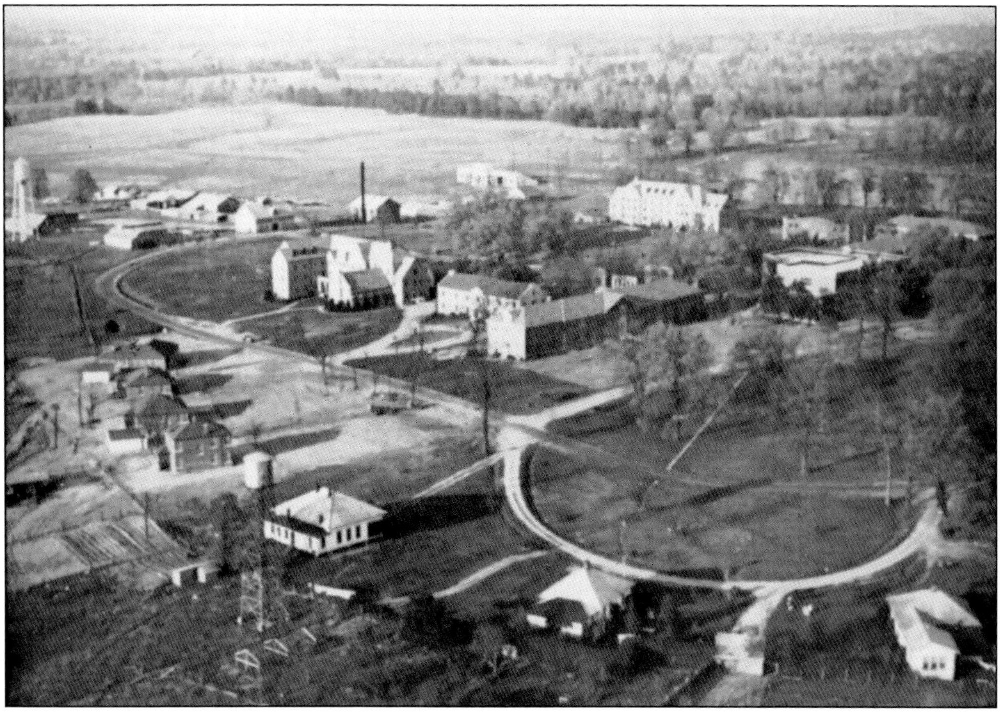

In the center of this 1938 aerial photograph of Arkansas A&M College is the famous huge cherry oak tree. To the right of it is Harris Hall. To the left is Horsfall Hall. The next year would see the construction of the science building (later called the Memorial Classroom Building) as a Public Works Administration project. (Courtesy of UAM Library.)

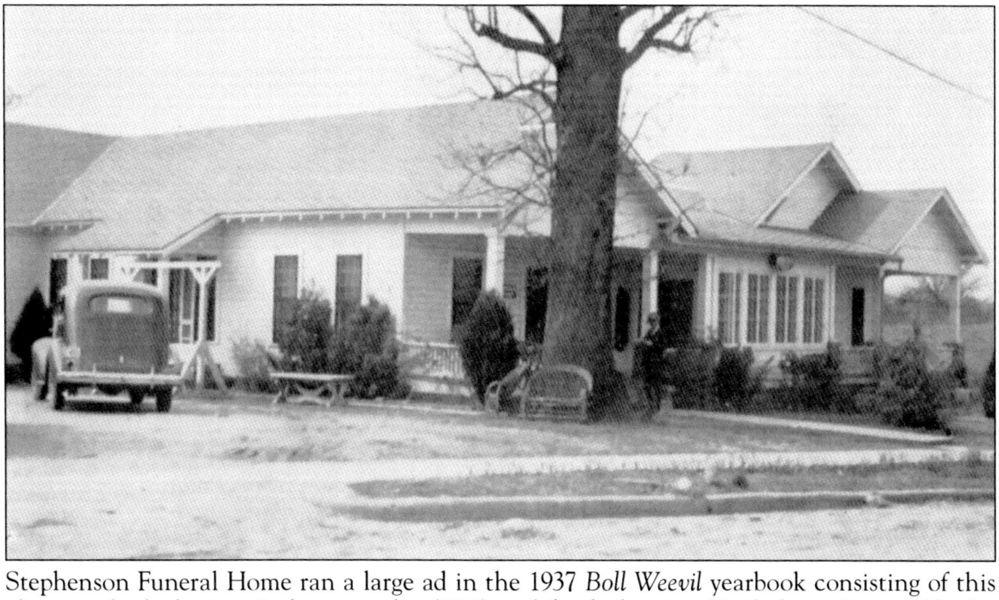

Stephenson Funeral Home ran a large ad in the 1937 *Boll Weevil* yearbook consisting of this photograph, the business's phone number ("71"), and the declaration "Ambulance Service." In the 1930s, Monticellonians had the opportunity to join the Monticello Burial Association, sponsored by Stephenson Funeral Home. For annual dues, citizens could be guaranteed certain basic services in the event that they passed away while active members. (Courtesy of UAM Library.)

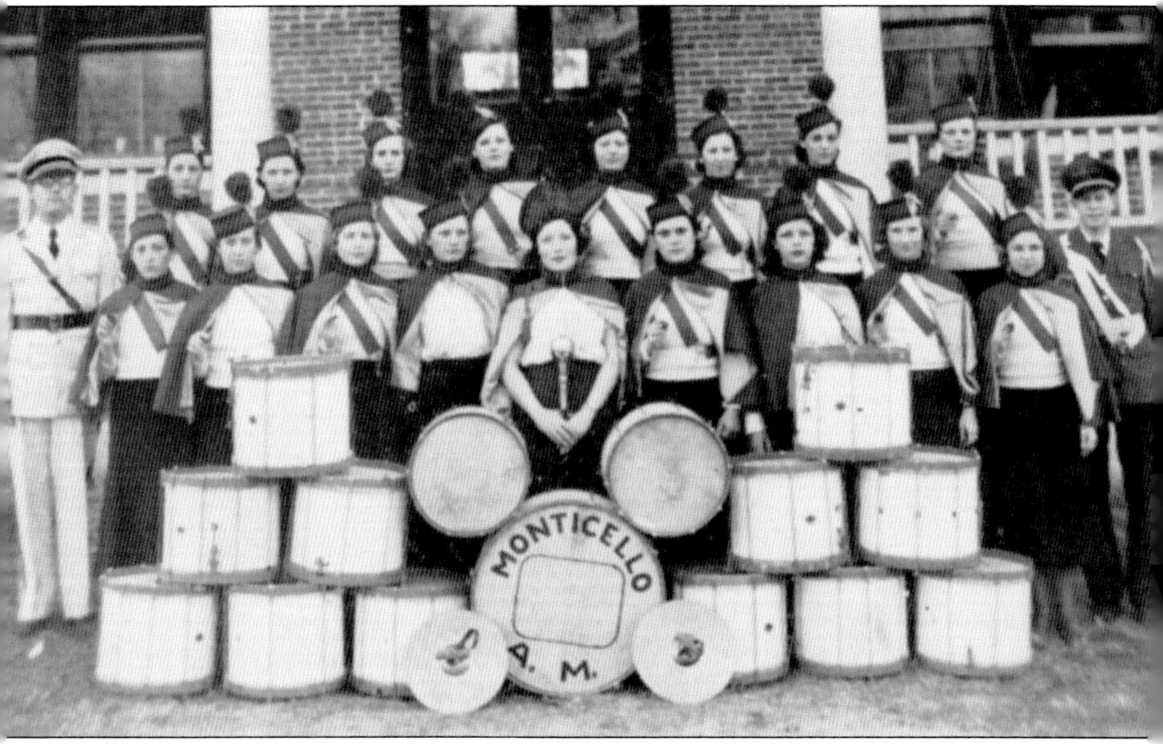

Lee O. Wallick is pictured here at far left, in his white uniform, with the 1933 Girls' Drum Corps of Arkansas A&M College. A prolific band builder, Wallick started a number of school and town bands throughout southern Arkansas, but his longest stint of service was from 1924 to 1951 at Arkansas A&M College. In 1935, while serving as a volunteer firefighter, Wallick lost his eyesight when a board in a burning building fell and struck him in the head. However, the disability had no apparent effect on his energy or ability to direct bands. Even after developing a heart condition and retiring from Arkansas A&M, he continued to direct the Monticello High School Band, operate his chain of Wallick Music Stores, and run the summer Dixie Music Camps, which were created in 1938 to benefit high school musicians and were held on the Arkansas A&M campus. (Courtesy of UAM Library.)

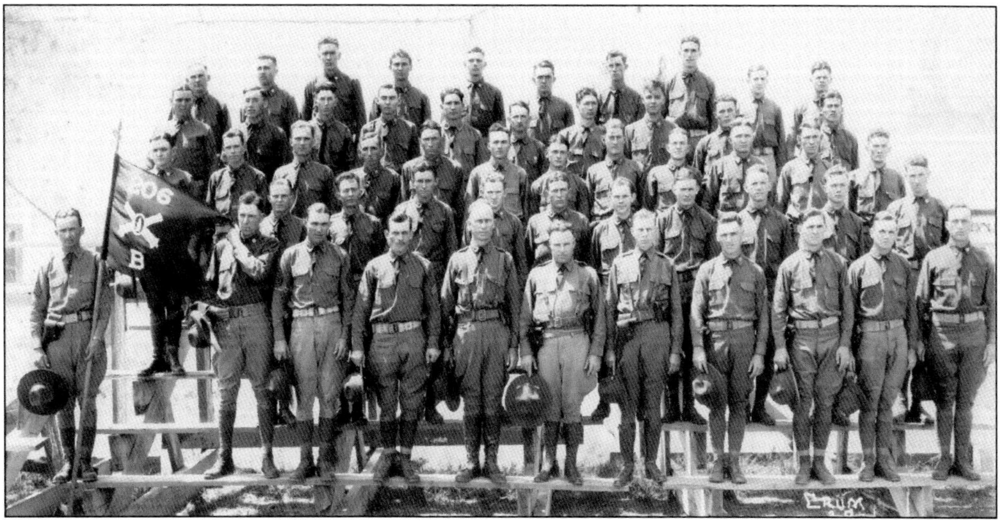

This picture from the 1930s shows the soldiers of the National Guard Unit Battery B of the 206th Coast Artillery. The battery was called to active duty and inducted into the US Army on January 6, 1941. (Courtesy UAM Library.)

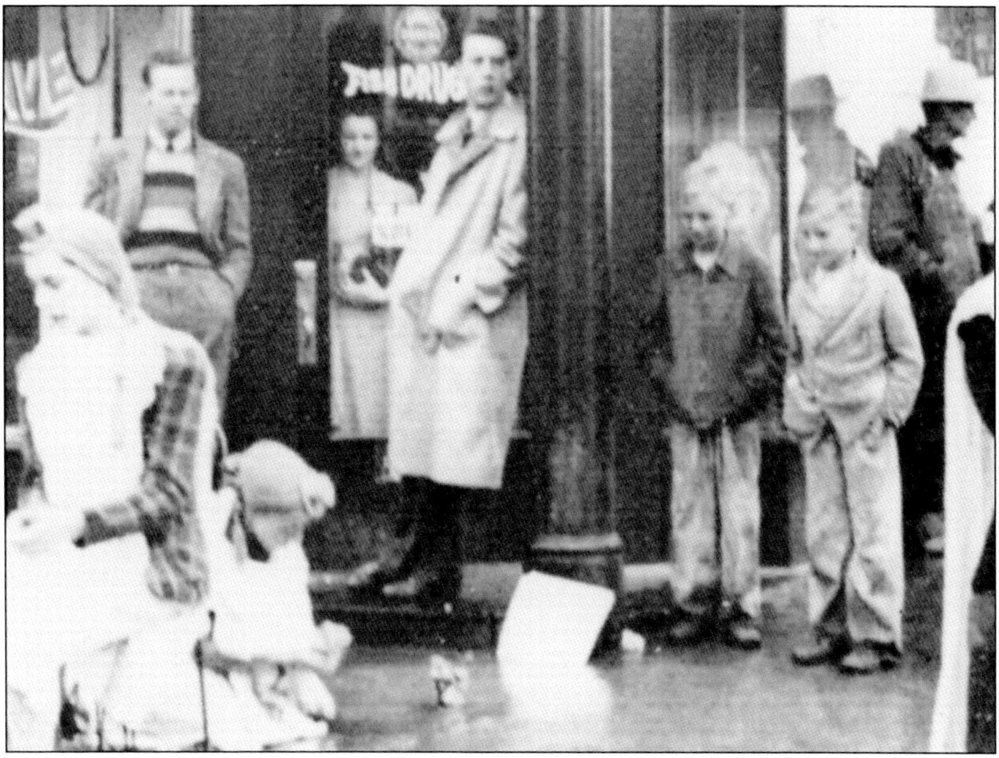

Children play a game in front of the Fish Drug Store just off the square in 1941. In addition to pharmaceuticals, the store sold veterinary supplies, gifts, and beauty aids. Many couples courted at the soda fountain. George and Jessie Fish ran the store from 1918 to around 1950. Their oldest daughter, Thelma Fish Giessen, worked in the store and was a member of the Arkansas A&M College class of 1934. Other college students, including Paul "Bear" Bryant, who became a legendary coach at the University of Alabama, got their start through employment at the store. (Courtesy UAM Library.)

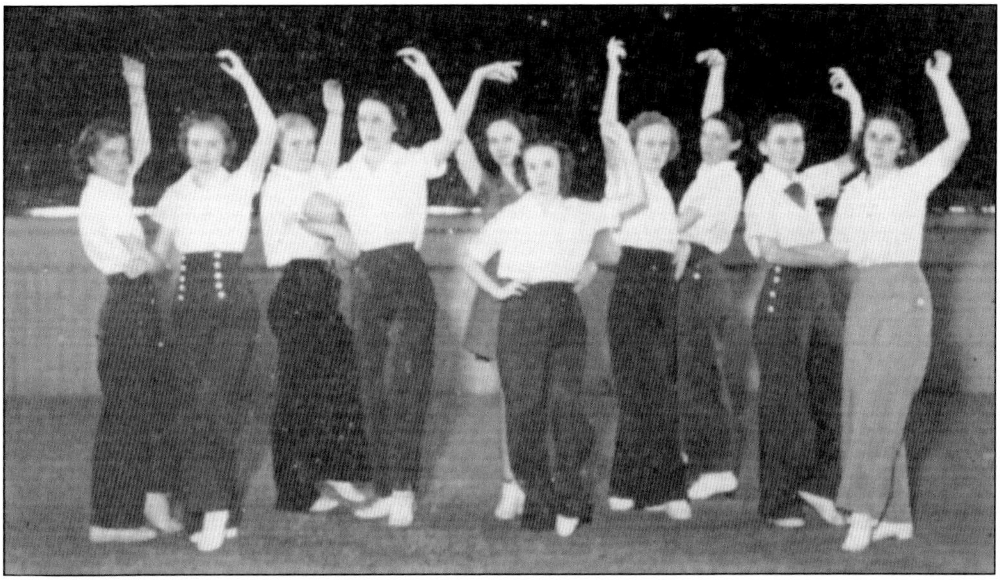

According to the 1939 yearbook, the Department of Physical Education at Arkansas A&M College instituted "new theory and teacher training courses" that year. (Courtesy of UAM Library.)

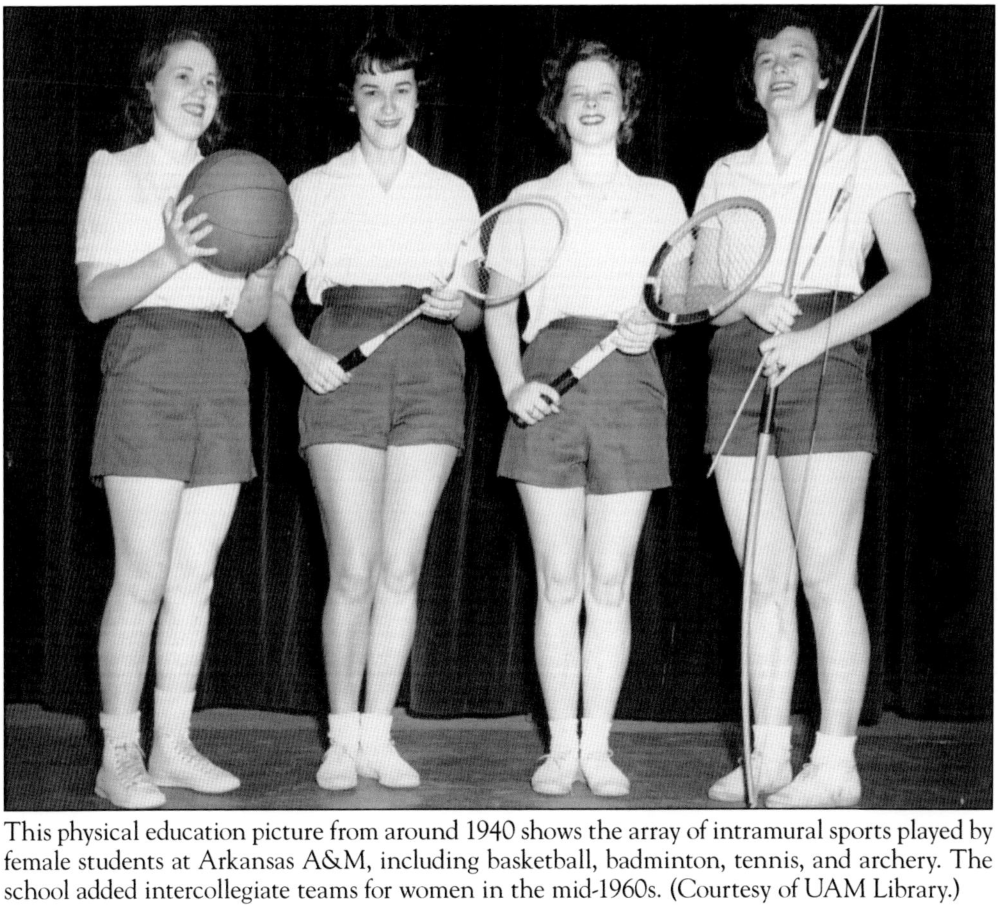

This physical education picture from around 1940 shows the array of intramural sports played by female students at Arkansas A&M, including basketball, badminton, tennis, and archery. The school added intercollegiate teams for women in the mid-1960s. (Courtesy of UAM Library.)

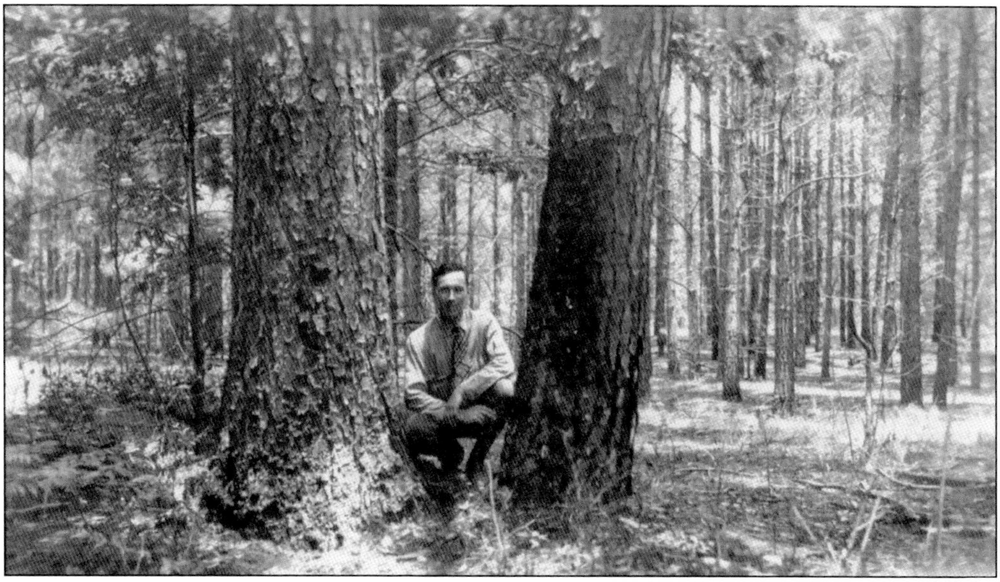

The forestry industry has long been critical to the economy of southeast Arkansas. Leslie K. Pomeroy and Eugene P. Connor pioneered the method of selective cutting, in which certain trees are selected for logging and others allowed to grow for future harvesting. L.K. Pomeroy is pictured between two trees selected for harvesting in 1929. (Courtesy of Michael Pomeroy.)

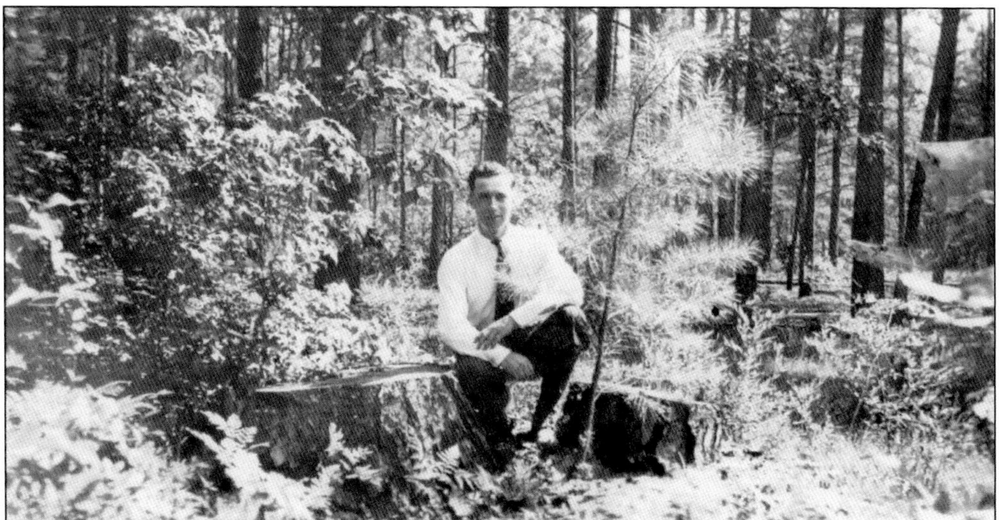

Here, L.K. Pomeroy is pictured in the same location five years later. The trees in the background have increased in size and young pine and oak trees have seeded naturally around the stumps of the original trees. (Courtesy of Michael Pomeroy.)

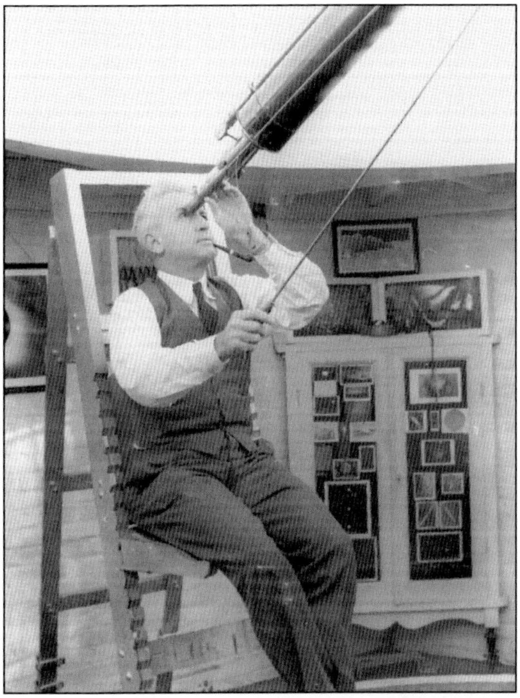

Adrian Williamson Jr., a Monticello attorney, is pictured here in 1938 gazing through his refracting telescope at the observatory he built on his property. From about 1933 to 1939, Williamson's friend L.K. Pomeroy shared his passion for stargazing and joined him on many occasions to record stellar observations in a log. (Courtesy of Michael Pomeroy.)

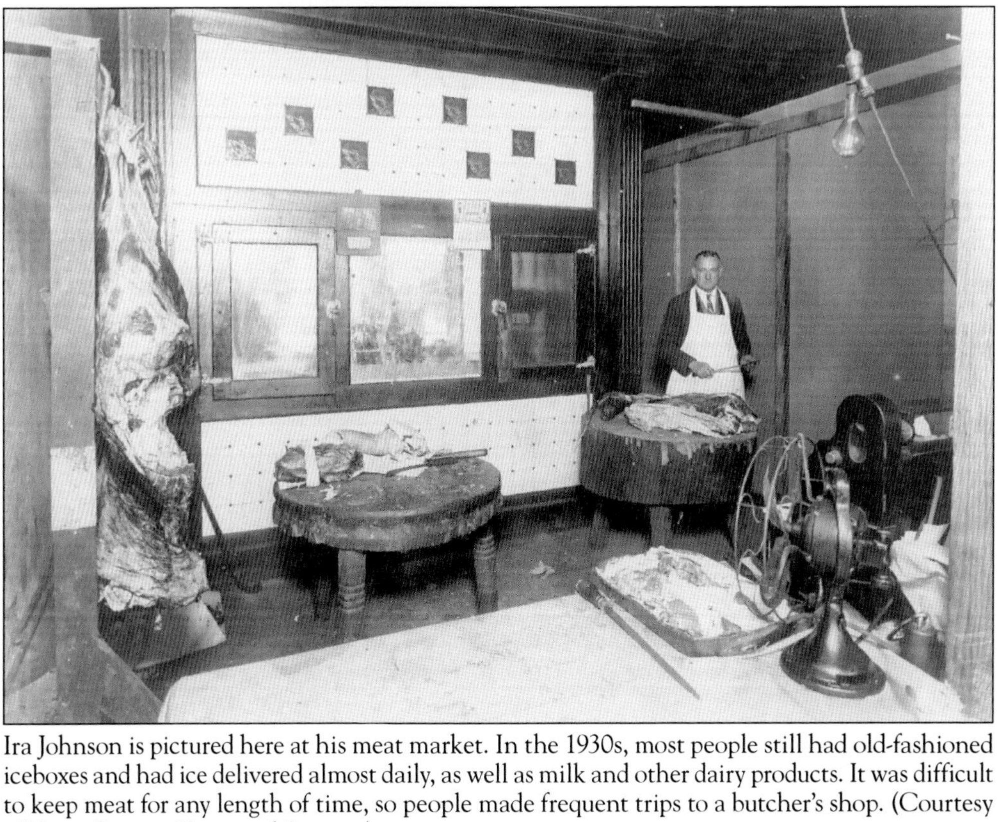

Ira Johnson is pictured here at his meat market. In the 1930s, most people still had old-fashioned iceboxes and had ice delivered almost daily, as well as milk and other dairy products. It was difficult to keep meat for any length of time, so people made frequent trips to a butcher's shop. (Courtesy of Drew County Historical Society.)

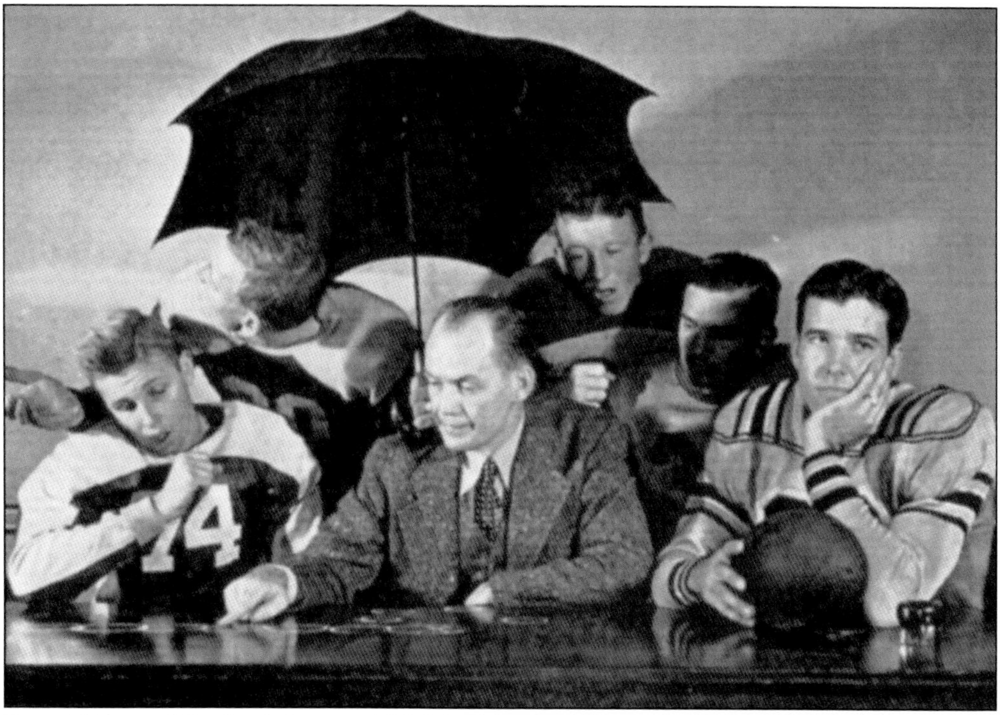

From 1939 to 1941, the Arkansas A&M College football team, the Wandering Weevils, were nationally famous—but not because they won a lot of games. In fact, they won only three of 33, but their coach, Stewart A. Ferguson, did not care. He abhorred "pressure" football and the prevailing ideology of winning at any cost. Ferguson envisioned a program in which players played for fun. The Weevils traveled all over America, putting over 40,000 miles on their green and white bus as they entertained crowds with gymnastics and slapstick comedy. They were known as "the Marx Brothers of Football." Coach Ferguson was quoted as saying, "We'll trade a laugh for a touchdown anytime." Ironically, this losing football team was one of the few American small-college teams that made money during the Great Depression. (Both, courtesy of UAM Library.)

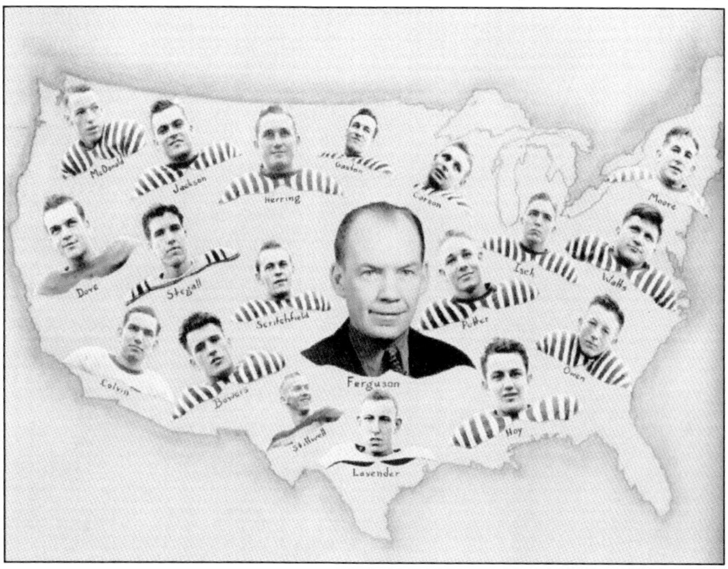

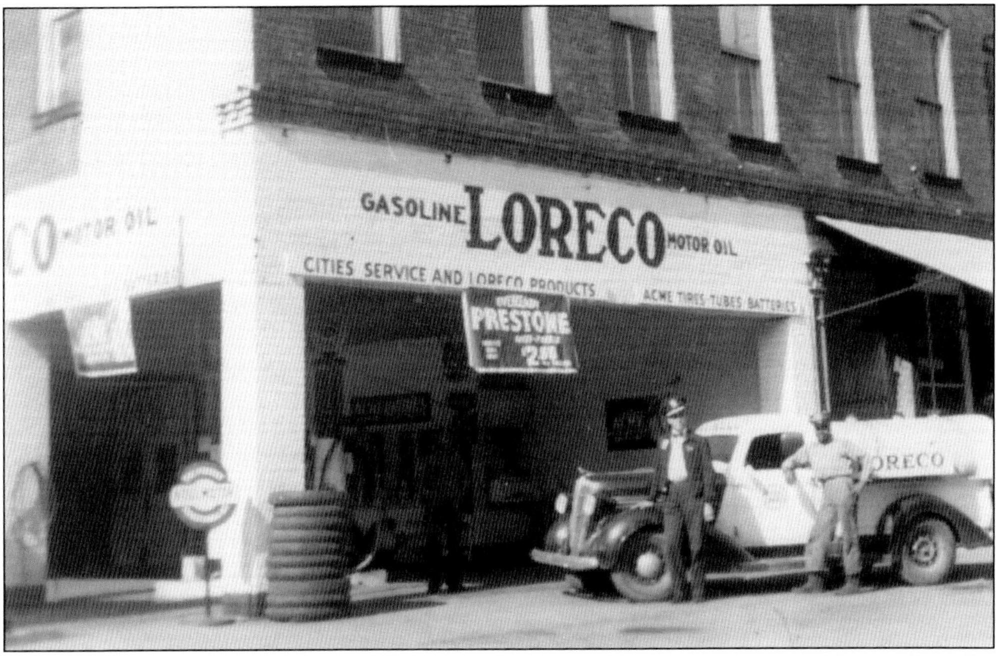

This photograph from the late 1930s shows Hellum Owen's service station, located on the corner of West McCloy and Church Streets. LORECO was a contraction of Louisiana Refining Company, which was eventually bought out by Cities Service. In 1939, Owen sold the service station to Wilbur White, who renamed it City Service Company. (Courtesy of Drew County Historical Society.)

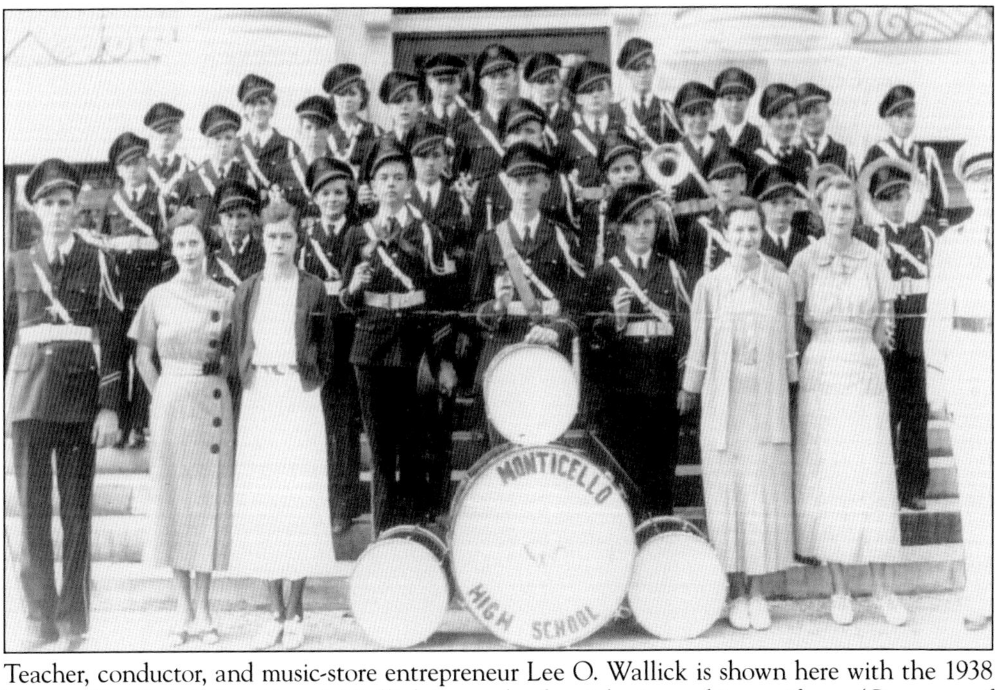

Teacher, conductor, and music-store entrepreneur Lee O. Wallick is shown here with the 1938 Monticello High School band. Wallick is on the far right in a white uniform. (Courtesy of Bob Boyd.)

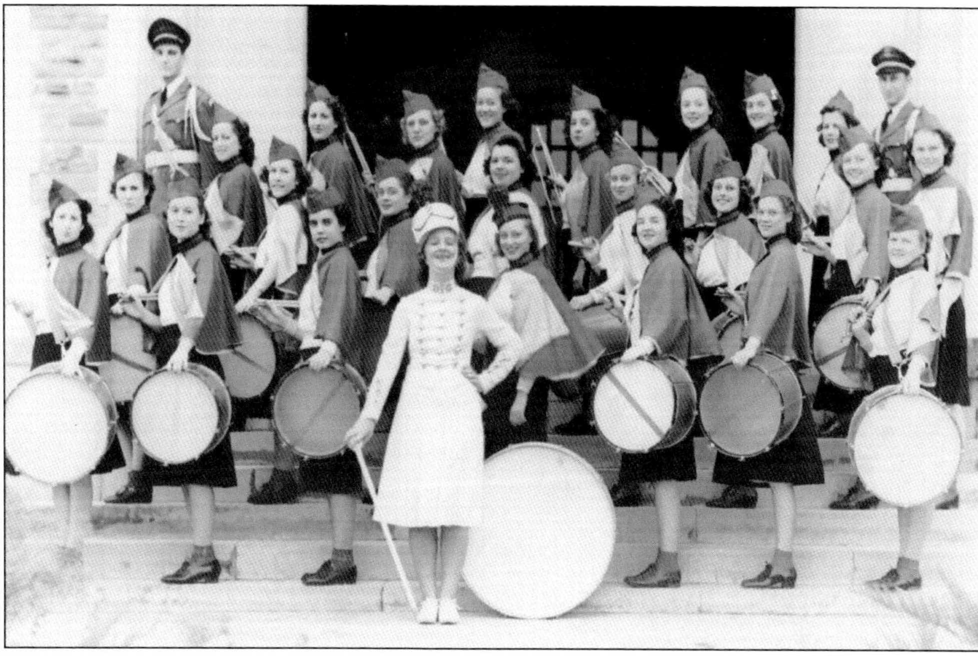

According to the Arkansas A&M yearbook, the band and the Girls' Drum and Bugle Corps were much in demand, playing in a number of towns throughout Arkansas and Mississippi. Pictured here is the 1939 Girls' Drum and Bugle Corps. (Courtesy of UAM Library.)

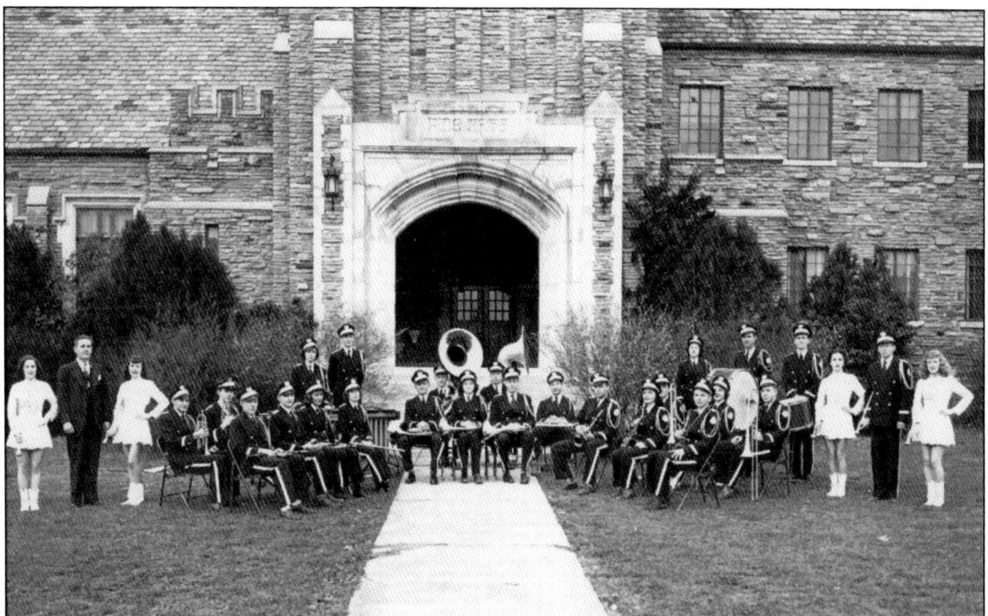

While the nationally famous Wandering Weevils were losing football games and winning laughs, the Arkansas A&M College concert band provided more refined entertainment to the college and community. The band performed twice a month, with different programs that varied from classical to popular music. The A&M concert band of 1940, directed by Lee O. Wallick, is pictured here. (Courtesy of UAM Library.)

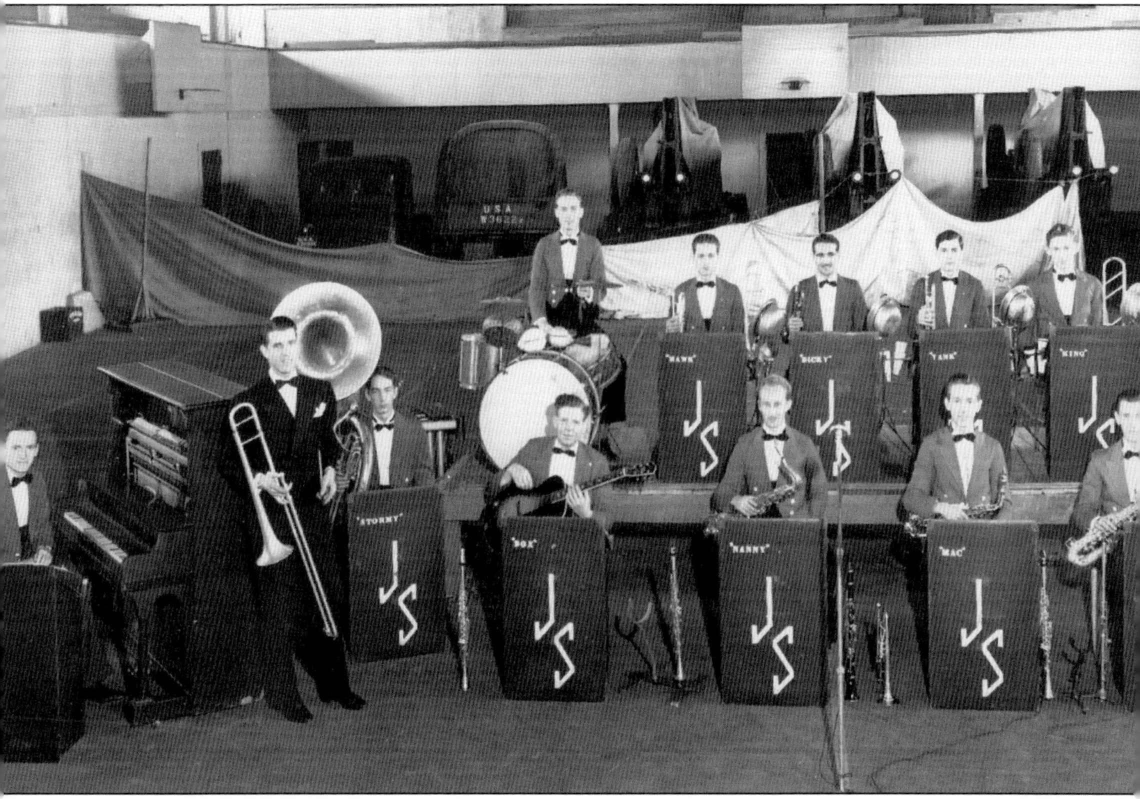

While the 1920s were known as the age of jazz, swing became the popular music of the 1930s. Big bands—like those of Tommy Dorsey, Duke Ellington, and Glenn Miller—were the rage. Arkansas A&M College's impressive and diverse music program included the concert band, the Girls' Drum and Bugle Corp, the marching band, and even a dance band. First known as the Southerners Dance Band, this group of swingsters later became known as the Collegians. Their director, Jack Shelton, put his name on their trailer and on each musician's music stand. Arkansas A&M's band program was suspended after the 1941–1942 school year because of World War II. However, music did not entirely disappear from campus. Many of the trainees in the Navy's V-12 program were accomplished musicians and Lee O. Wallick, the college's band director, organized them for occasional concerts. The band roster frequently changed during the war because of the soldiers' constant rotation in and out of the lineup. Wallick resumed the college's band program in the 1945–1946 school year. (Courtesy of UAM Library.)

Four

The World at War

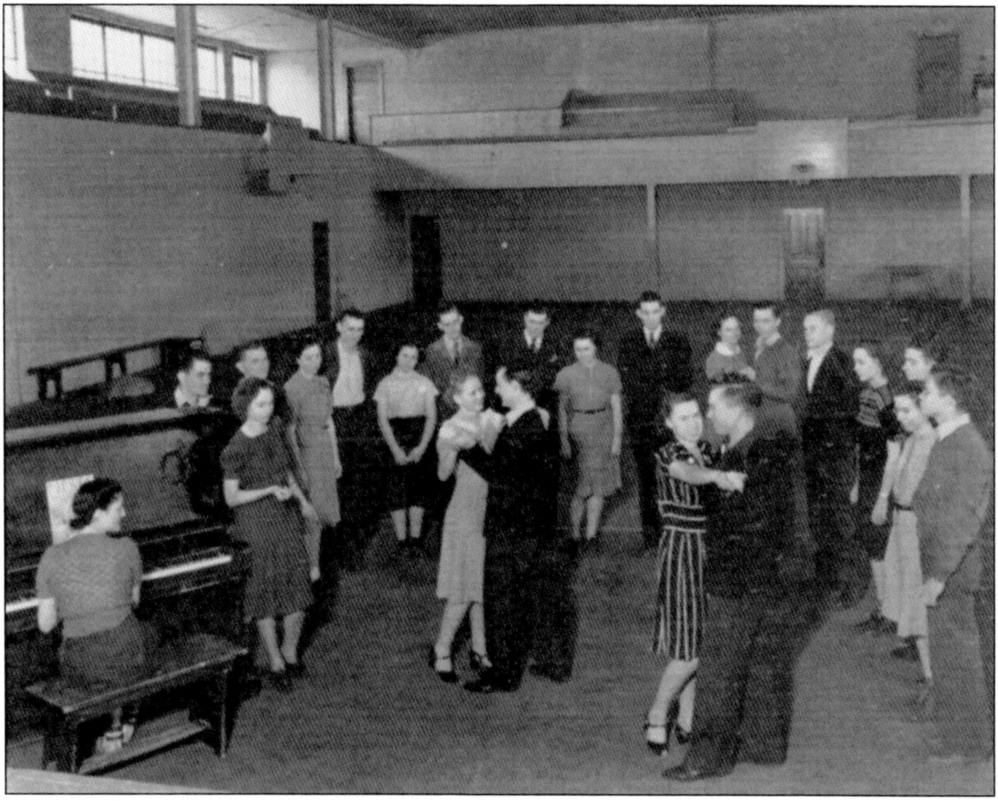

Peggy Wallick instructs Arkansas A&M students in ballroom dancing in 1940. That year, the folk dance group attended the College Folk Festival at Henderson in Arkadelphia. The innocence of this image is a reminder of how far Monticellonians were removed from the war raging in Europe. France was among the countries occupied by Germany in 1940 and England was enduring frequent bombing raids. (Courtesy of UAM Library.)

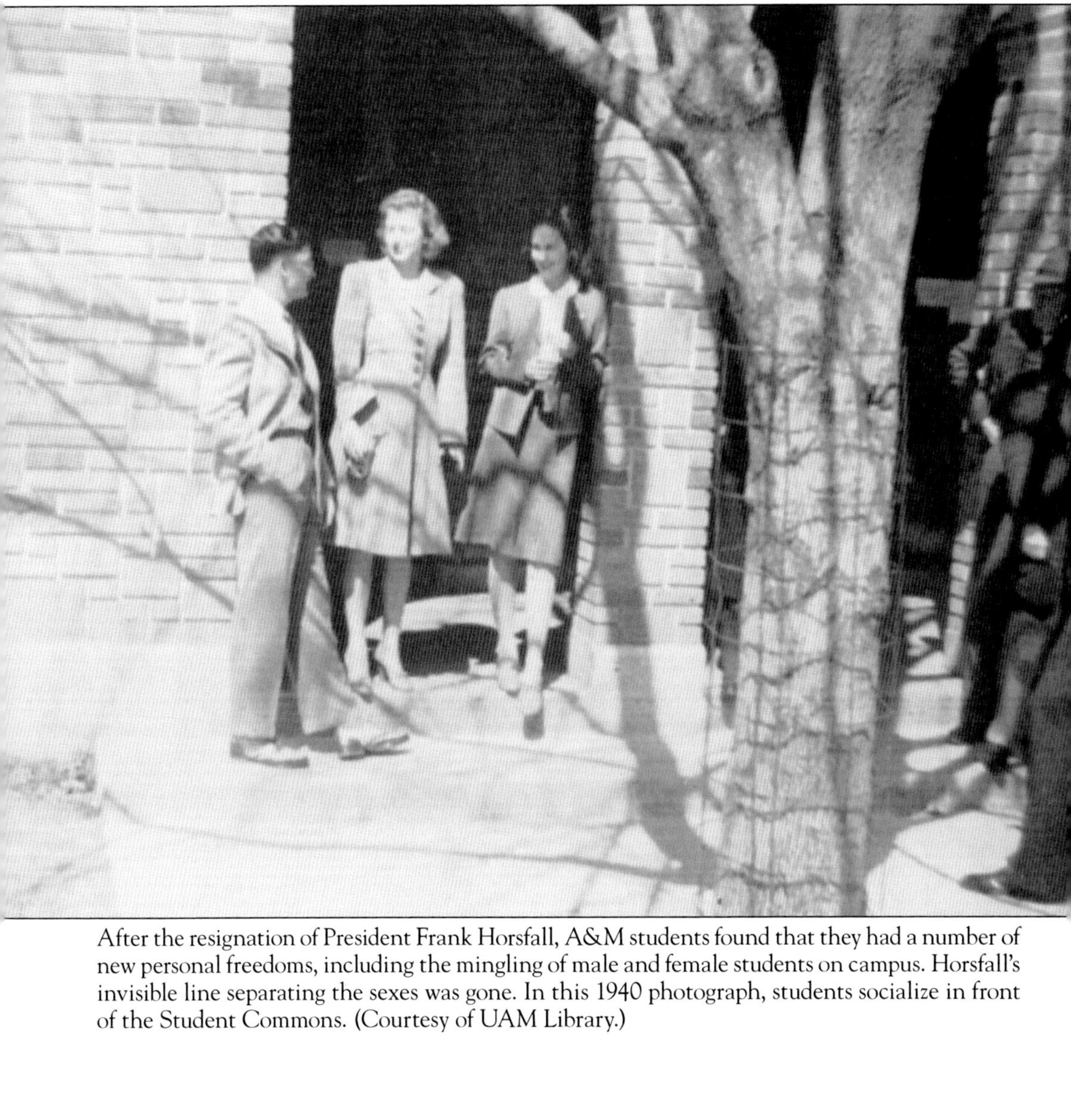

After the resignation of President Frank Horsfall, A&M students found that they had a number of new personal freedoms, including the mingling of male and female students on campus. Horsfall's invisible line separating the sexes was gone. In this 1940 photograph, students socialize in front of the Student Commons. (Courtesy of UAM Library.)

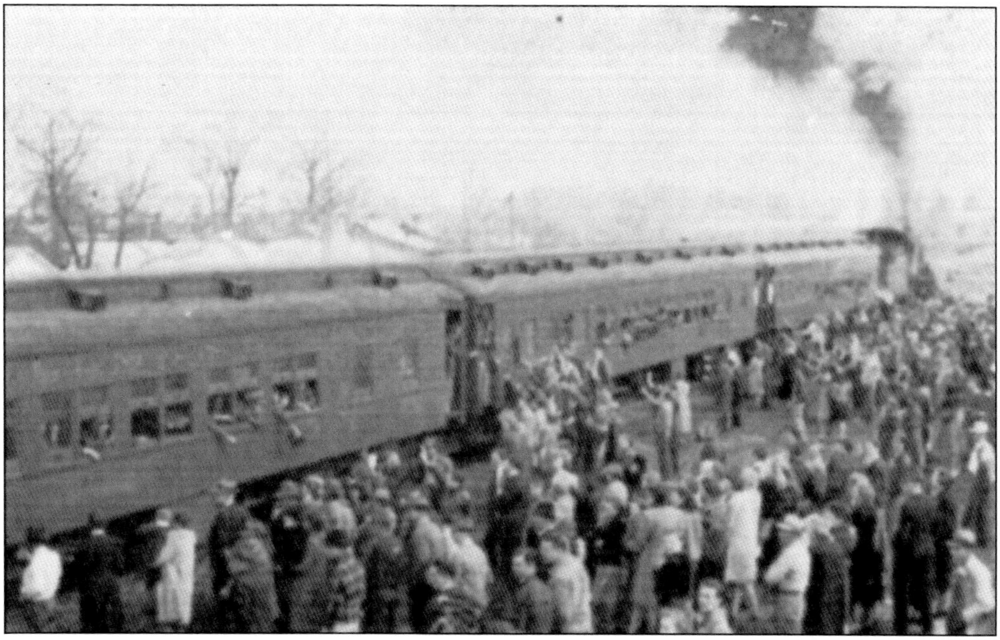

Although automobiles became more affordable and common and more roads were paved throughout the 1920s and 1930s, passenger trains continued to provide a relatively fast and safe means of travel for Monticellonians. This image is from 1941. The trains would soon be crowded with GIs. (Courtesy of UAM Library.)

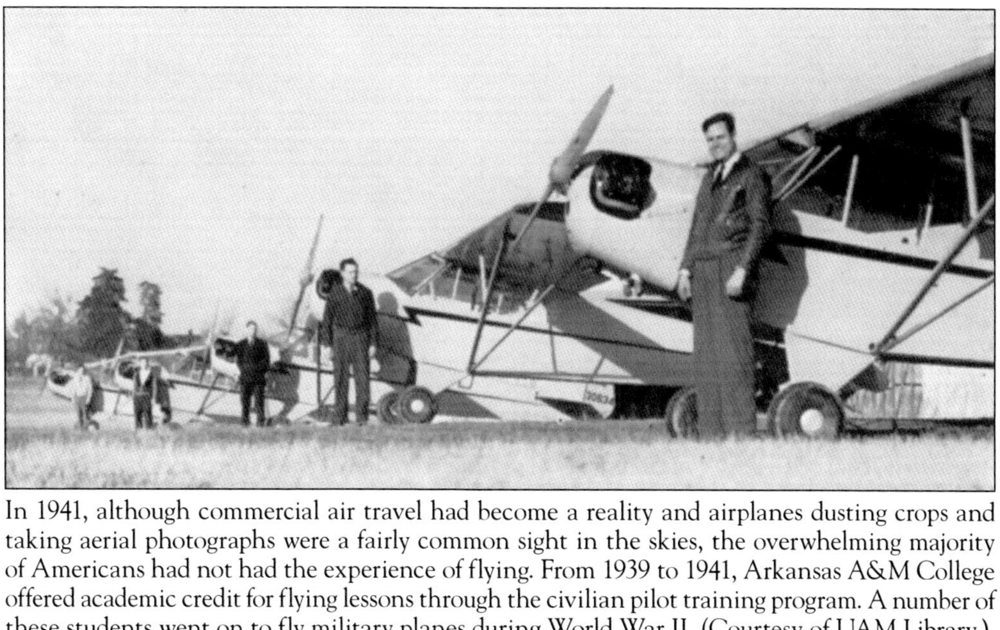

In 1941, although commercial air travel had become a reality and airplanes dusting crops and taking aerial photographs were a fairly common sight in the skies, the overwhelming majority of Americans had not had the experience of flying. From 1939 to 1941, Arkansas A&M College offered academic credit for flying lessons through the civilian pilot training program. A number of these students went on to fly military planes during World War II. (Courtesy of UAM Library.)

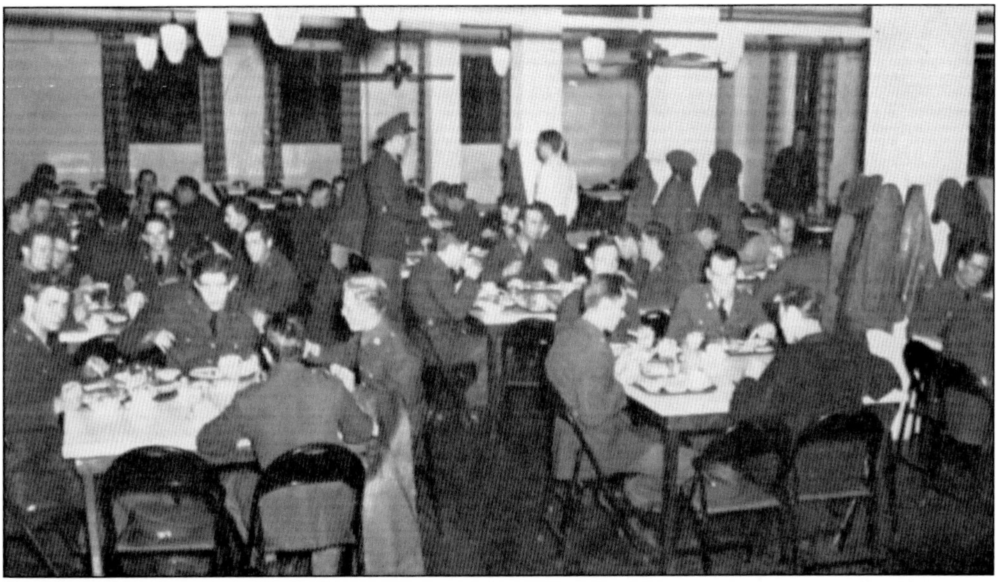

During World War II, it was common to see men in Army, Navy, and Marine uniforms on the campus of Arkansas A&M College and in town. The Navy's V-12 program trained officers on campus, and Monticello hosted a prisoner-of-war camp for Italian soldiers. The nearby community of Jerome (originally known as Blissville) was the site of a Japanese American internment camp. In this photograph, soldiers have a meal in the college's cafeteria. (Courtesy of UAM Library.)

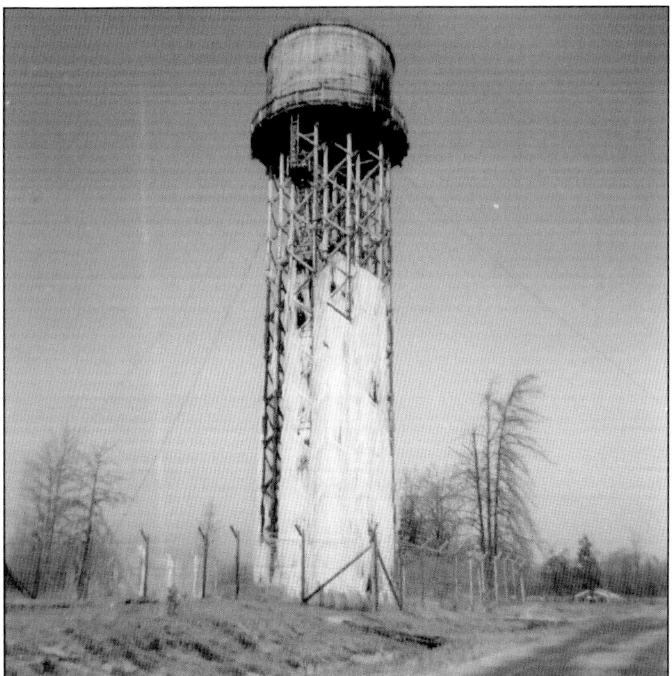

During the cold winter days of late December 1943 or early January 1944, this water tower leaked, forming cascades of frozen water down its base. As war time rations made finding metal to construct the tower difficult, the engineers built the tower out of wood. That may have contributed to its tendency to leak. The water tower serviced the Italian prisoner-of-war camp near Monticello. (Photograph taken by Ed Pomeroy; Courtesy of Michael Pomeroy.)

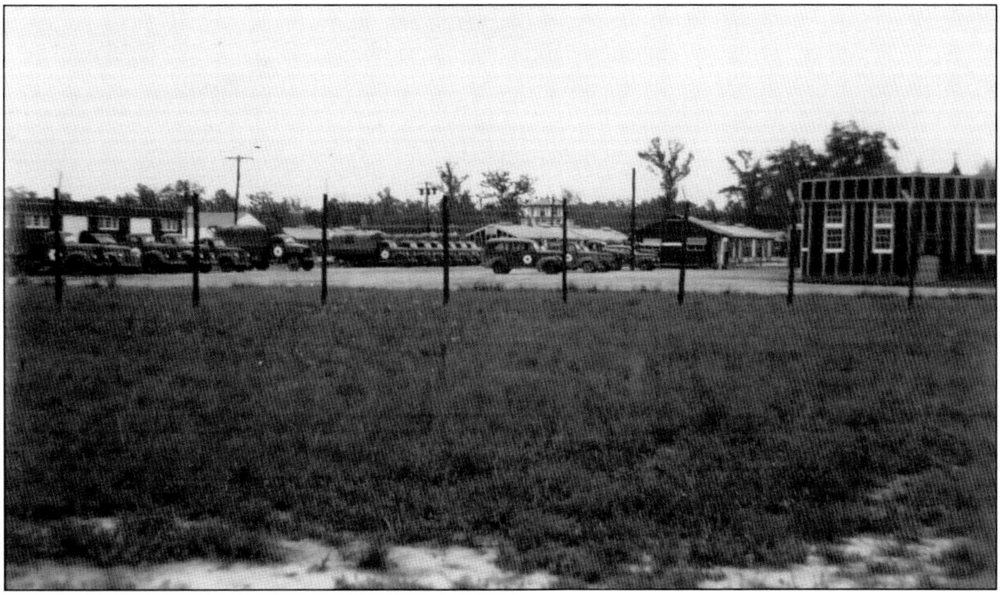

Camp Monticello incarcerated Italian prisoners during World War II. Prisoner-of-war camps were established in the United States largely in response to a British request that America help alleviate the POW housing shortage in Great Britain and North Africa. About 425,000 Axis troops were shipped to the United States for internment in approximately 500 camps. Arkansas accommodated nearly 23,000 Germans and Italians. POWs were required to work in and around the camp and earned 80¢ a day, with which they could purchase various items such as cigarettes, candy, and beer. Arguably, the standard of living of POWs on American soil exceeded that of many American citizens, who were still recovering from the Great Depression and were now subject to wartime rationing. (Both, photographs by L.K. Pomeroy; courtesy of Michael Pomeroy.)

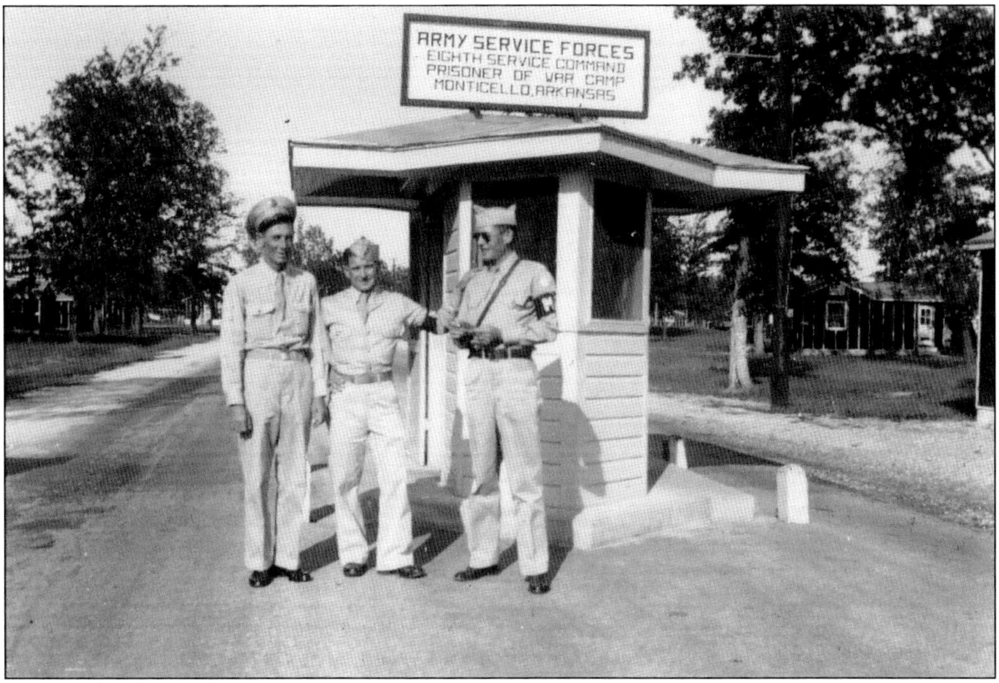

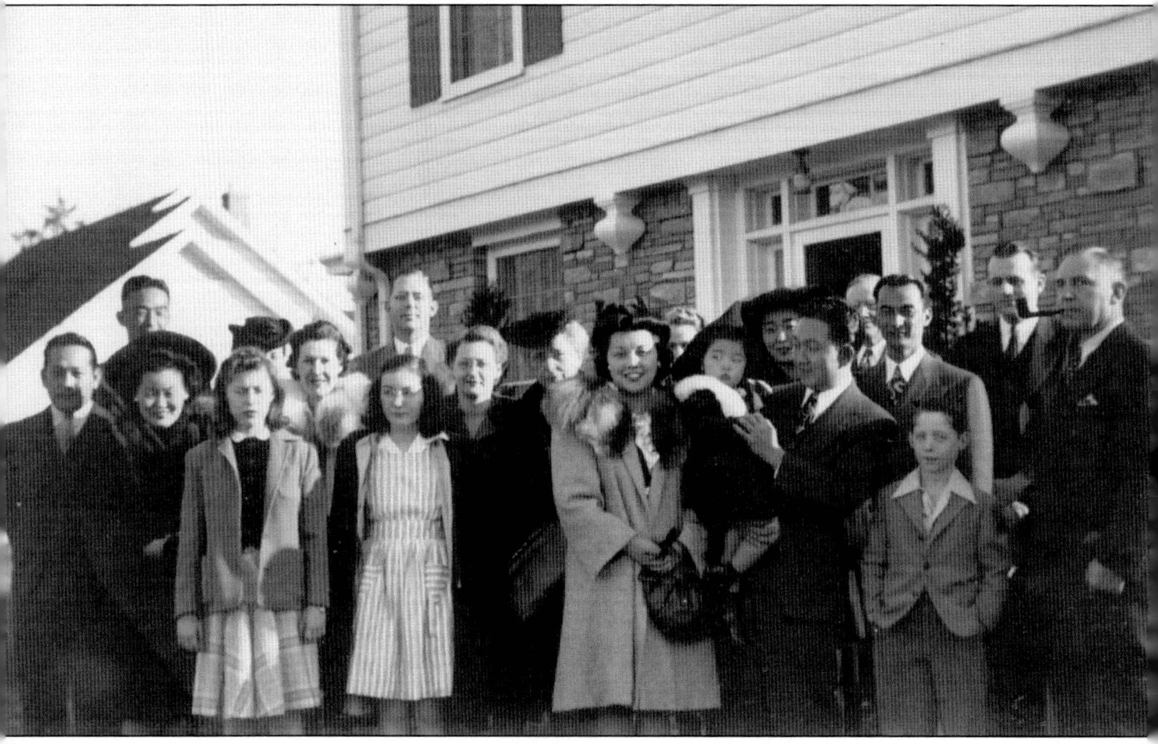

Two years after America's entry into World War II, the Japanese Americans in this 1943 photograph were internees at the Rowher Relocation Center in Desha County. They were on furlough for the day to attend the First Presbyterian Church in Monticello. After church, they lunched at the home of L.K. Pomeroy and his family. Together, the Rowher camp and Jerome Relocation Center in Drew County housed 16,000 Japanese Americans who were forcibly removed from the West Coast in accordance with "military necessity." These two camps were the easternmost relocation facilities in the United States. Jerome was in operation for 634 days, the fewest of any of the camps. Rowher, on the other hand, was in operation the longest of all the camps, from September 18, 1942, until November 30, 1945. (Photograph by L.K. Pomeroy; courtesy of Michael Pomeroy.)

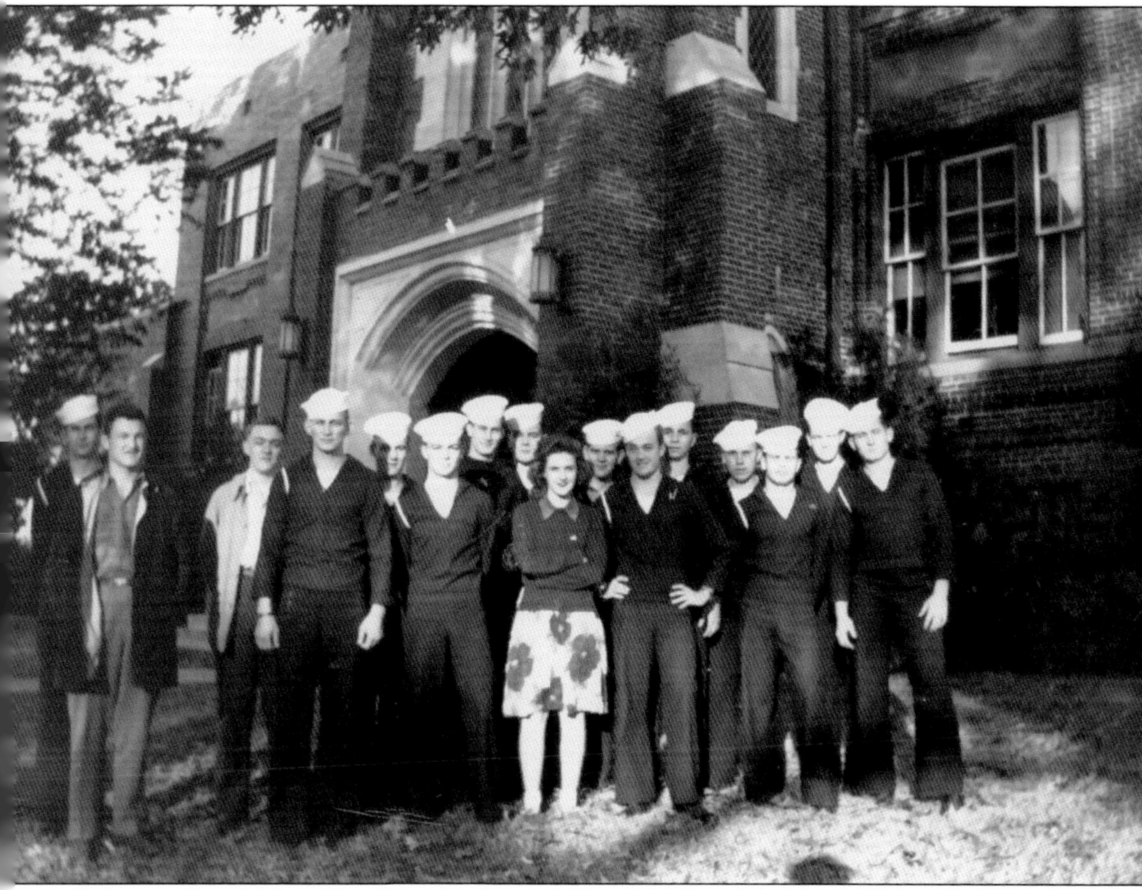

Clara Kennan's English class stands in front of the administration building on the Arkansas A&M campus. From 1943 to 1945, the college hosted the only Navy V-12 unit in the state, which provided training for US Navy and Marine Corps officers. (Courtesy of UAM Library.)

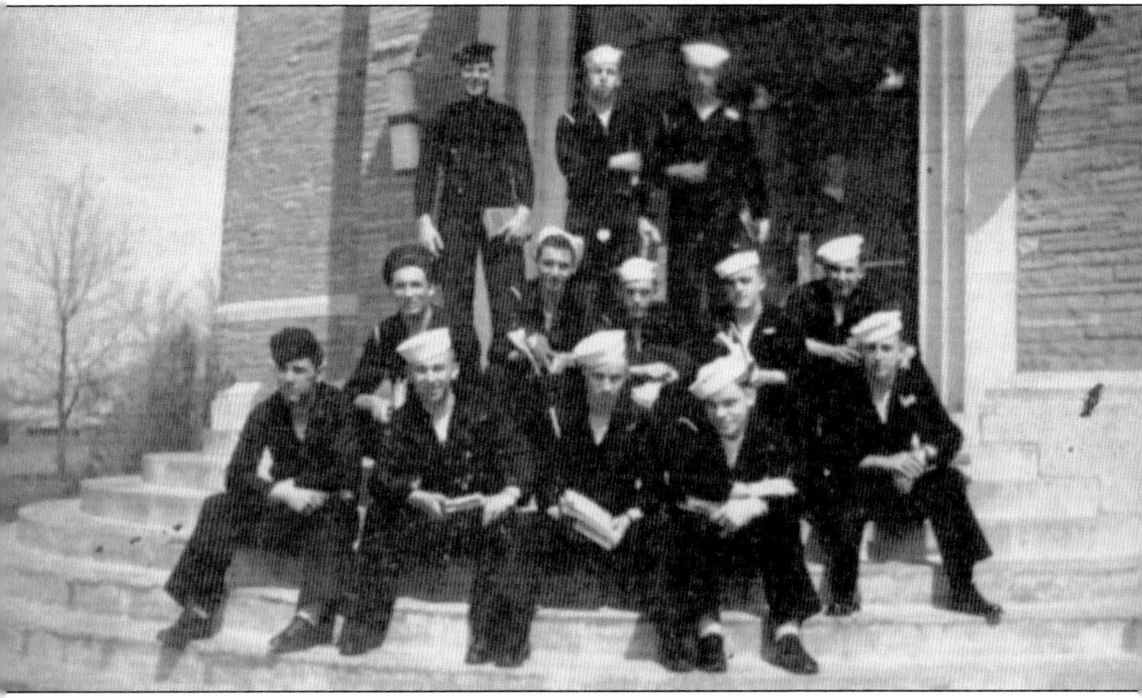

These V-12 trainees sit on the steps of the science building at Arkansas A&M College in early 1945. In Europe, Allied troops were moving into Germany and would soon arrive in Berlin. Germany surrendered on May 8, 1945. The war in the Pacific continued until August 15, when the Japanese unconditionally surrendered. After the war, veterans taking advantage of the educational benefits of the GI Bill flooded colleges like Arkansas A&M. (Courtesy of UAM Library.)

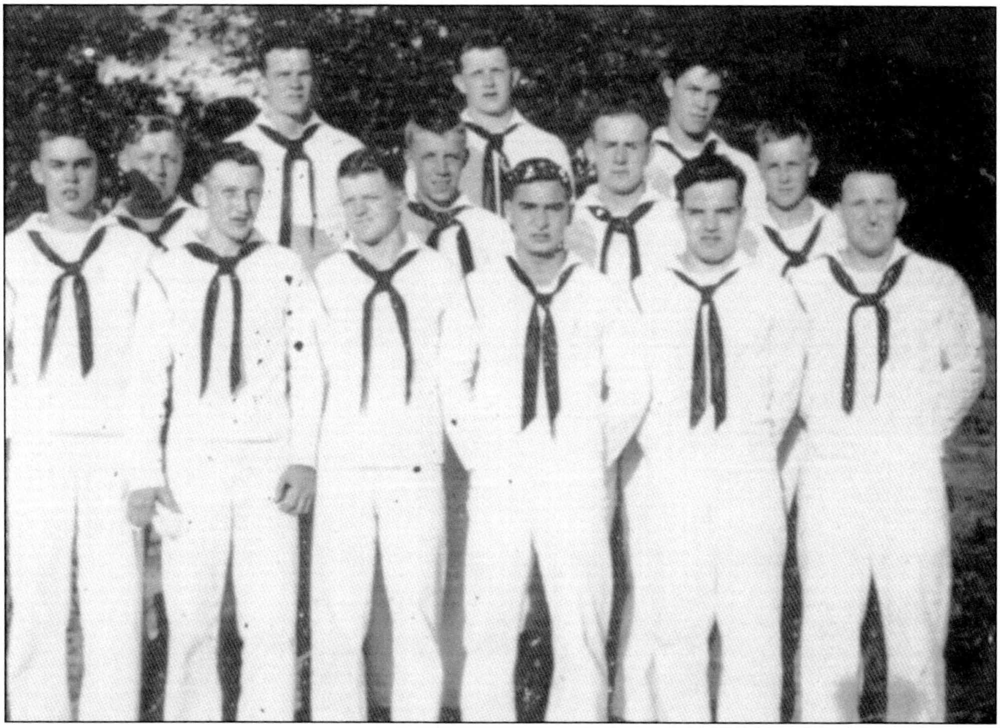

In 1945, with the Germans and the Japanese defeated, these V-12 trainees attending Arkansas A&M College during the 1945–1946 academic year could focus on fighting as members of the school's boxing team. (Courtesy of UAM Library.)

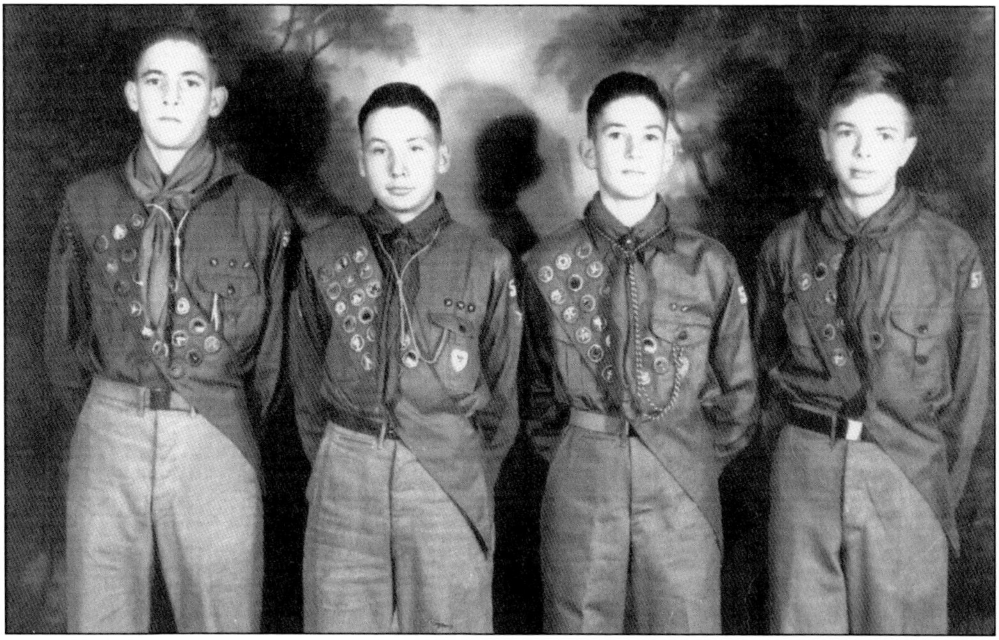

This 1946 photograph shows members of BSA Troop 57, the first Eagle Scouts from Monticello. The Eagle Scouts are, from left to right, Bobby Boyd, Thomas Deal, Edgar Spencer, and Yates Trotter. (Courtesy of Bob Boyd.)

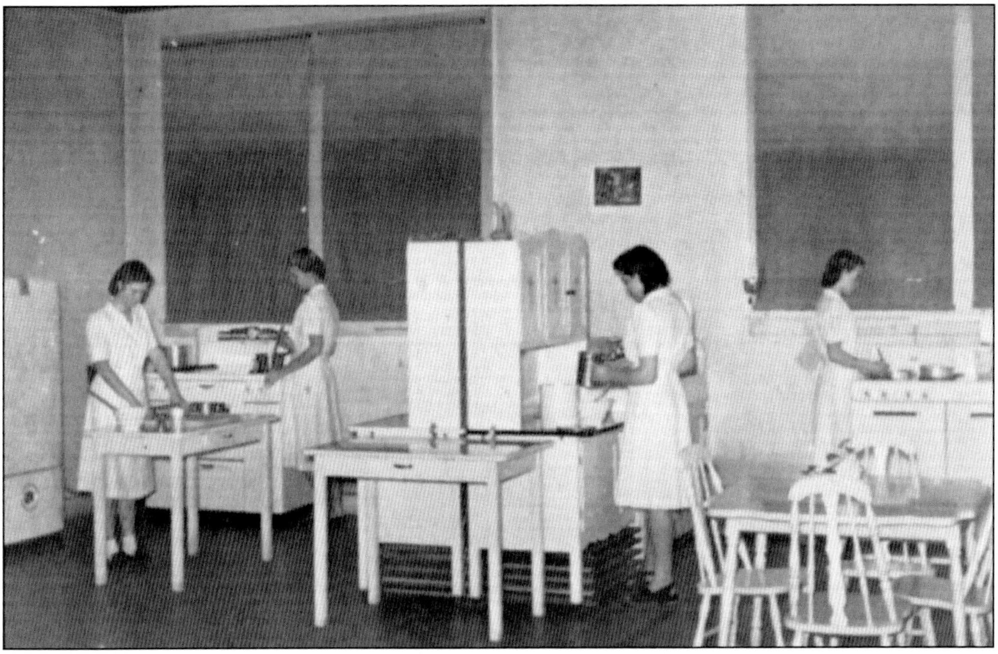

During World War II, women joined the workforce in unprecedented numbers, with many working in war-related industries. Following the end of the war and the return of the men, women returned to the home. In this 1948 photograph, Arkansas A&M College coeds work on their home economics skills. (Courtesy of UAM Library.)

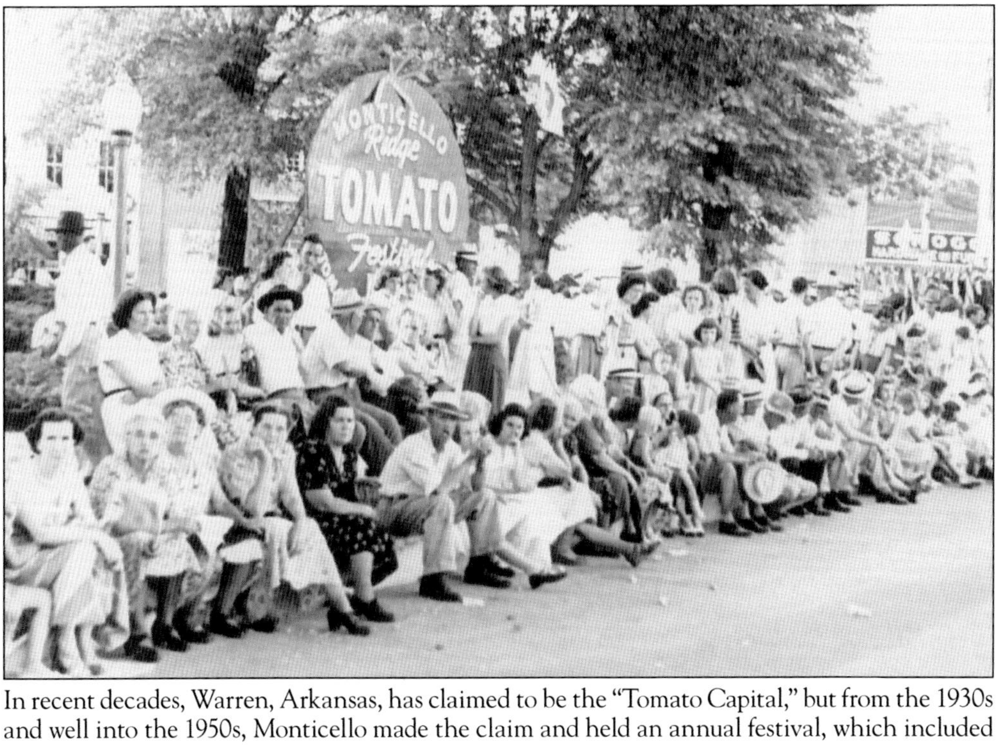

In recent decades, Warren, Arkansas, has claimed to be the "Tomato Capital," but from the 1930s and well into the 1950s, Monticello made the claim and held an annual festival, which included a parade. (Courtesy of Edgar W. Spencer.)

As is the case at UAM in 2011, Arkansas A&M College in the 1940s provided students with the opportunity to learn how to use the latest technologies. Here, a student practices on a business machine. (Courtesy of UAM Library.)

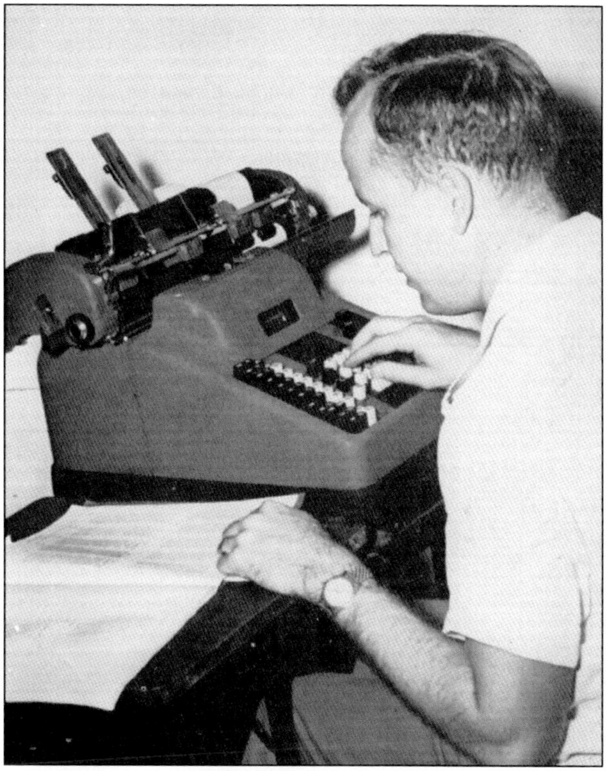

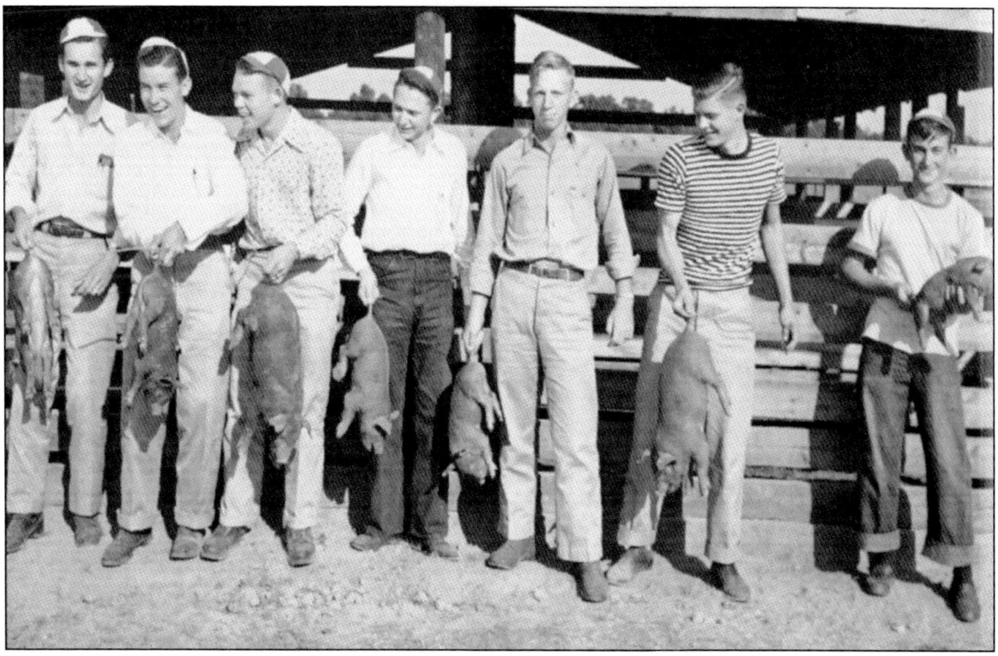

Who ever thought a person could go to college and play with pigs? In 1949, forty years after its founding, Arkansas A&M was still very much in touch with its roots as an agricultural-training school. The freshmen among these agriculture students are easy to identify by their beanies. (Courtesy of UAM Library.)

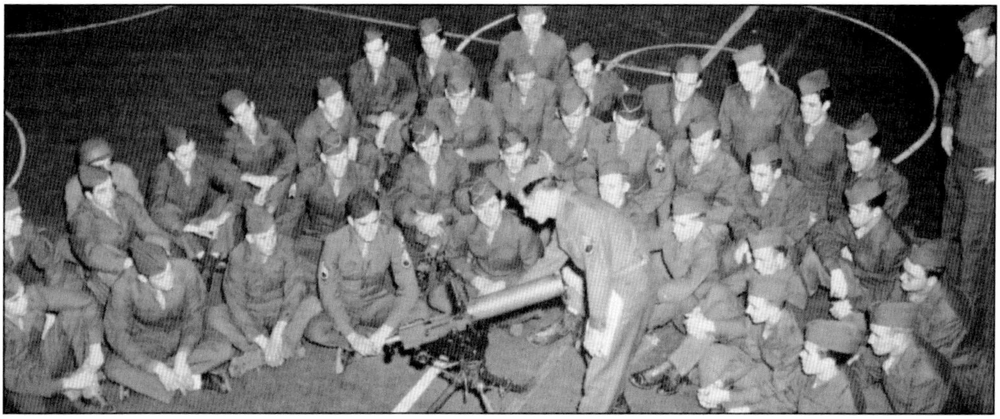

This 1949 photograph of a National Guard class on the campus of Arkansas A&M is a reminder of the Cold War with the Soviet Union, which commenced as soon as World War II ended, and the coming Korean War, which began in 1950. (Courtesy of UAM Library.)

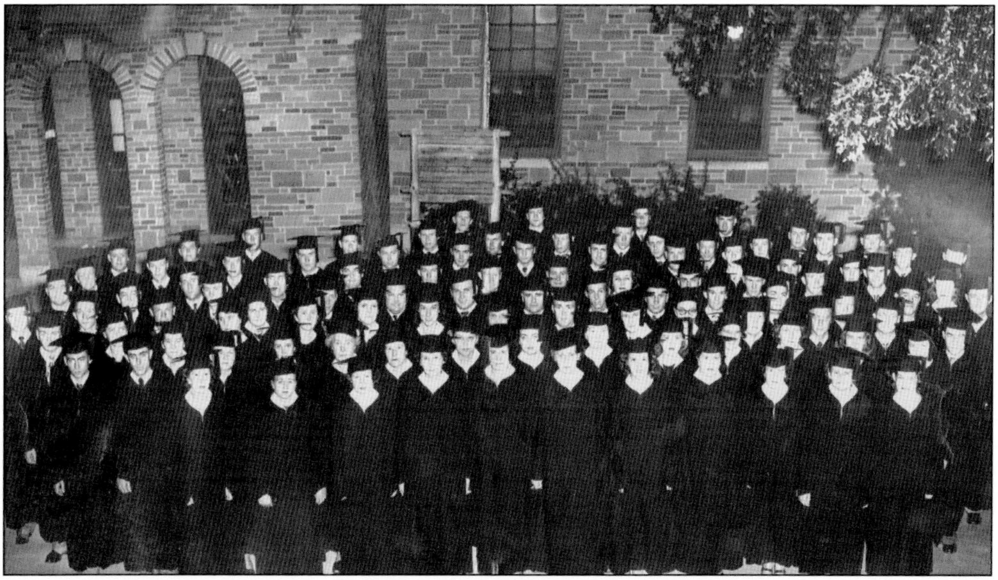

The graduating class of Arkansas A&M is pictured here in 1949. The Student Commons building is in the background. (Courtesy of Bud Bulloch.)

Five

Rock 'n' Roll

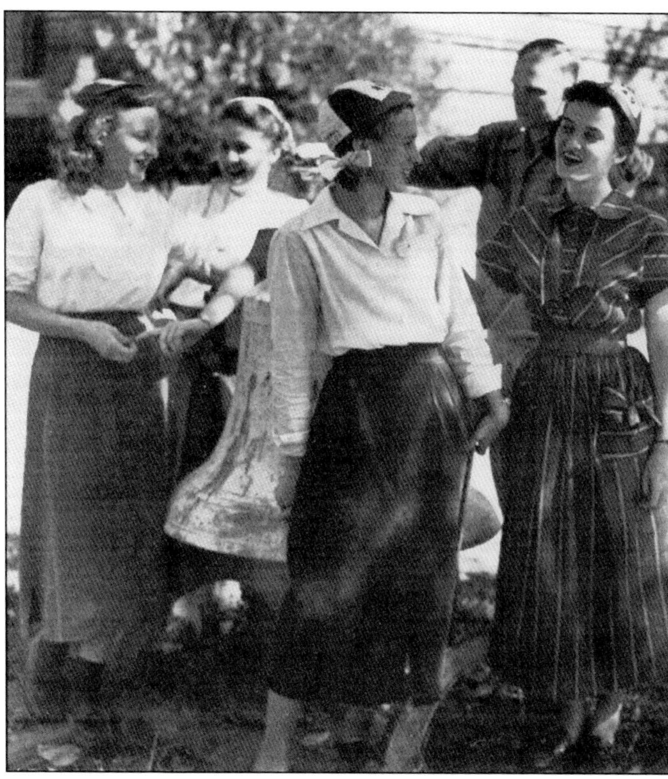

Although beanies were required attire for freshmen at Arkansas A&M in 1950, these students standing by the "French castle" courthouse bell near the administration building show no embarrassment or temerity about being "frosh." (Courtesy of UAM Library.)

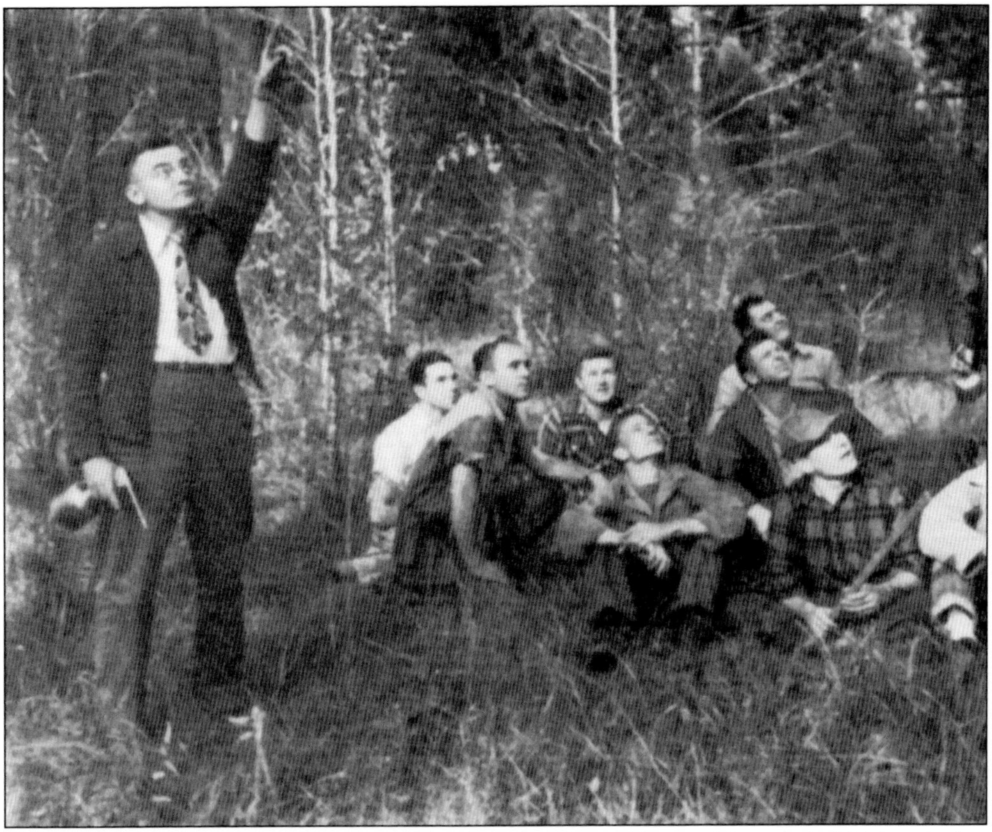

In 1945, Arkansas A&M president Marvin Bankston hired noted forester Henry "Hank" Chamberlin, who established the college's forestry program that eventually evolved into the state's only School of Forestry. This image from 1950 shows Chamberlin in the field with students. (Courtesy of UAM Library.)

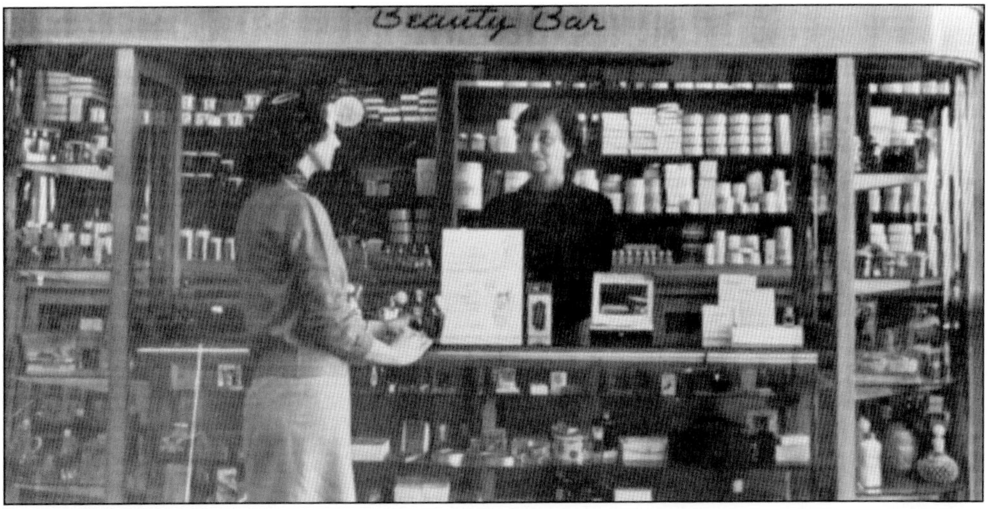

After World War II, America saw unprecedented growth and prosperity in the late 1940s and throughout the 1950s. Monticello Drug, shown in this 1951 photograph, was one of the thriving businesses in downtown Monticello. (Courtesy of UAM Library.)

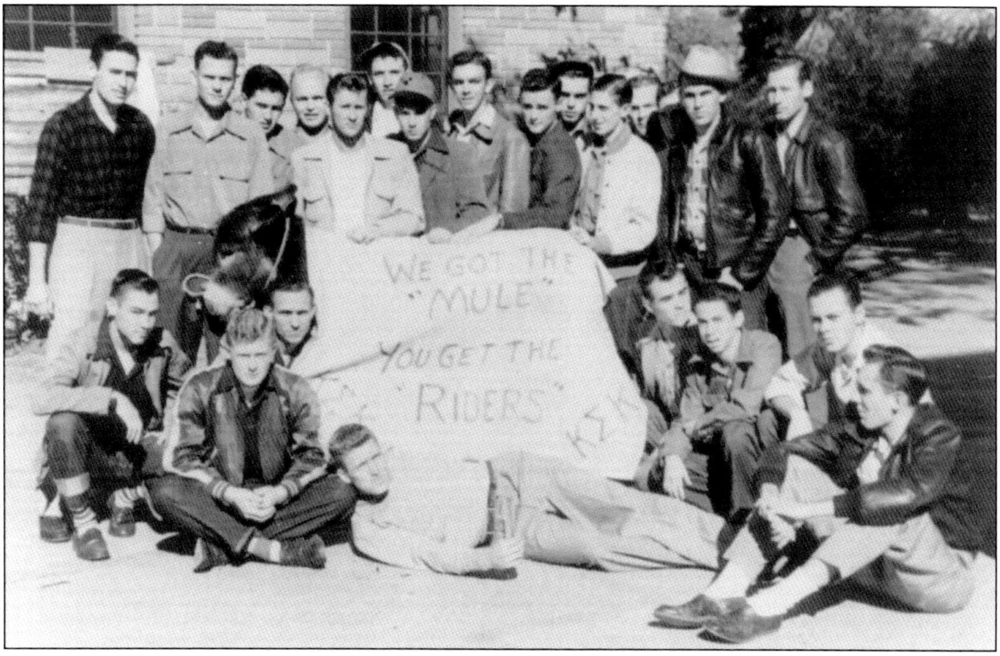

In 1950, a group of Arkansas A&M students kidnapped the mascot of Southern State College. Surely, the kidnapping was an attempt to demoralize the "Mule Riders" of Magnolia, Arkansas. The culprits from A&M hid the stolen mule on the Carson family's cattle farm in Monticello until the homecoming game between the fierce rivals. In this picture taken the day after the heist, the students are, from left to right, as follows: (first row) Albert Rodgers, Max Gates, Willard Pyle, Erwin Jones, Gerald Guidry, Buddy Clifton, Charles Purvis, and David "Tex" Graham; (second row) Bob Merrifield, Jack Gardner, Stanford Stanley, Joe Bob Glover, Ben "Pee Wee" Clark, Eddy Guinee, Homer Cogbill, Harold Humphries, James "Red" Carnley, Dick Young, Bobby Johnson, Arnold Wardlow, Albert "Red" Favors, Cecil Scaife, and Craig Beard. In 1983, more than 30 years after the famous heist, some of the criminals reunited to gleefully reminisce. (Both, courtesy of Richard A. Young.)

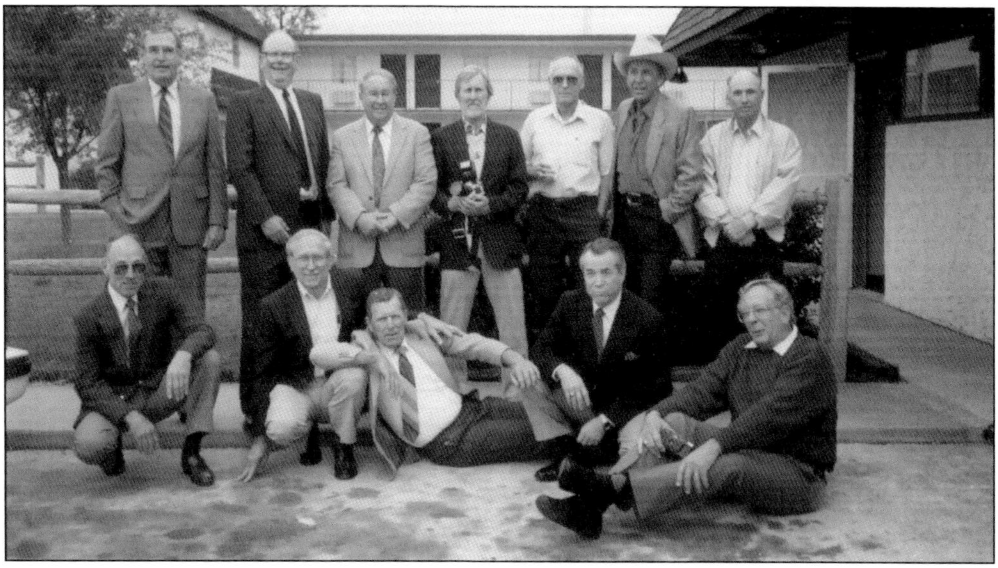

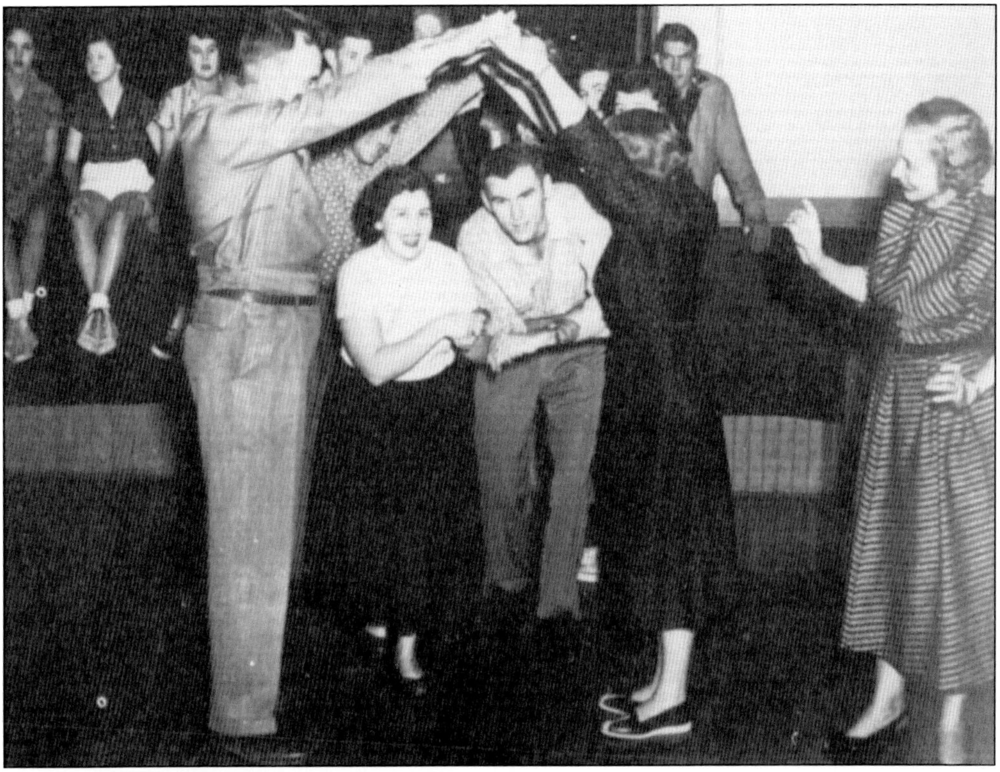

The Arkansas A&M dance students of Peggy Wallick are pictured here during a country-dance sequence. (Courtesy of UAM Library.)

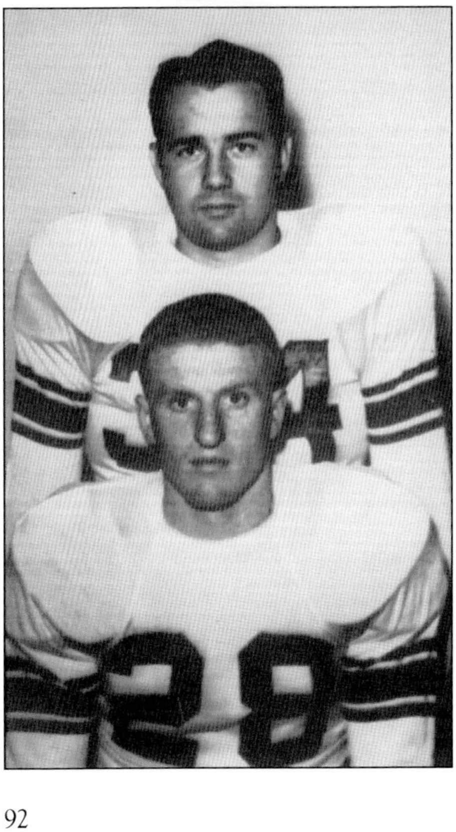

Charles Selman, cocaptain (rear), and Jimmy Parker, halfback, are pictured here in 1951. Jimmy "Red" Parker was a star athlete for the Arkansas A&M Weevils from 1949 to 1952. Parker was the Weevils head coach from 1961 to 1965, before moving on to lead the football programs at The Citadel and, subsequently, Clemson University. (Courtesy of UAM Library.)

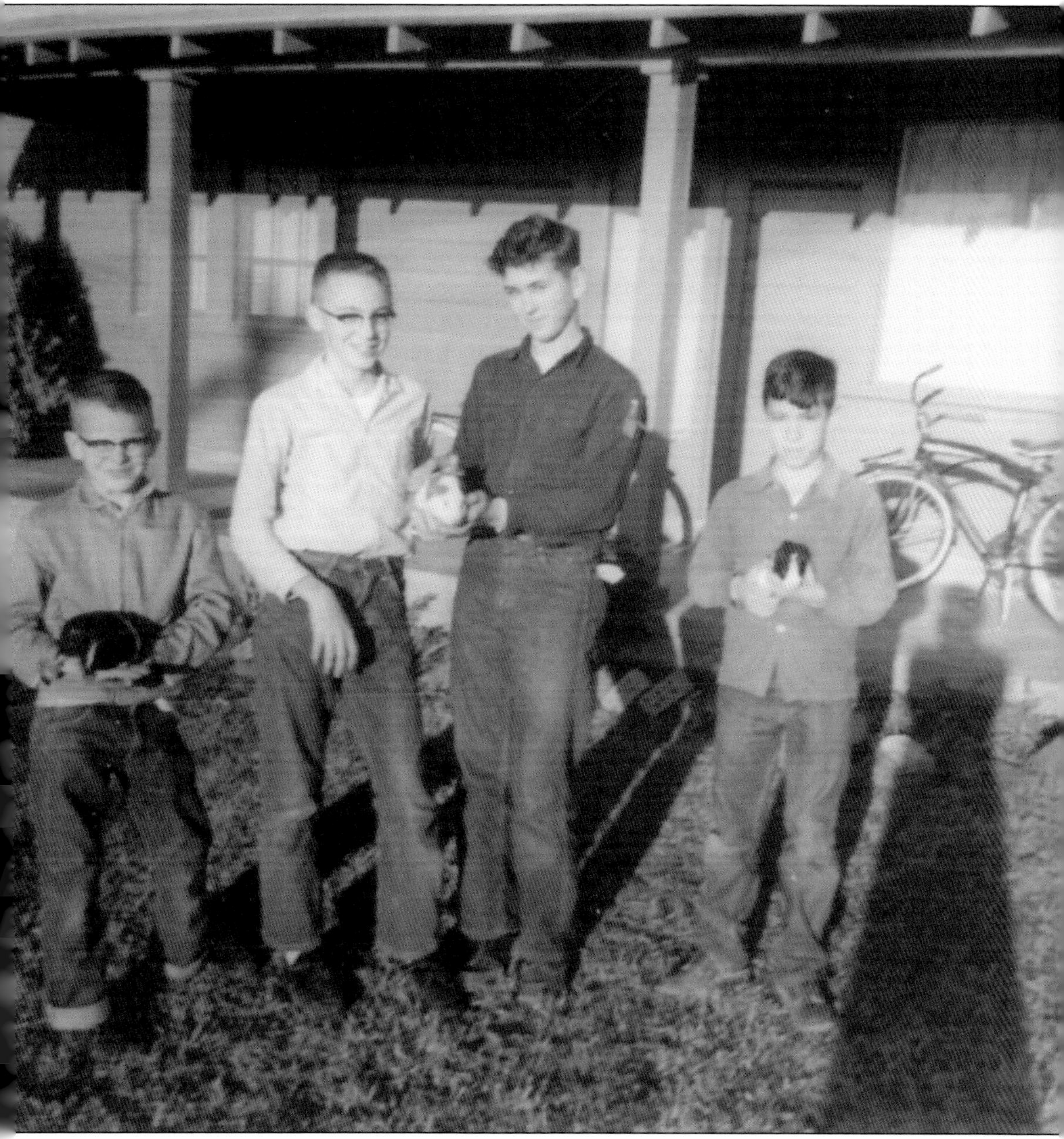

Longtime Monticello resident Aileen Coston used this image to relate a humorous story about raising her children in the 1950s. A neighbor boy mentioned to Coston that he would not be going on vacation with the rest of his family because he had to stay home and take care of his guinea pigs. Feeling sorry for the boy, Coston assured him that she and her sons would take care of his pets while he was away. She told him to just place their beds on her back porch. Expecting two or three animals, she was shocked to find herself caring for 40 guinea pigs, to which her sons became rather attached. Pictured in front of the Coston home on East Gabbert Street are, from left to right, Ken Coston, Dan Coston, Butch Burton, and Troy Burton. (Courtesy of Aileen Coston.)

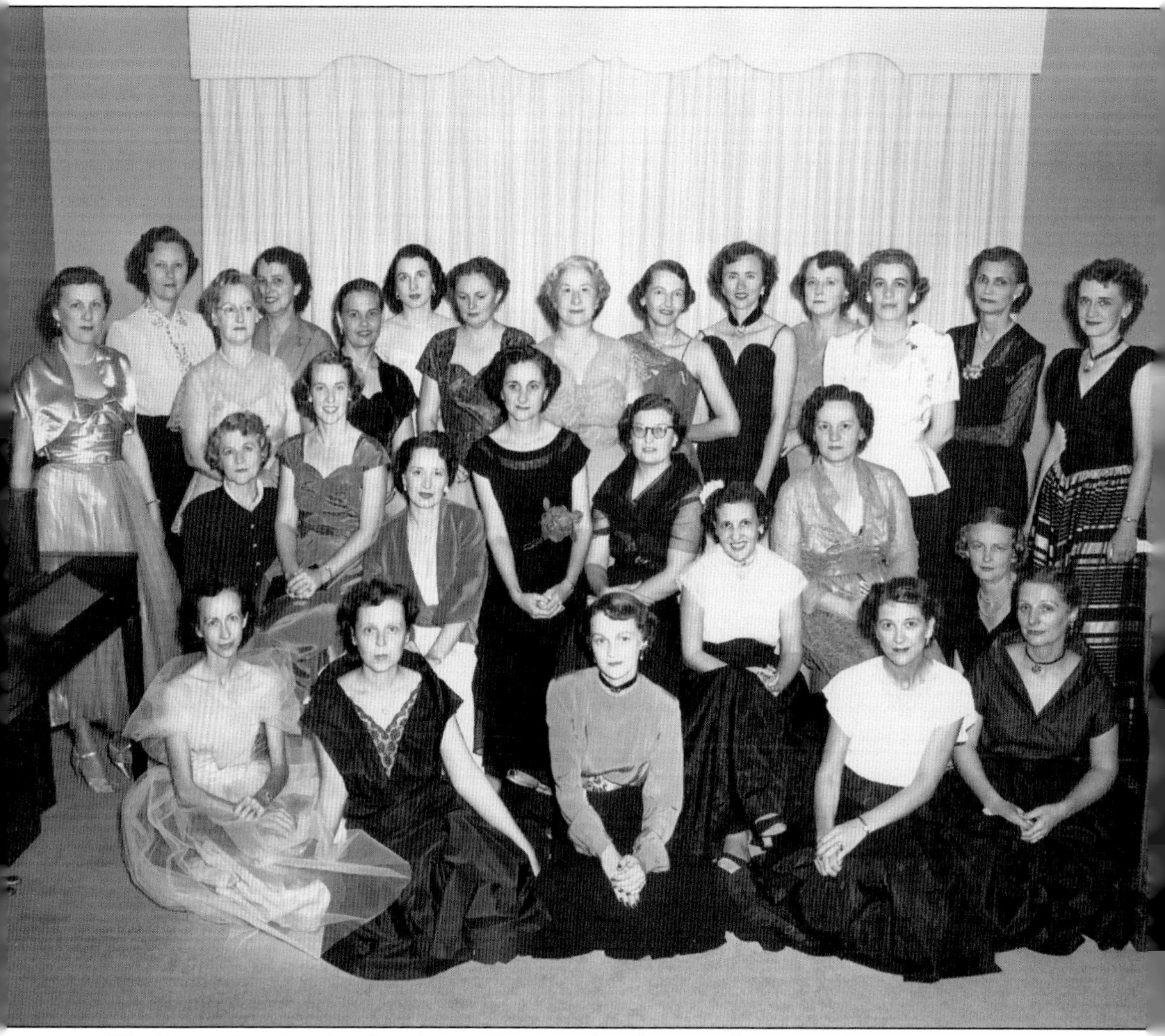

The Junior Auxiliary has long been a bastion of tradition and community service in Monticello. Pictured here in 1951 are, from left to right, (front row) Edna Davis, Kathryn Wells, Frances Stephenson, Ethel Mae Stephenson, and Margaret Daniels; (second row) Calie Porter, Ruth Moffatt, Virginia Edwards, Wanda Hyatt, Carolyn Hancock, Molly Ross, Pauline McClendon, and Margaret Wells; (third row, standing) Dulcie Daroux, Flossie Daniels, Fay Pomeroy, Virginia Lucky, Liz Towler, Virginia Ryburn, Frances Hyatt, Martha Howlett, Bernice Holder, Virginia Johnson, Corinne Campster, Margaret White, Pat Trotter, and Florence Carmical Vardaman. (Courtesy of Drew County Historical Society.)

In this 1951 photograph, Arkansas A&M coeds focus on skills that will make them good secretaries. According to the yearbook caption, "It's much harder to translate shorthand than it is to write it." (Courtesy of UAM Library.)

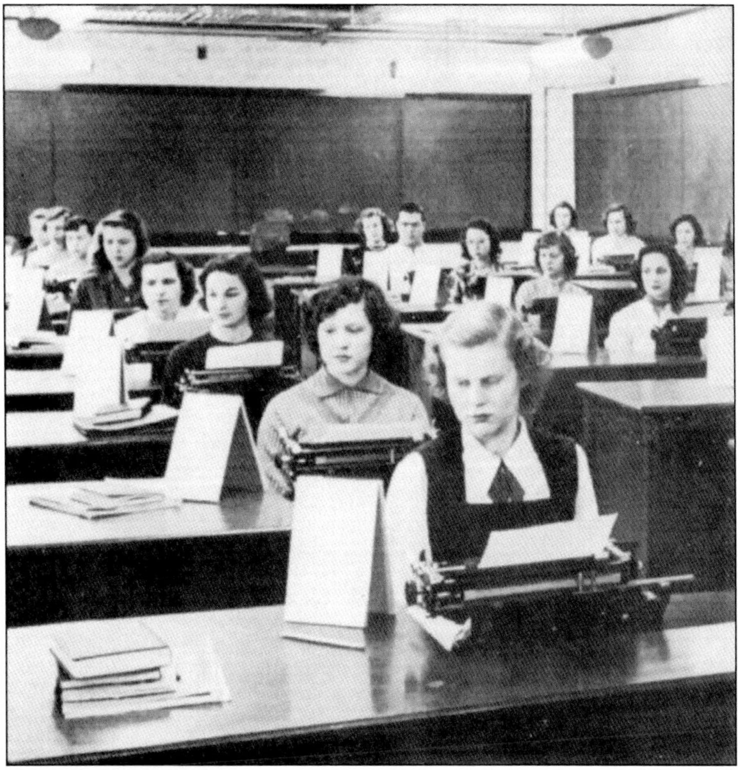

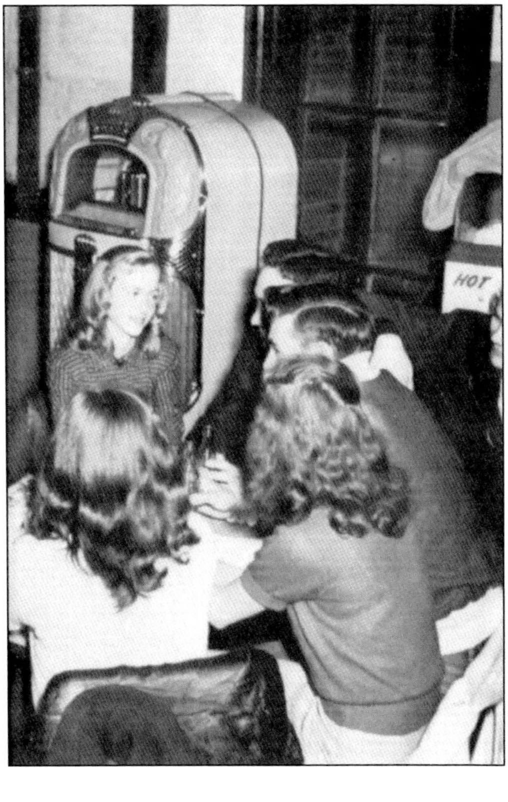

Arkansas A&M College students enjoy socializing in the student commons. The jukebox was central to recreation and entertainment on and off campus. The three most popular songs of 1951 were "Tennessee Waltz" by Patti Page, Nat King Cole's "Too Young," and The Weavers' rendition of "On Top of Old Smokey." (Courtesy of UAM Library.)

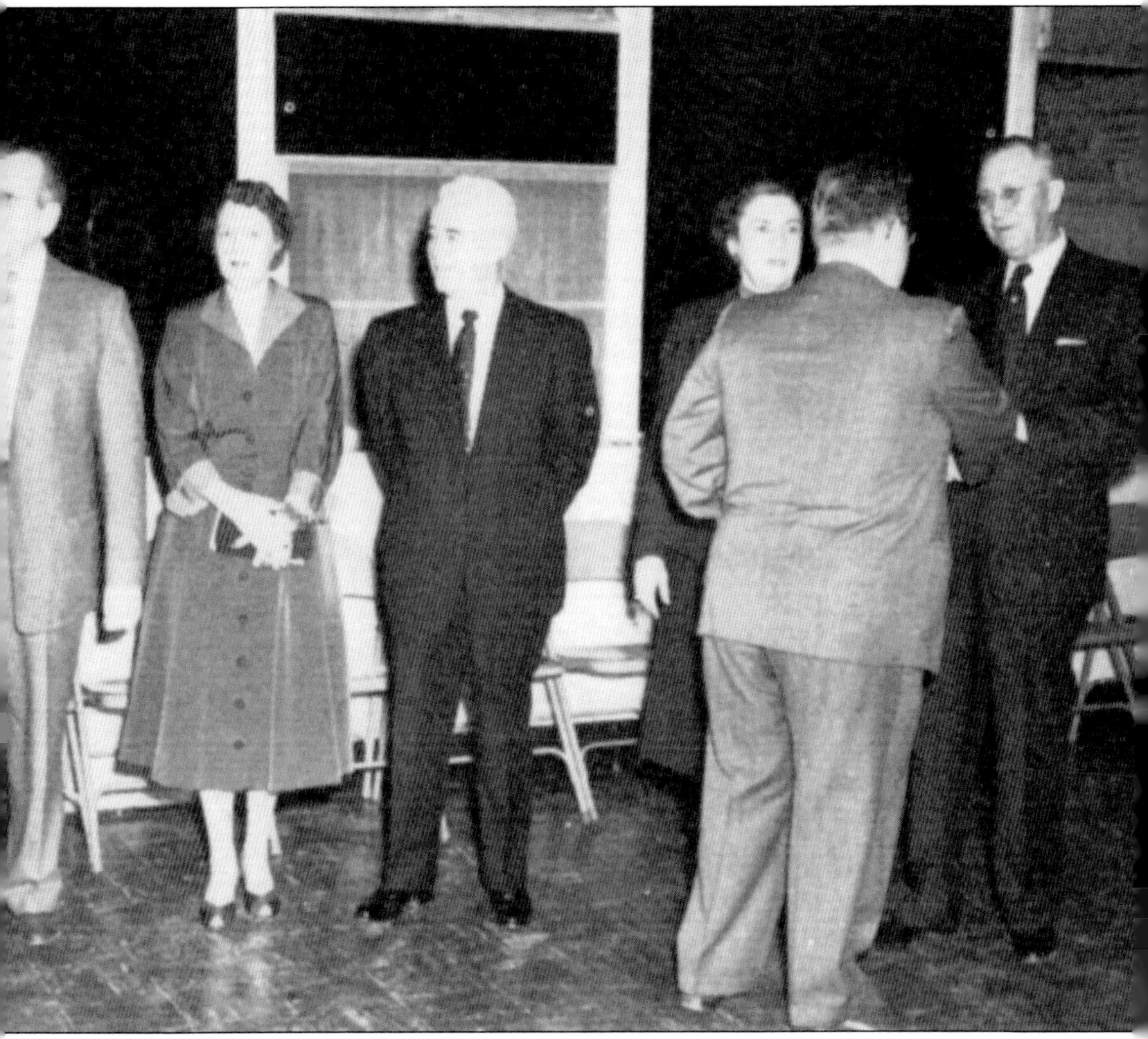

Francis Cherry (center), the governor of Arkansas from 1953 to 1955, was on the Arkansas A&M campus to address January 1954 graduates. Little known before running for governor, Cherry benefited from being a new face in state politics and had a catchy campaign slogan: "Pick a Cherry." His election was seen as a break from old-style Arkansas politics, which had become associated with corruption and scandal in the public's mind. However, Cherry's lack of political competence allowed for a return of the old guard after he had served only one two-year term; Arkansas did not see political reform until the election of Winthrop Rockefeller in 1966. (Courtesy of UAM Library.)

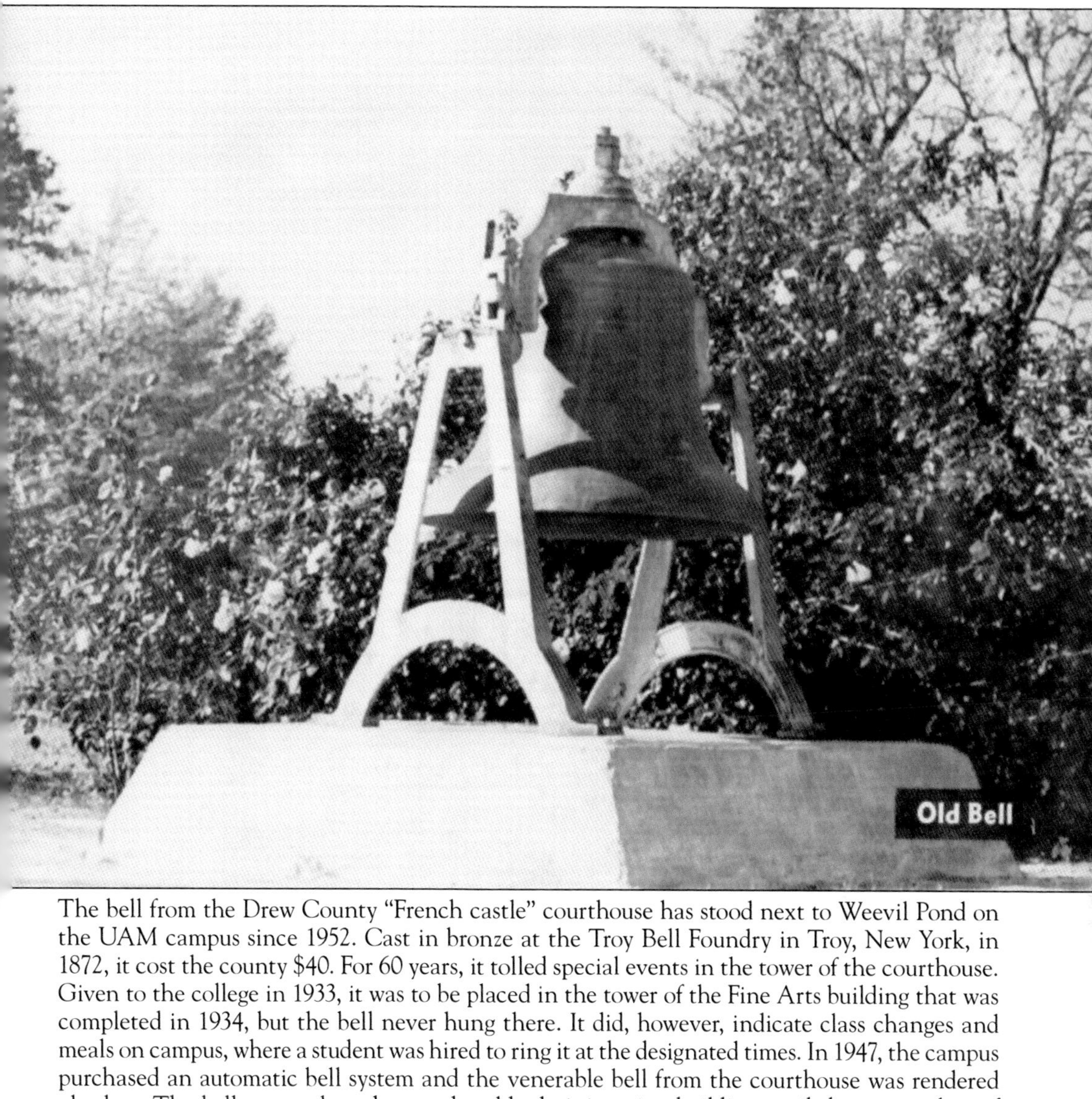

The bell from the Drew County "French castle" courthouse has stood next to Weevil Pond on the UAM campus since 1952. Cast in bronze at the Troy Bell Foundry in Troy, New York, in 1872, it cost the county $40. For 60 years, it tolled special events in the tower of the courthouse. Given to the college in 1933, it was to be placed in the tower of the Fine Arts building that was completed in 1934, but the bell never hung there. It did, however, indicate class changes and meals on campus, where a student was hired to ring it at the designated times. In 1947, the campus purchased an automatic bell system and the venerable bell from the courthouse was rendered obsolete. The bell sat, neglected, near the old administration building until the senior class of 1952 constructed a base for it on the west bank of Weevil Pond, moved it to that spot, and placed a marble plaque inscribed "Class of 1952" on the base. (Courtesy of UAM Library.)

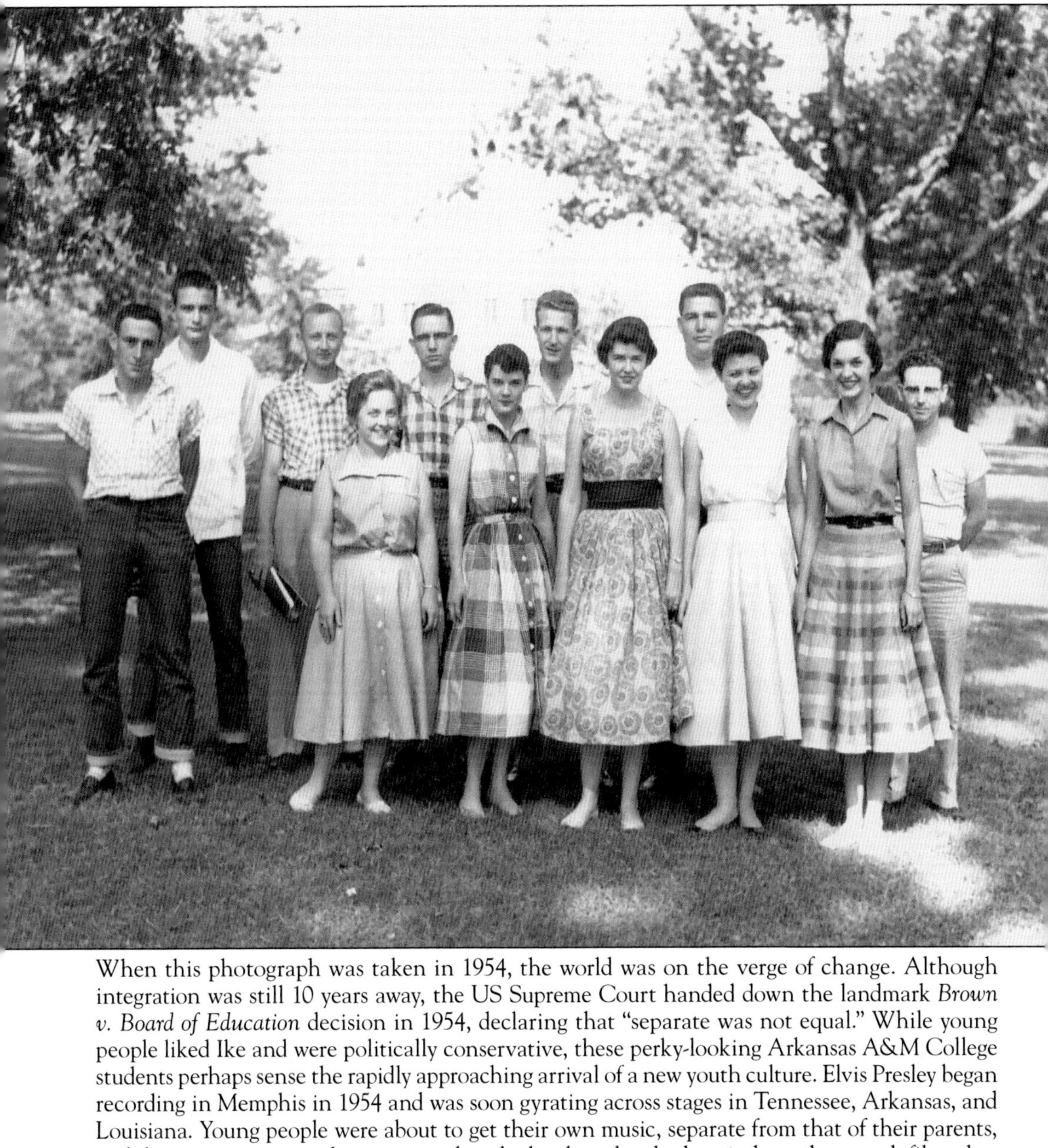

When this photograph was taken in 1954, the world was on the verge of change. Although integration was still 10 years away, the US Supreme Court handed down the landmark *Brown v. Board of Education* decision in 1954, declaring that "separate was not equal." While young people liked Ike and were politically conservative, these perky-looking Arkansas A&M College students perhaps sense the rapidly approaching arrival of a new youth culture. Elvis Presley began recording in Memphis in 1954 and was soon gyrating across stages in Tennessee, Arkansas, and Louisiana. Young people were about to get their own music, separate from that of their parents, and their own movies and movie stars, largely thanks to low-budget, independent youth films that integrated rock 'n' roll music, leather-jacketed young rebels, seething but never explicit sexuality, and—more often than not—invasions from outer space. (Courtesy of UAM Library.)

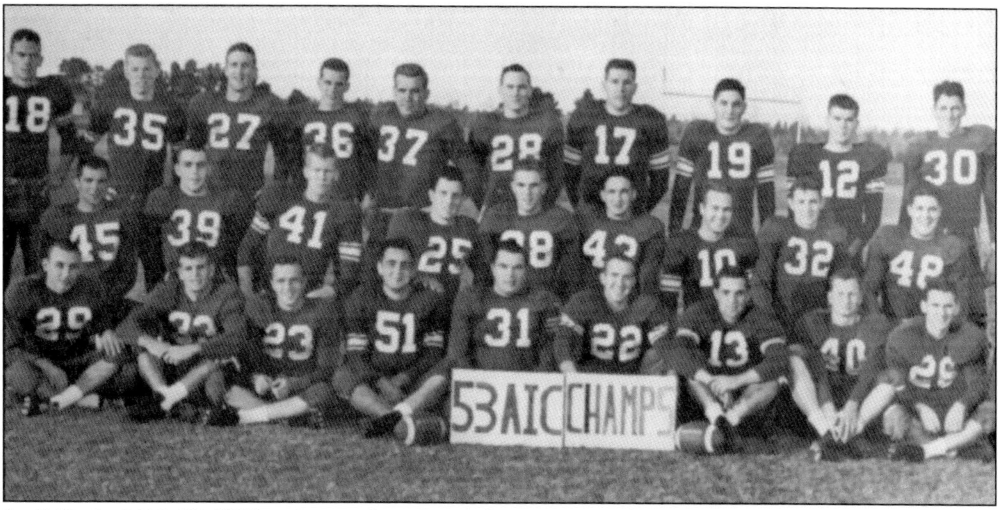

In 1953, the UAM Boll Weevils won their first Arkansas Intercollegiate (AIC) football championship. The team, which no one expected to win the title that year, became known as coach Jim Benton's "gridiron wonders." (Courtesy of UAM Library.)

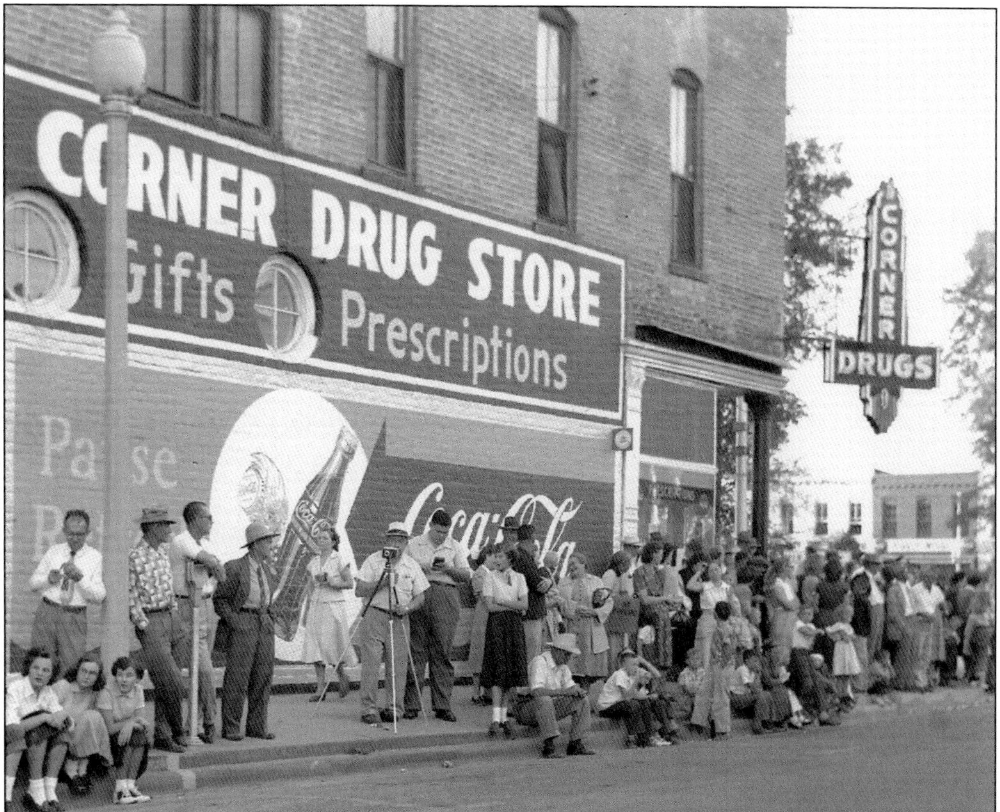

A crowd waits for a parade coming from South Main Street in the early 1950s. (Courtesy of Tuell White.)

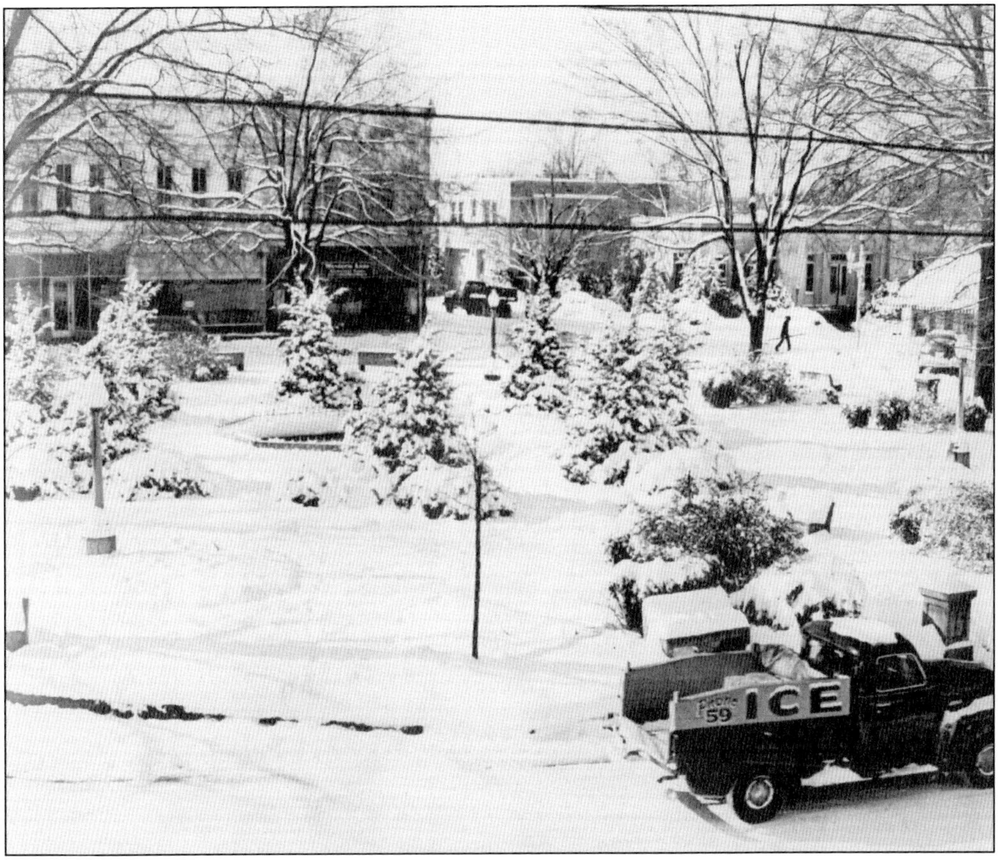

Heavy snowfalls are rare in southeast Arkansas. This one, which occurred on January 30, 1949, turned the downtown square into a winter wonderland. Note the ironic detail of an ice truck and the two-digit phone number on the truck. (Courtesy of UAM Library.)

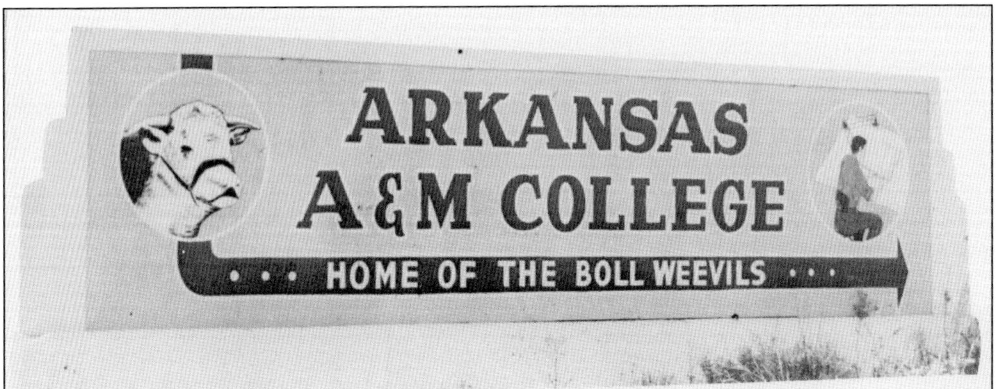

The cow and the draftsman on this 1956 sign represent Arkansas A&M's tradition of providing agricultural and mechanical training, but the school had long been offering teacher training and an array of programs in the arts and sciences. (Courtesy of UAM Library.)

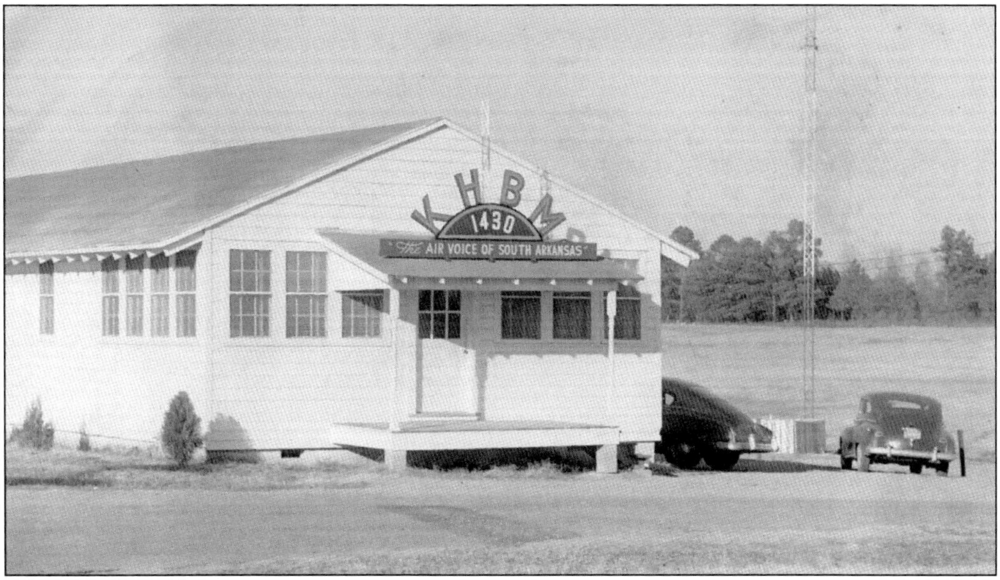

KHBM, at 1430 on the AM radio dial, was located on the campus of Arkansas A&M College and advertised itself as "*the* air voice of south Arkansas." This photograph is from 1956. (Courtesy of UAM Library.)

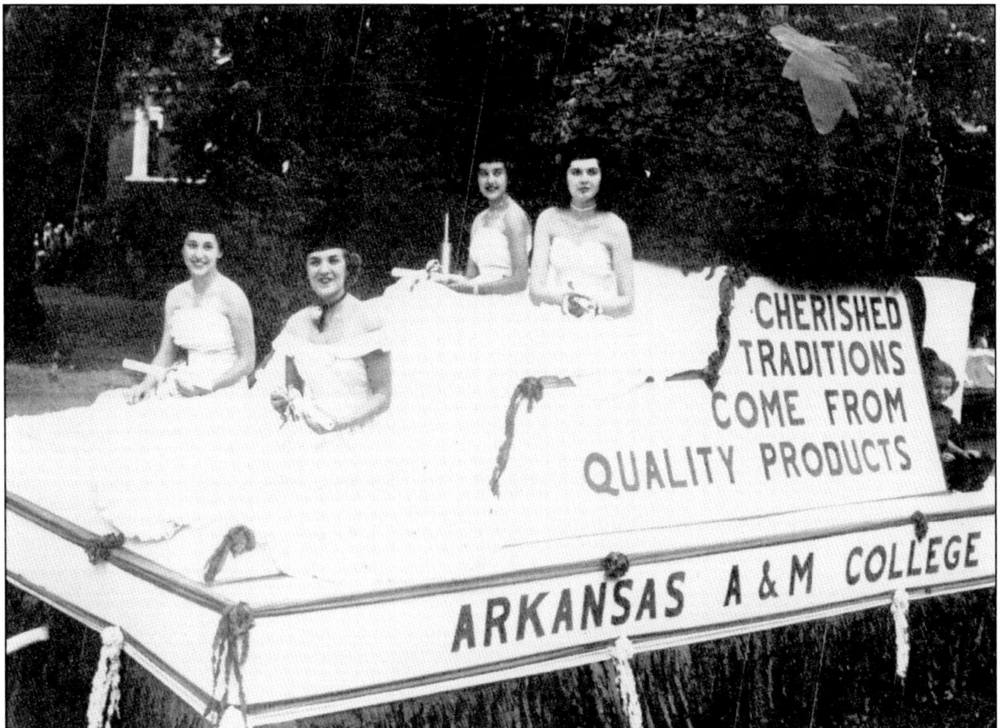

From the 1930s through the 1950s, Monticello claimed to be a tomato capital, if not *the* tomato capital. Always aware that what was good for Monticello was good for the college, faculty and students at Arkansas A&M regularly participated in town celebrations. Here, the college's float appears in the 1956 Tomato Festival parade. (Courtesy of UAM Library.)

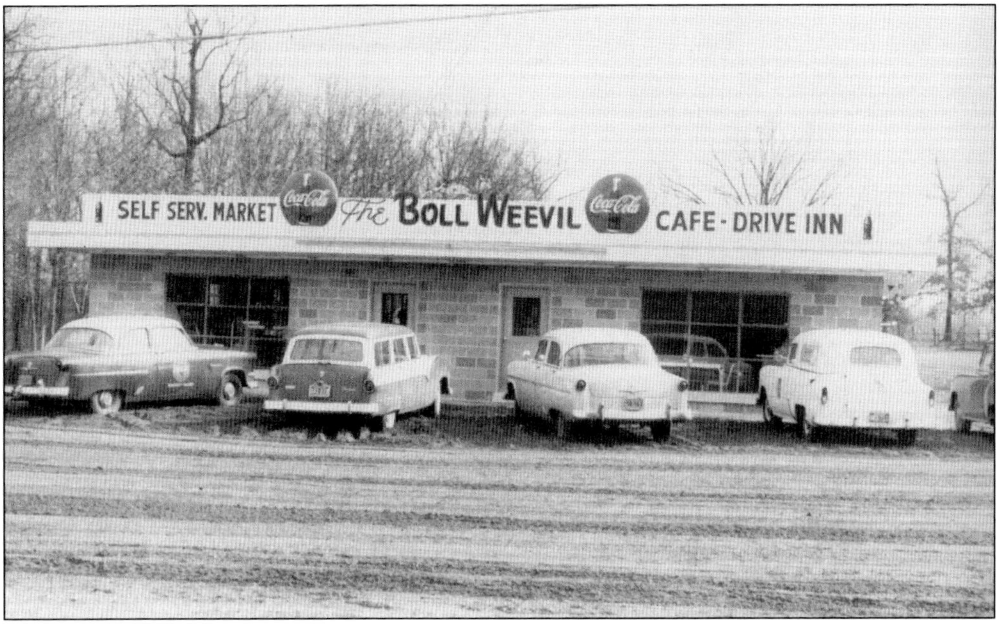

The self-serve grocery store represented a transition between the old full-service store and the modern-day supermarket. There is also perhaps some foreshadowing of strip malls in the grocery's connection to a cafe and drive-in. (Courtesy of UAM Library.)

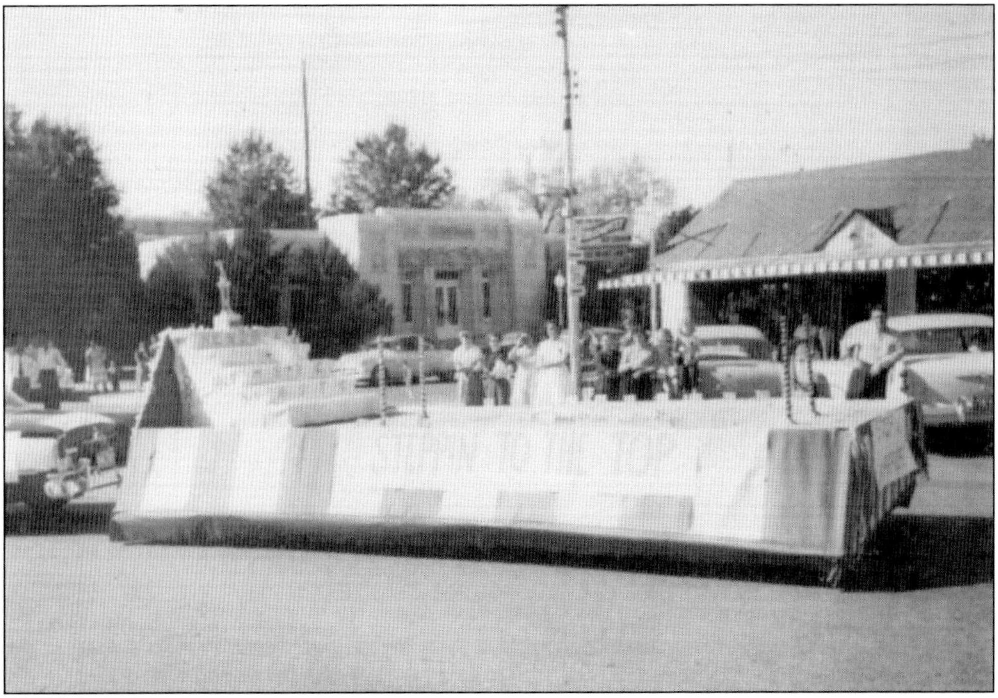

Arkansas A&M homecoming was not just celebrated by the college students and alumni, but by the whole town. Here, a homecoming float in the 1955 parade makes its way around the square, passing Jolley's Café and the Monticello post office. (Courtesy of UAM Library.)

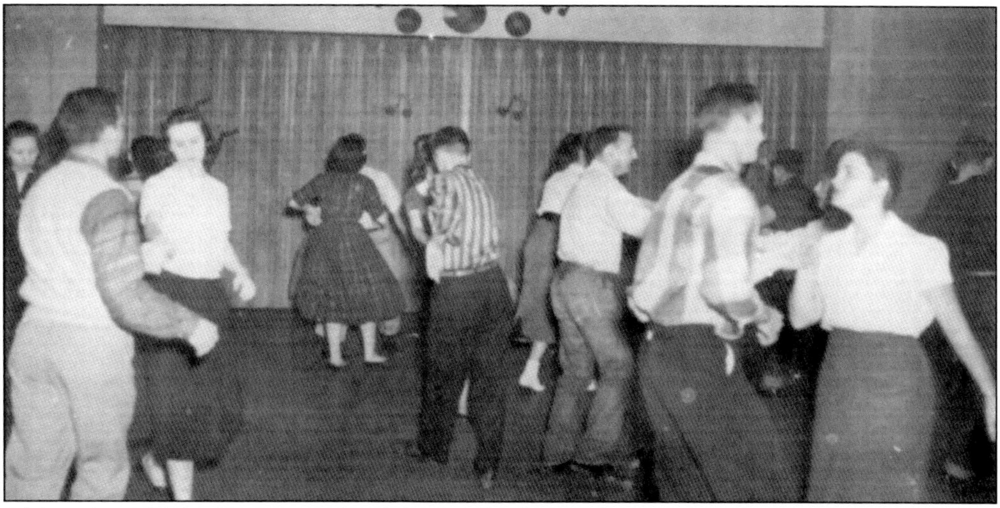

Although rock 'n' roll was considered downright obscene by some members of older generations, by 1957 it was quickly coming to dominate the musical tastes of the young. (Courtesy of UAM Library.)

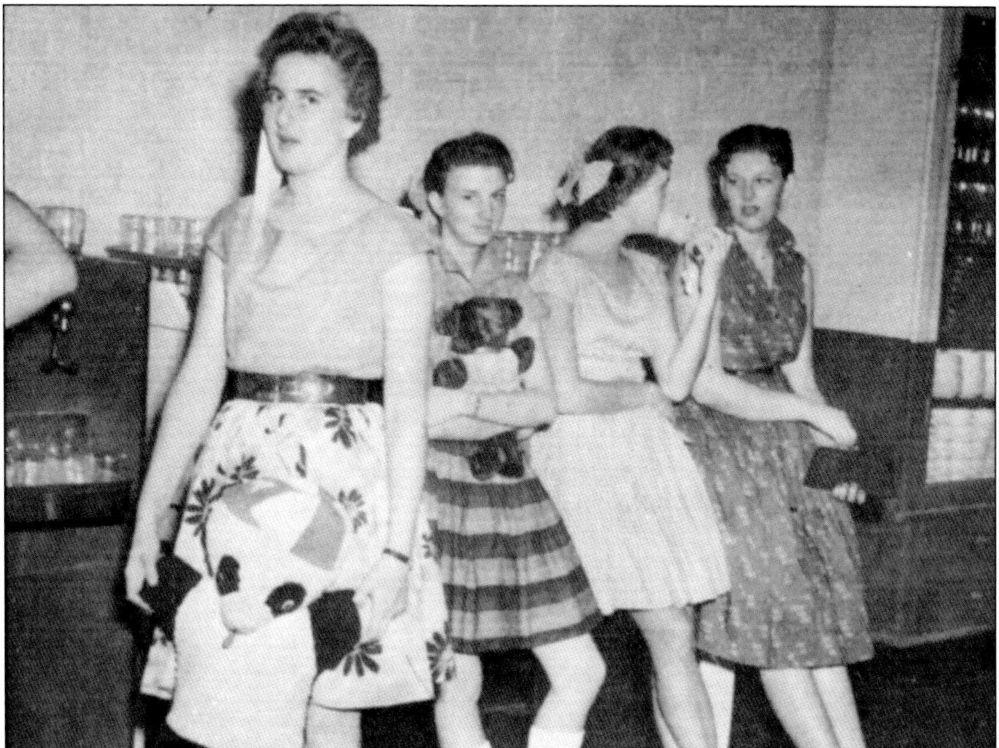

At a college dance, these Arkansas A&M coeds hold teddy bears in homage to Elvis Presley's 1957 number-one hit, "(Let Me Be Your) Teddy Bear." It was Presley's third number-one hit of four that year. (Courtesy of UAM Library.)

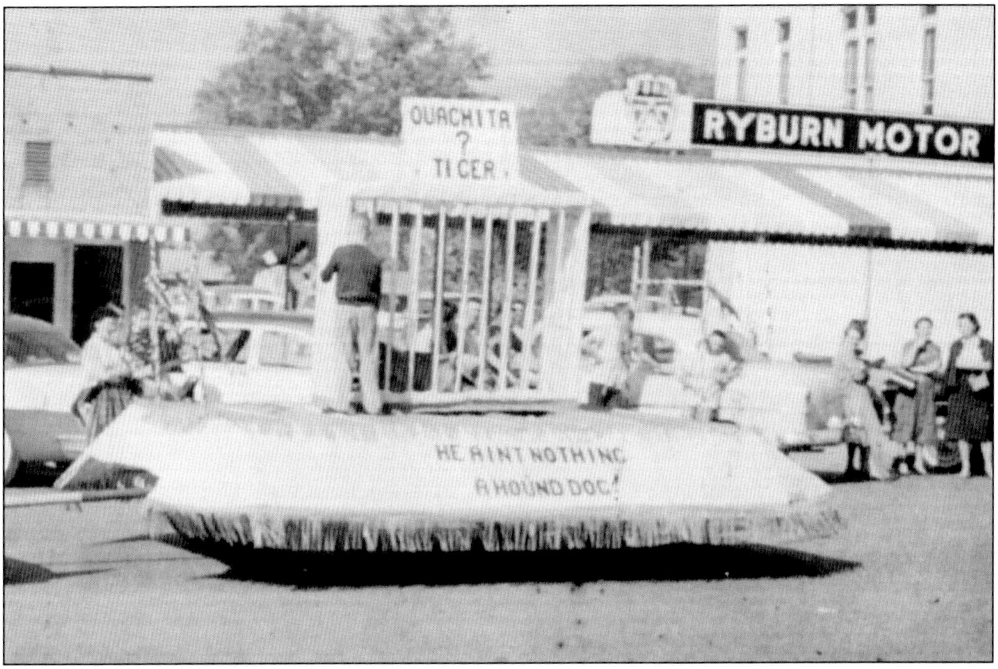

This 1956 Arkansas A&M homecoming float, shown passing Ryburn Motor Company, uses an Elvis Presley hit to disparage the Ouachita College tiger: "He ain't nothing but a hound dog." (Courtesy of UAM Library.)

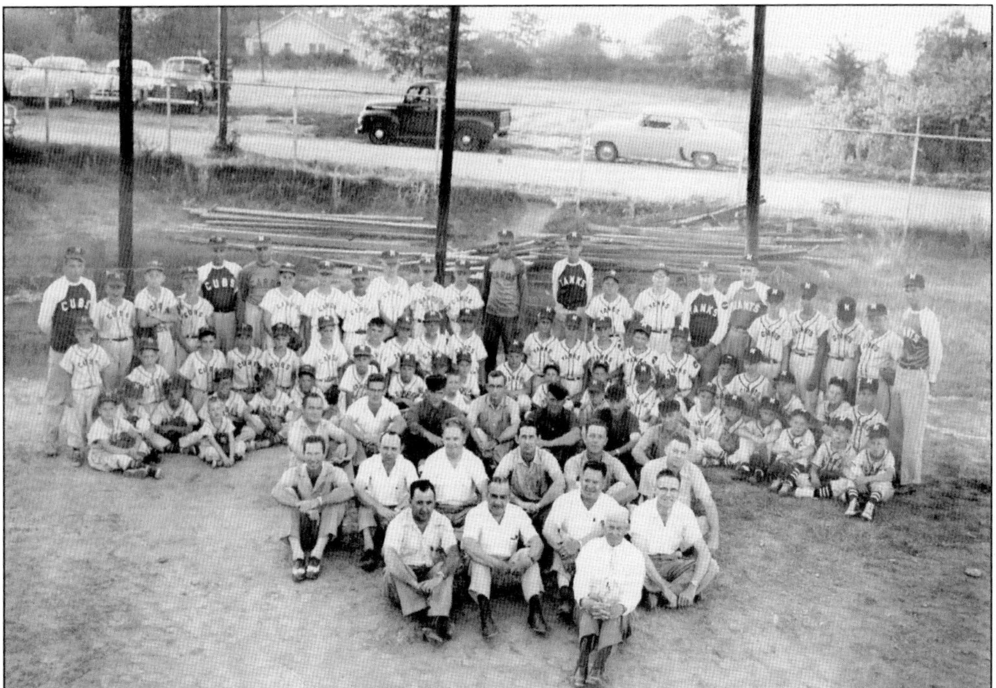
Pictured here in 1953 are the team members, coaches, and mentors of the organized Little League teams. (Courtesy of Drew County Historical Society.)

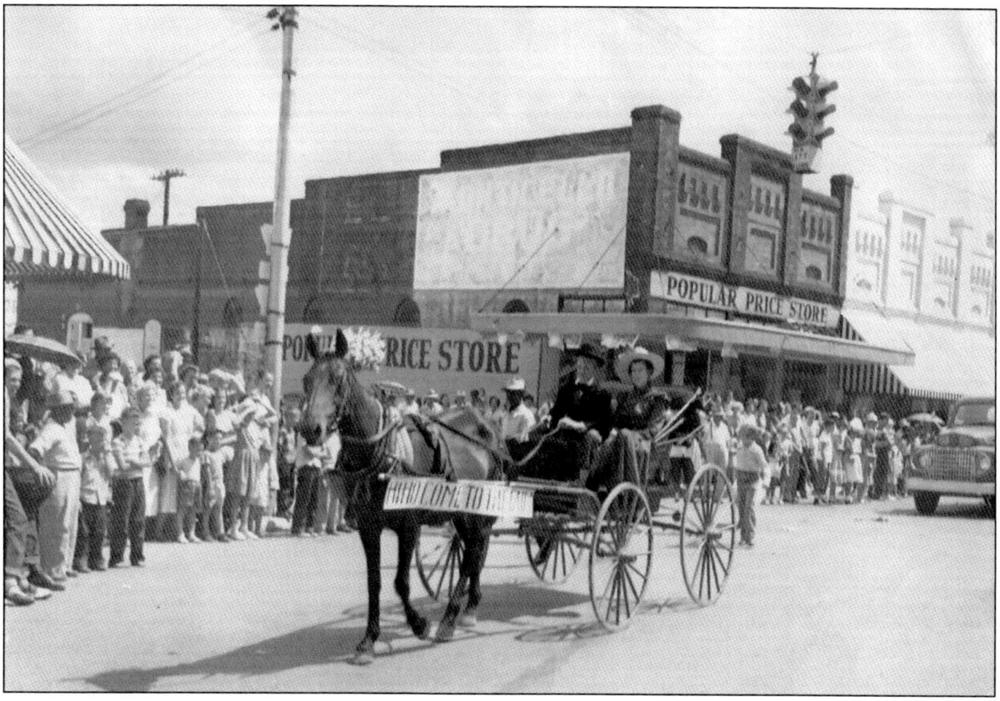

The 1951 Drew County Fair parade on the square featured the juxtaposition of a horse-drawn buggy followed by a 1950s-era truck. Bill Ward and Anita Higgason ride in the buggy. (Courtesy of Drew County Historical Society.)

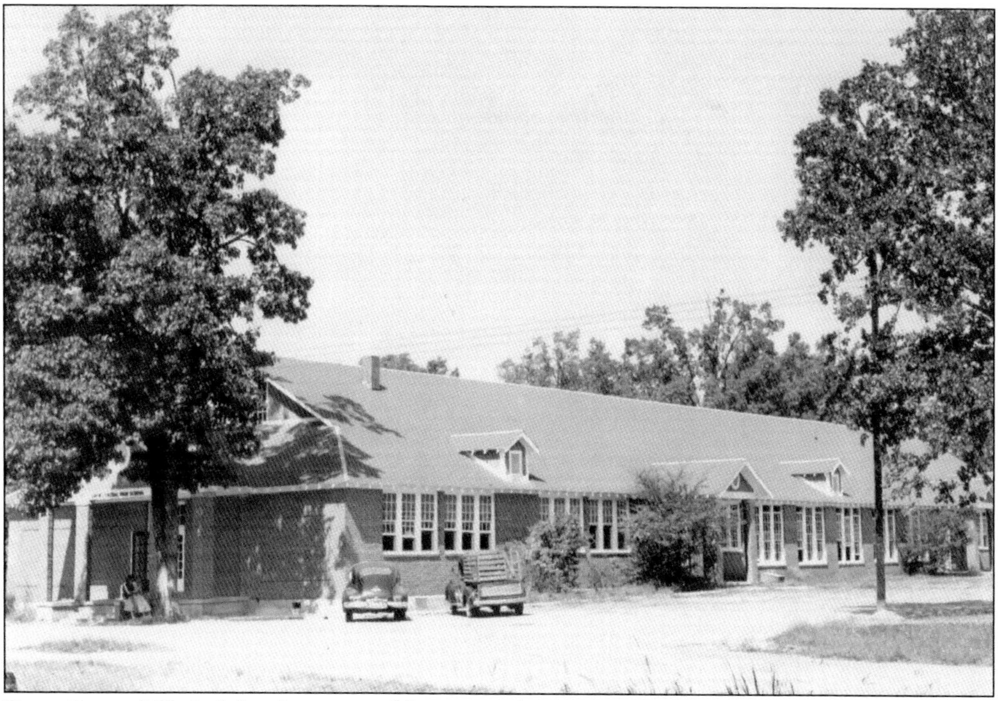

Drew Central High School is pictured here in 1950. Pre-service teachers received their training at this school. (Courtesy of UAM Library.)

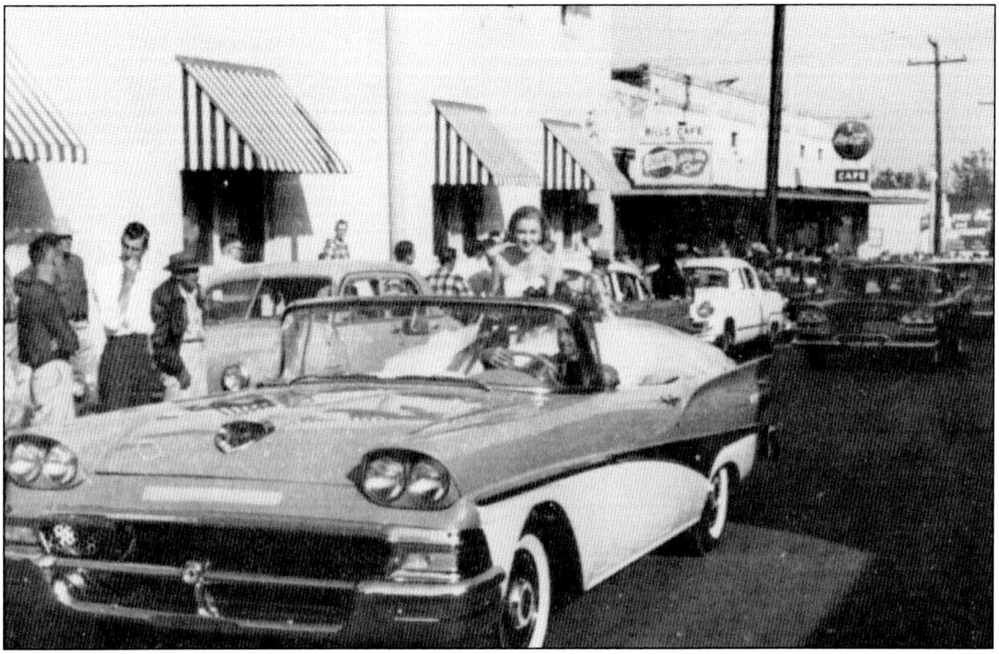

By 1958, as automotive designers took cues from jet airplanes and rocket ships, fashion called for fins, along with wide whitewalls and a lower, wider, two-tone look. Automobile manufacturers advertised that the fins enhanced stability on the new highways stretching across much of America (but not near Monticello). Bill's Café is visible in the background. (Courtesy of UAM Library.)

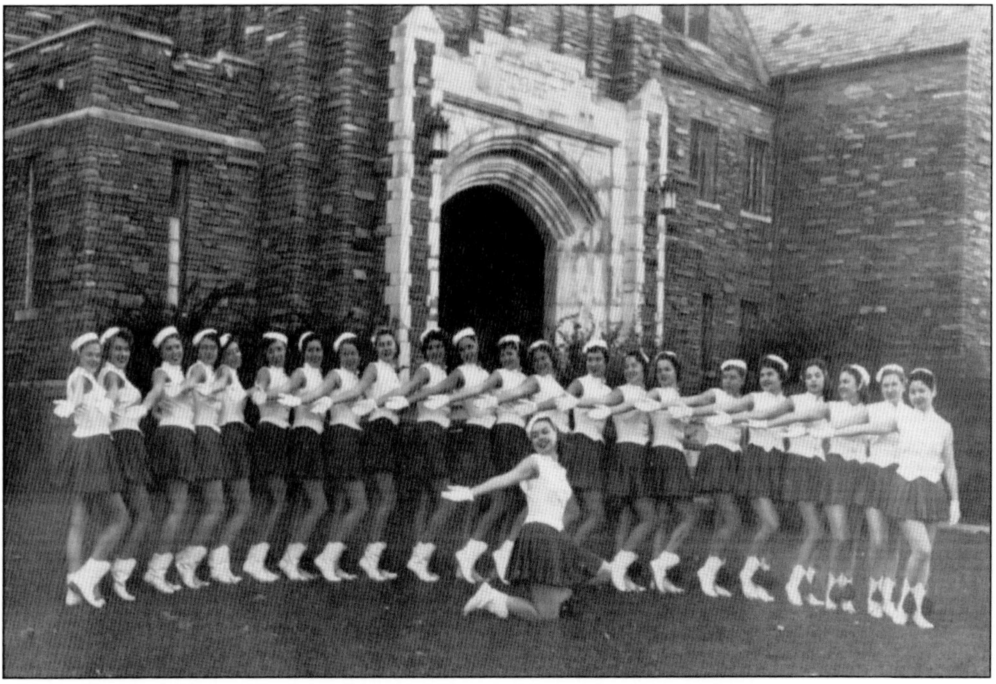

The Gothic-style Fine Arts building provides a somewhat ironic background for this stunning photograph of the very modern-looking Arkansas A&M Weevilettes of 1958. (Courtesy of UAM Library.)

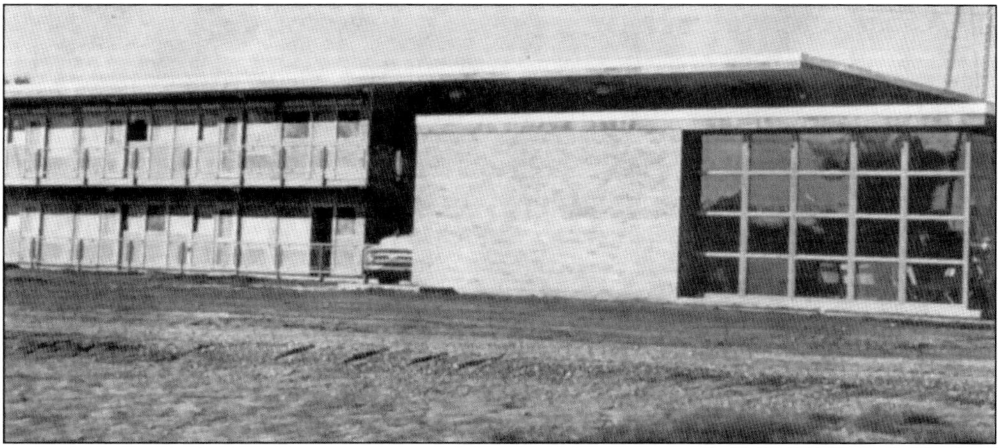

In the 1950s, the construction of Jeter Hall represented expansion, progress, and the introduction of contemporary architecture on the campus of Arkansas A&M College, whereas its demolition represented progress in 2011, making room for a new wing of the Forest Resources building. (Courtesy UAM Library.)

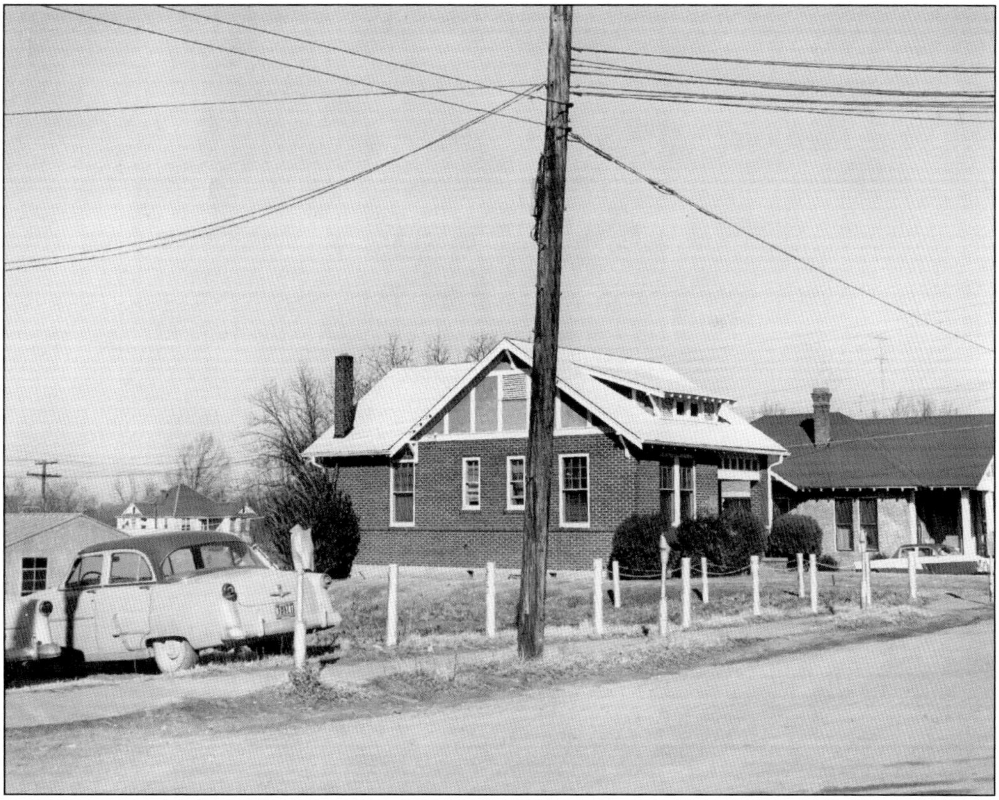

What looks like a modest private residence was actually the Southwestern Bell Telephone building, pictured here in 1959. Inside the building, operators worked at switchboards to connect calls. When telephones jangled inside the homes of Monticello, residents picked up the headset to hear a live operator announcing a call. Party lines, the sharing of a single line by two or more telephone customers, were also the rule of the day. A truly private conversation was never certain. (Courtesy of Jody Gladden.)

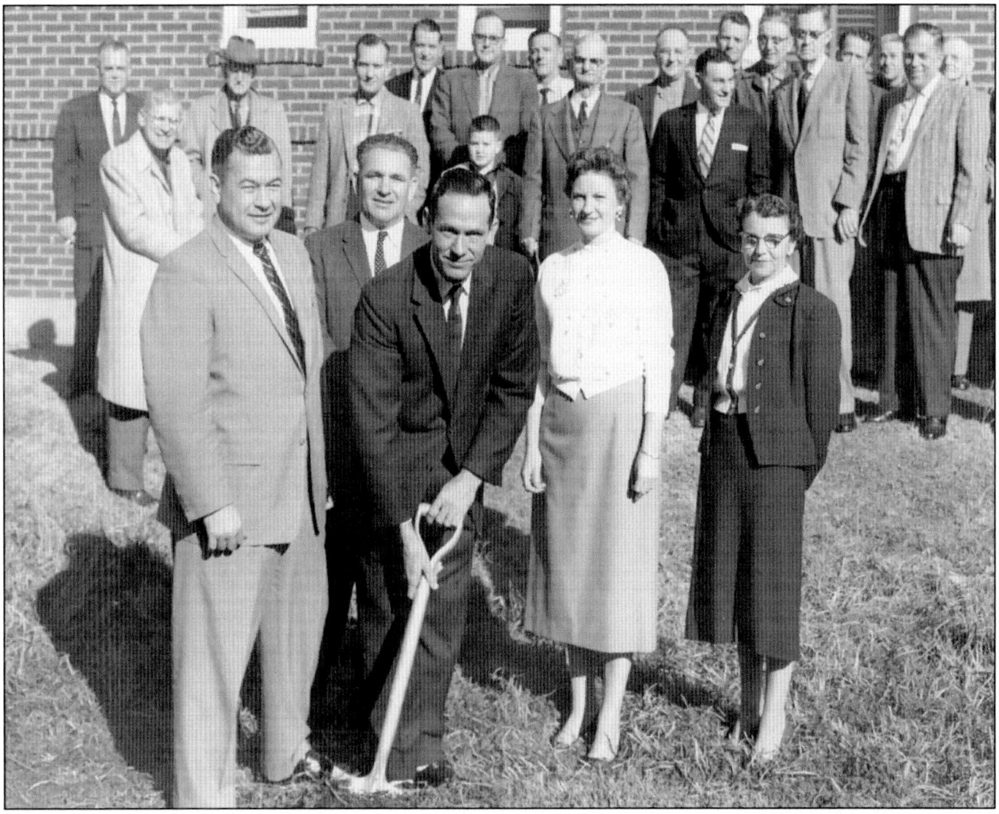

Mayor Henry Ross, who held office from 1959 through 1969, turns the first spade of ground at the 1959 ground-breaking ceremony for the $450,000 dial telephone building, which would end switchboard and operator-assisted telephone service in Monticello. The individuals in the foreground are, from left to right, Jack Keith of Little Rock, general commercial contractor; George Pruett, wire chief of the Monticello telephone office; Mayor Ross; Margaret Ann Barnes, chief operator; and Kathleen Stephens, service representative for the telephone company. Until 1959, when residents of Monticello picked up a telephone, they did not hear a dial tone. Instead, they heard a live switchboard operator say, "Number please." (Both, courtesy of Jody Gladden.)

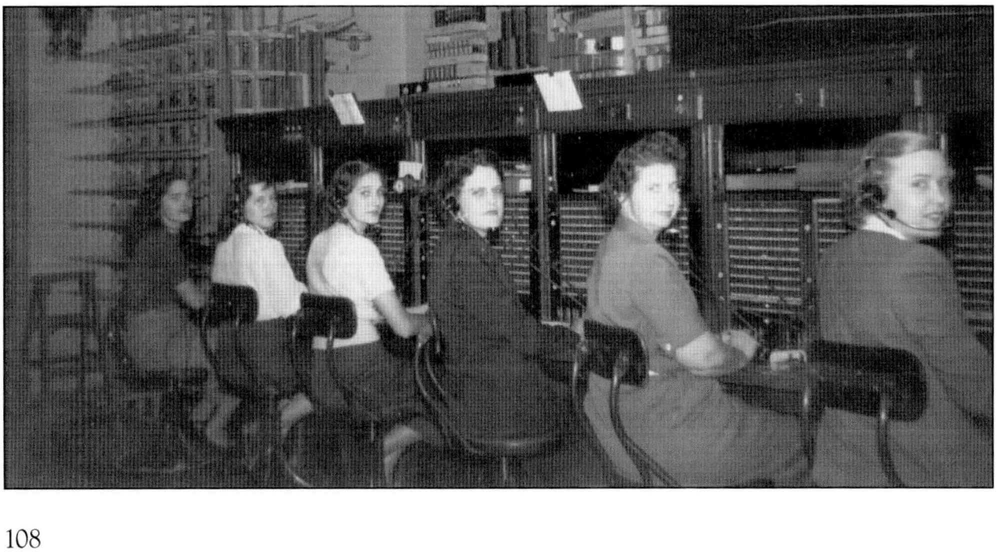

Six

THE WINDS OF CHANGE, THE MARCH OF TIME

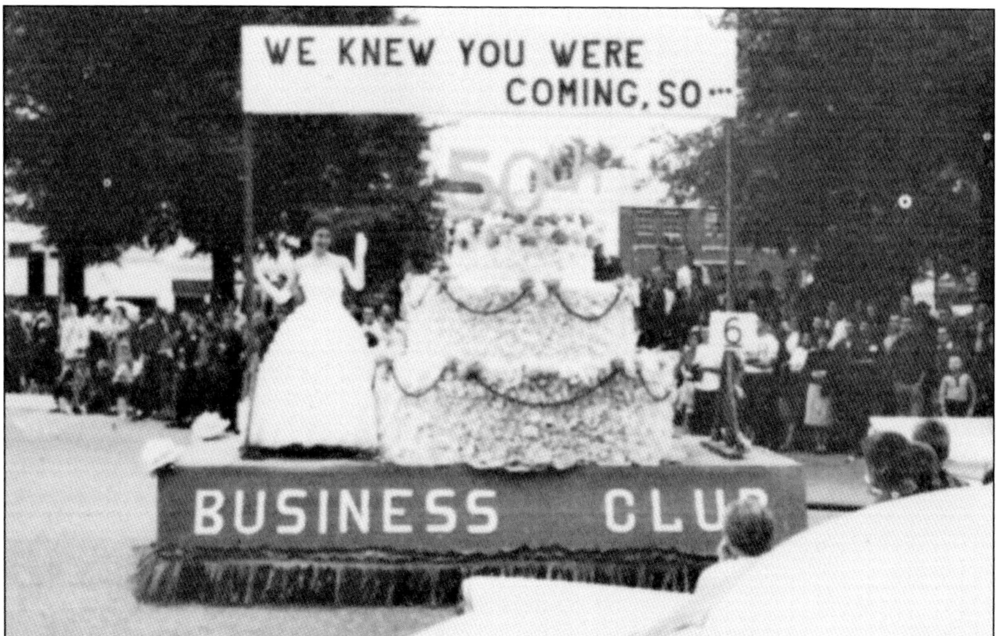

The Business Club's homecoming float of 1960 celebrates the college's 50th year in existence with a giant birthday cake. The institution had grown from agricultural training school to two-year college to four-year college. (Courtesy of UAM Library.)

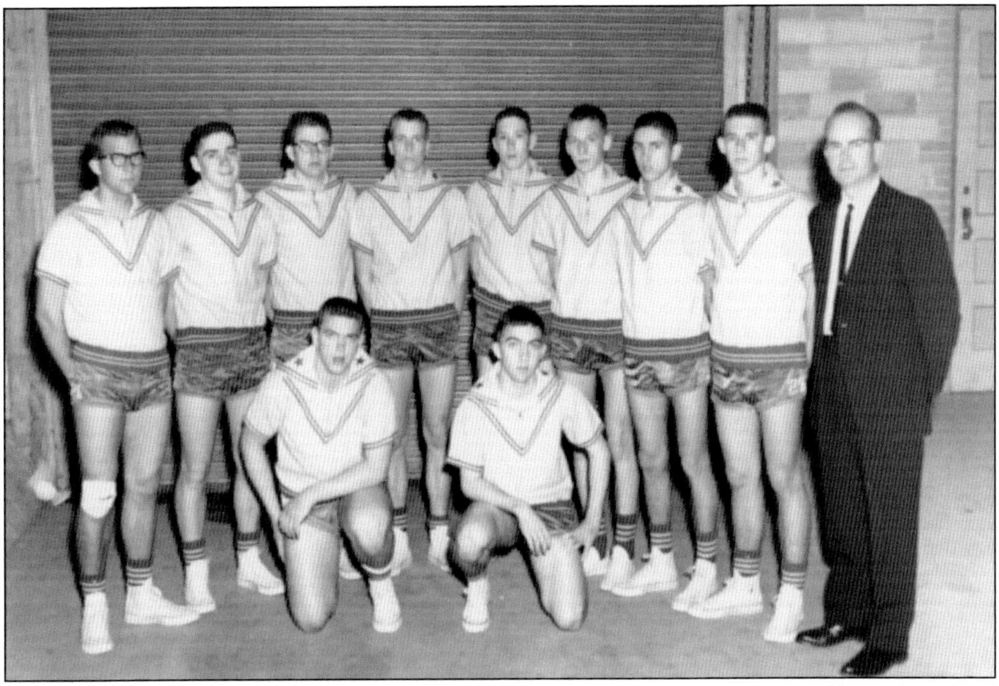

Dan Coston was named Arkansas Coach of the Year in 1963 after his Monticello High School basketball team won the Class A State Championship. In the mid-1950s, he was named Teacher of the Year at Monticello High School, and in 1975 he was honored for his 29 years as a teacher and coach in the Monticello school system when the MHS field house was named for him. (Courtesy of Aileen Coston.)

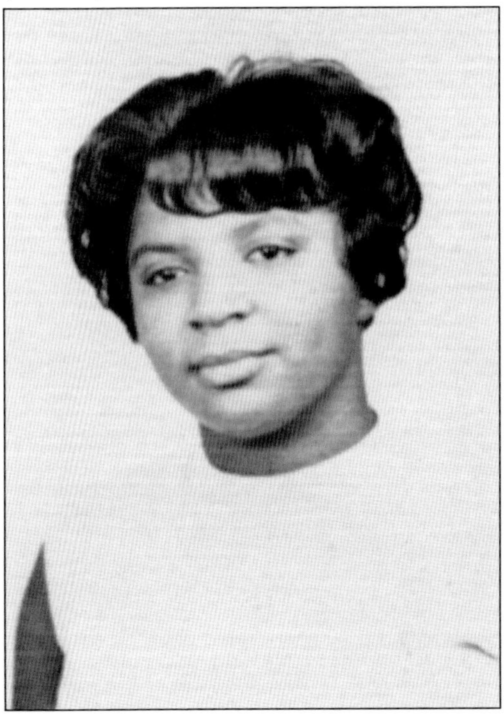

In 1964, the first African American students attended Arkansas A&M College. In 1967, Barbara Ann Blanks Gathen became the first African American to graduate from A&M. A 1963 graduate of Drew High School, she received a B.S.E. degree in English. For over 40 years, she has taught grades seven through 12 in southeast Arkansas schools. (Courtesy of UAM Library.)

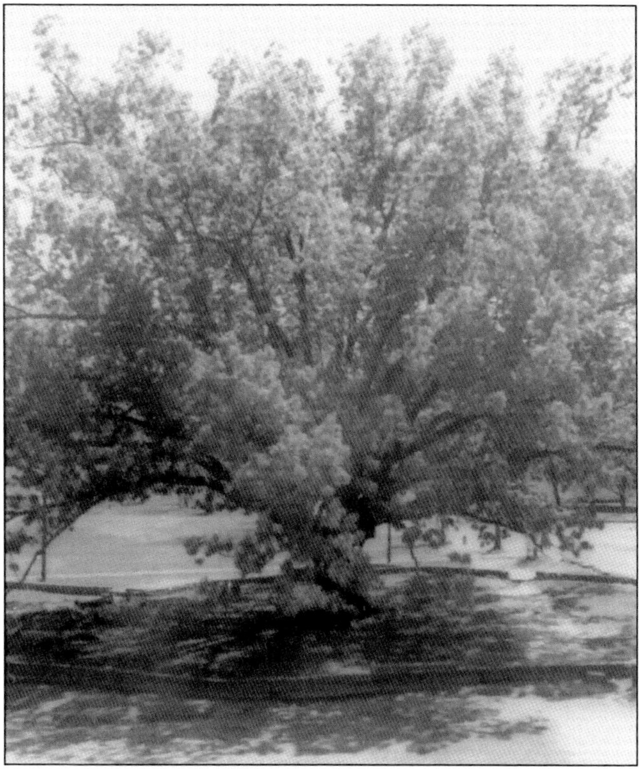

A symbol of the college for decades, the giant oak tree that once stood near the center of the UAM campus is a sentimental and evocative image for many alumni. Its significance in the history and culture of the school is underscored by the fact that UAM's national literary magazine bears the name *The Foliate Oak*. By some estimates, the 300-year-old oak—which was huge, at 20 feet in circumference and with a limb spread of 113 feet—was the oldest of its kind in the state. It was cut down in September 1983 after two large limbs fell and school officials determined that the diseased tree had become a hazard to campus safety. Below, in 1963, freshmen raise their beanies in tribute as they approach the hallowed tree. (Both, courtesy of UAM Library.)

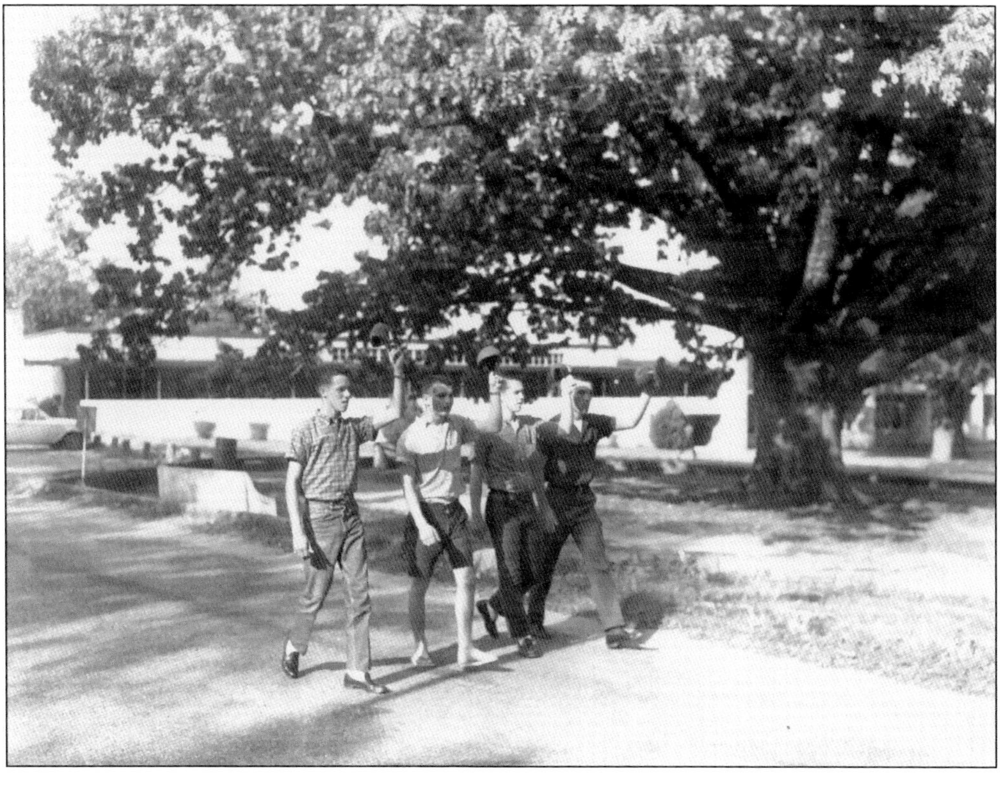

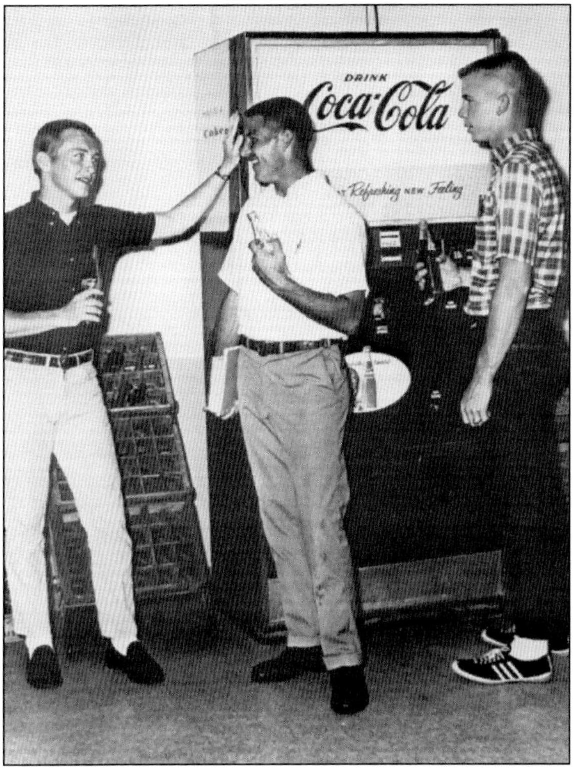

This 1966 photograph, taken on the Arkansas A&M College campus, could serve as a Coca-Cola advertisement. Next to the vintage 1960s Coke machine is a crate for empty eight-ounce bottles. The students in the photograph are perhaps athletes, or "Beatles haircuts" had not yet made it to Monticello. (Courtesy of UAM Library.)

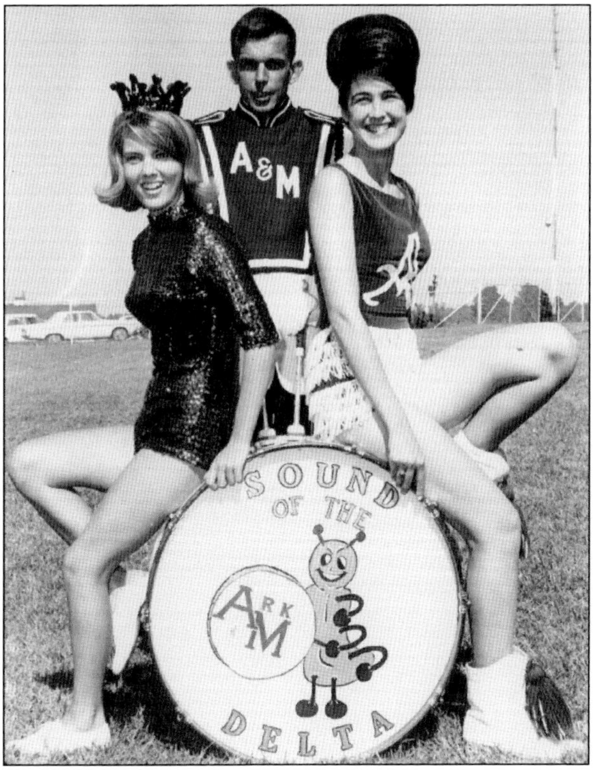

In 1967, the Arkansas A&M marching band billed itself as "the sound of the Delta." Pictured here are Pam Ainsworth (left), Joe Ogden, and Kyla Kolb. (Courtesy of UAM Library.)

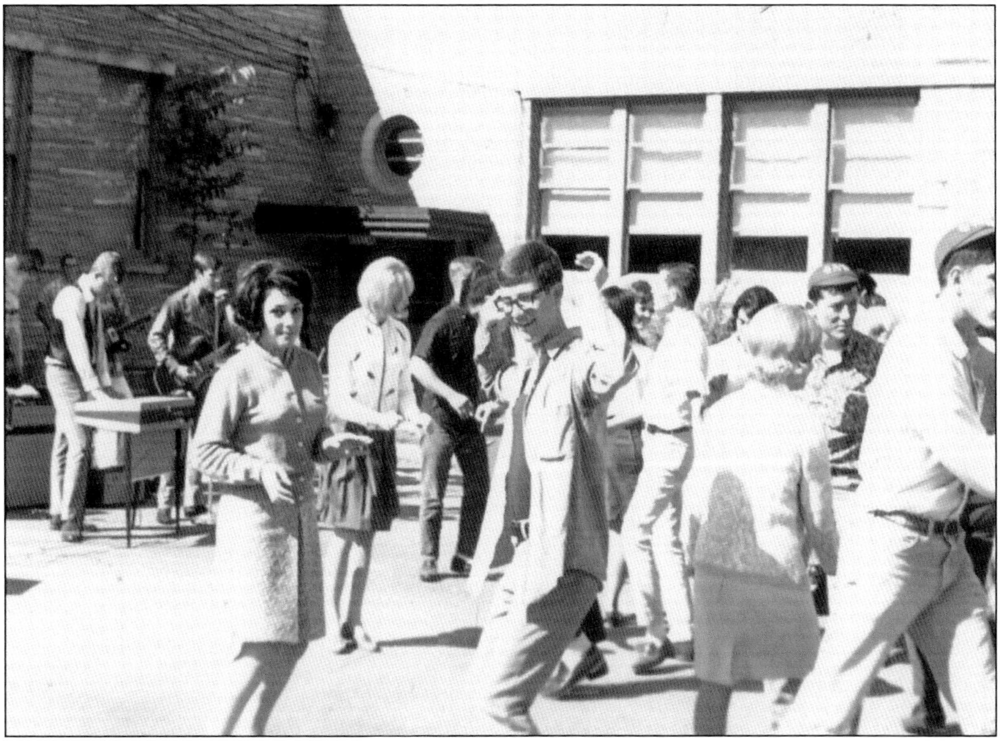

In this c. 1968 image, Arkansas A&M students get funky in the parking lot behind the Memorial Classroom Building while a live band performs. Some of the male students are wearing fraternity pledge caps. (Courtesy of UAM Library.)

Myrtle Ireland Boyd and her husband, Alaga Harrison Boyd, pictured here in 1970, spent most of their lifetimes in Monticello. After Alaga graduated from the University of Missouri, the Boyd family moved to Monticello in 1927. Alaga served as a medic in the US Army during World War I and as a lieutenant in the A&M National Guard unit until 1939. As a civil engineer, he was instrumental in directing the building projects on campus during the 1930s and 1940s. After working at Arkansas A&M for 44 years, Alaga retired in 1970 from his post as the chairman of the Department of Natural Sciences and Mathematics. Myrtle taught Latin, mathematics, and English in the Monticello school system. She also wrote the words to the UAM alma mater in the early 1930s. (Courtesy of Bob Boyd.)

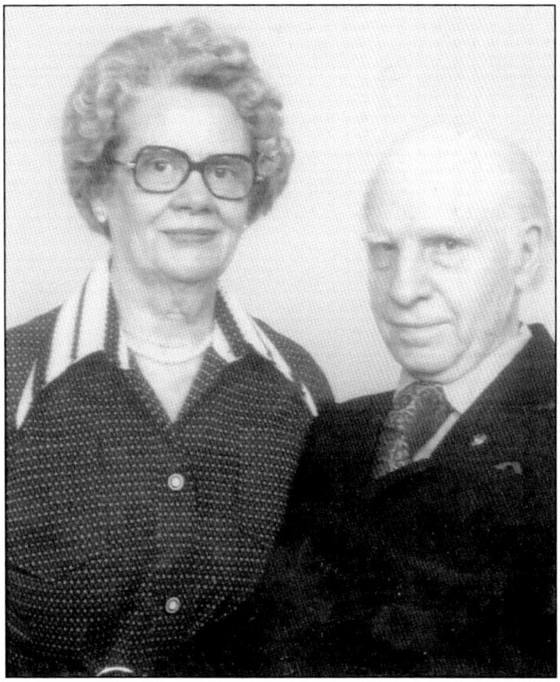

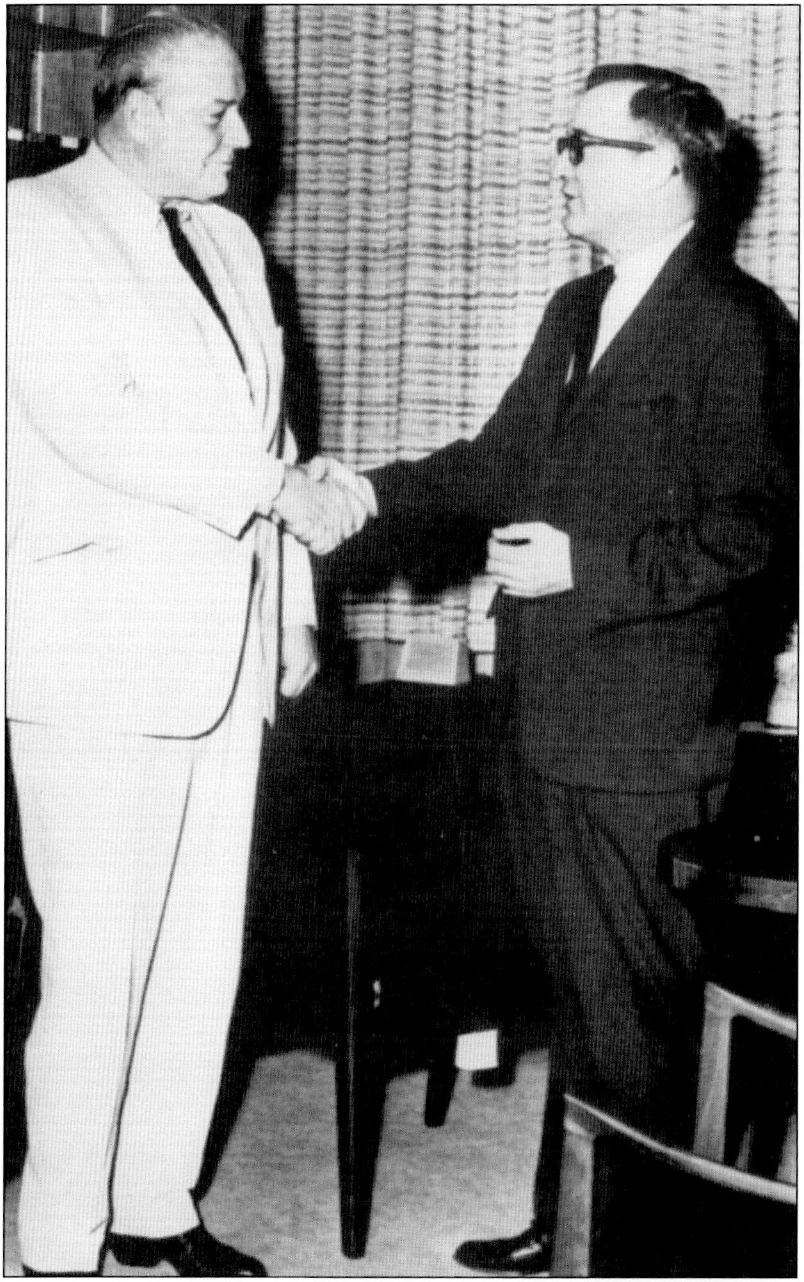

Dr. Claude Babin (right), president of Arkansas A&M College, shakes hands with Arkansas governor Winthrop Rockefeller in 1968. Originally from New York City and the grandson of Standard Oil Company founder John D. Rockefeller, Winthrop Rockefeller moved to Arkansas in the 1950s. The 1966 election of Rockefeller, a relatively liberal candidate, marked a turning point in Arkansas politics and culture. After defeating a traditional segregationist candidate who refused to shake hands with African Americans, Rockefeller paved the way for the election of other moderate politicians in Arkansas, such as Bill Clinton. It was under the Rockefeller administration that Arkansas A&M became the University of Arkansas at Monticello. (Courtesy of UAM Library.)

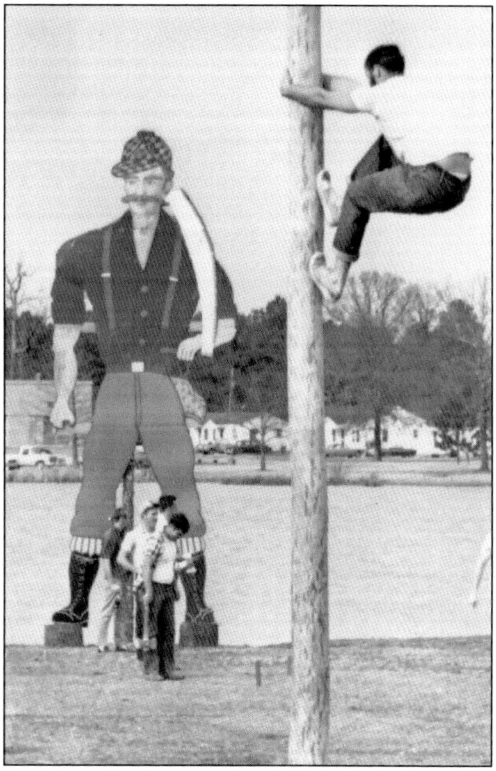

Arkansas A&M College became the University of Arkansas at Monticello in 1971. The college also hosted and won the 1971 Association of Southern Forestry Clubs Conclave. The competition tests students' technical and physical forestry skills. As of 2011, UAM foresters have won the competition 31 times, 22 more than their closest rival, Stephen F. Austin State University, of Texas. Here, a student competes in the pole-climbing competition, with a plywood cutout of Paul Bunyan in the background. Also pictured is Henry "Hank" Chamberlin, professor of forestry, standing next to a larger-than-life statue of a lumberjack. (Both, courtesy of UAM Library.)

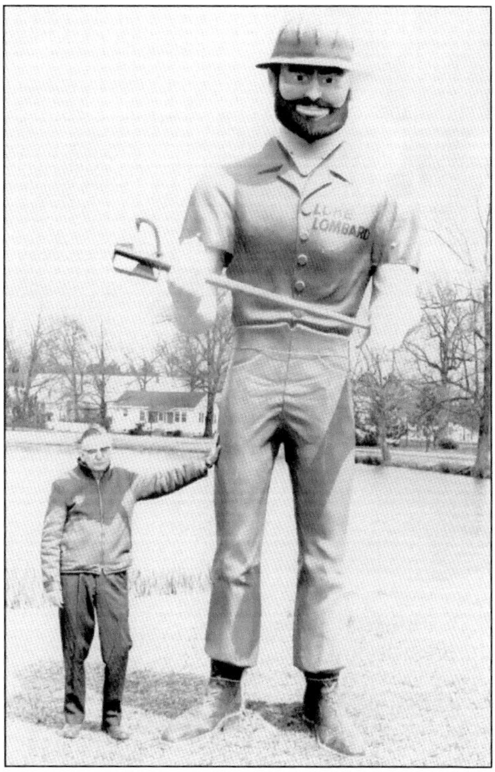

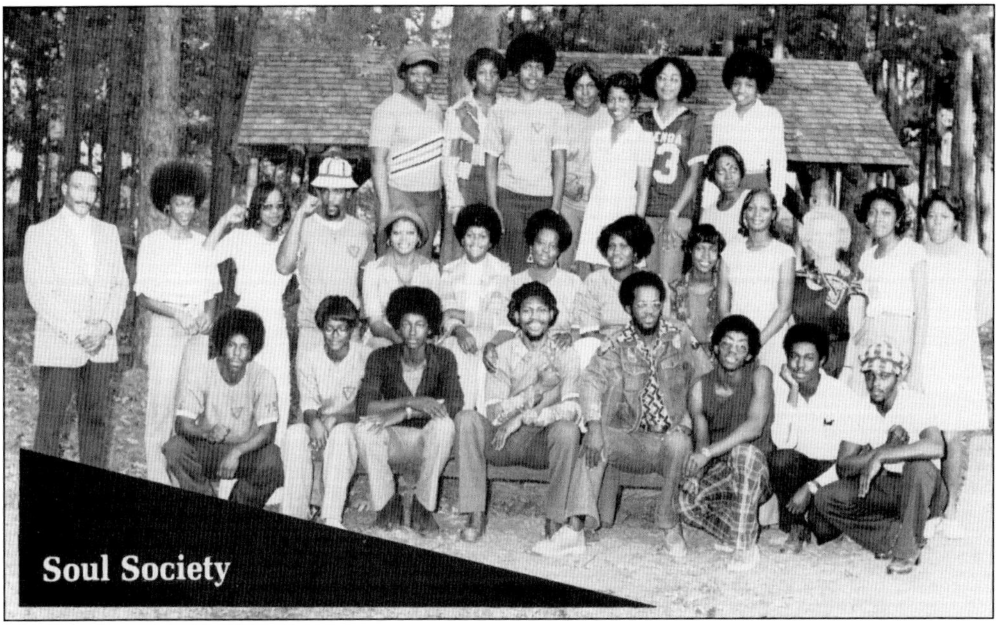

The first student organization for African Americans on campus was the Soul Society, organized in 1969. Its aims were to give African American students the opportunities to encourage each other to succeed. The group is pictured here in 1976. Standing to the left of the group is Louis Dunlap, the first full-time African American professor at UAM. (Courtesy of UAM Library.)

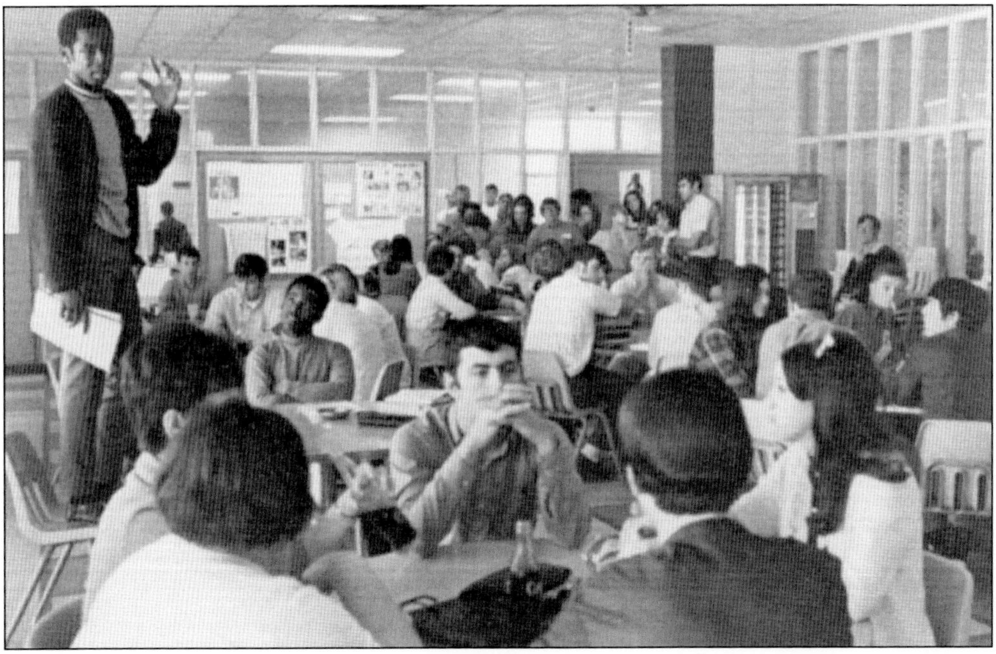

In 1971, members of the Soul Society organized a peaceful march on campus. They presented UAM Pres. Claude Babin with a list of demands including requests for African American instructors, African American dorm mothers, and African American security officers. In 1972, Ernestine Stanley became the first African American dorm mother; Louis Dunlap became the first full-time African American professor in 1973. (Courtesy of UAM Library.)

Pictured here in 1969 are Arkansas A&M coeds in mod fashions and pantsuits. The 1969 yearbook notes that the Student Senate passed a bill that year giving female students permission to wear slacks. After the campus became a university two years later, more casual dress would become the norm. (Courtesy of UAM Library.)

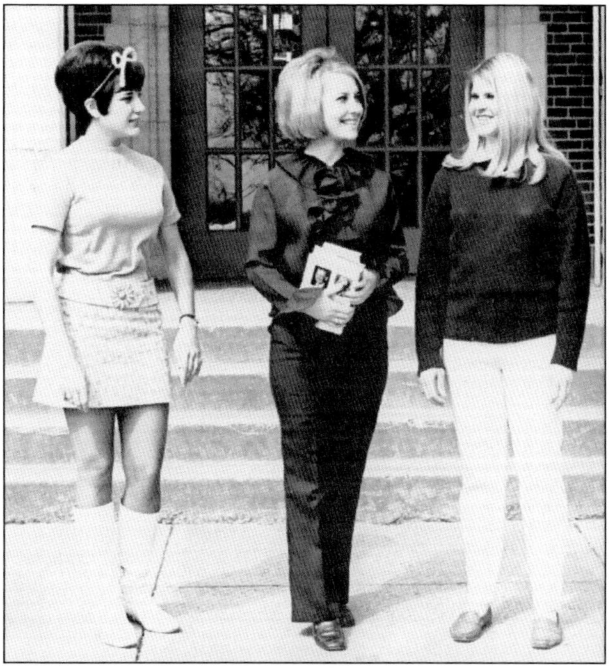

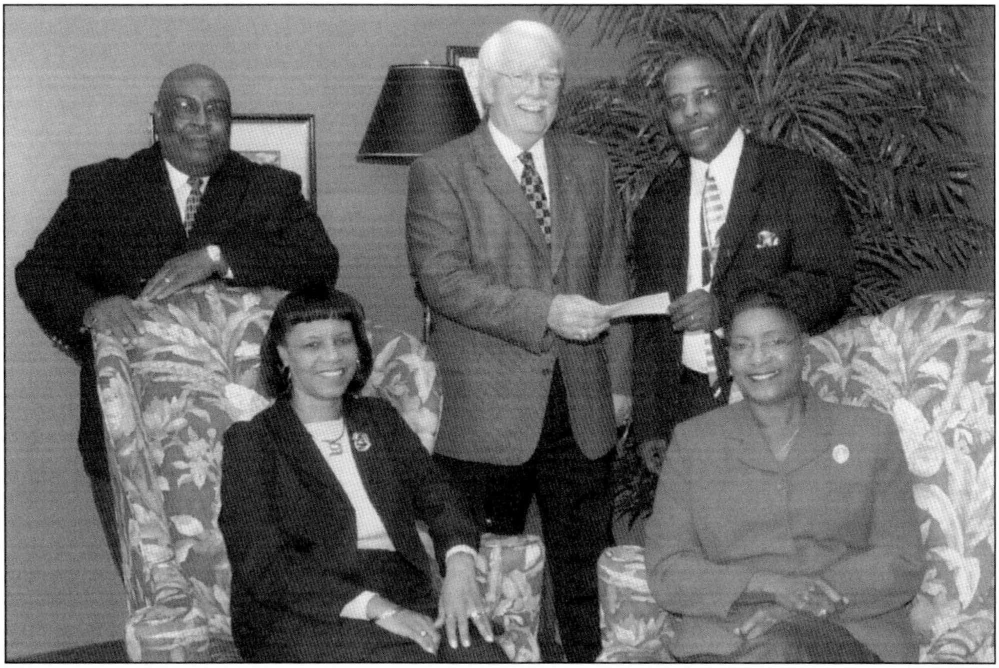

In 2006, members of the UAM African American Alumni Association presented a gift to the UAM Foundation Fund, represented by Chancellor Jack Lassiter (center). Classie Jones-Green (seated at left) graduated in 1972 as the first African American student to receive a degree in nursing from UAM. Standing at left is Al Peer, one of the founding members of Kappa Alpha Psi, the first African American fraternal organization on campus. Seated at right is Mary Hollins of Lake Village, and standing at right is Shay Gillespie, the first African American sports editor of the student newspaper and the yearbook. (Courtesy of UAM Media Services.)

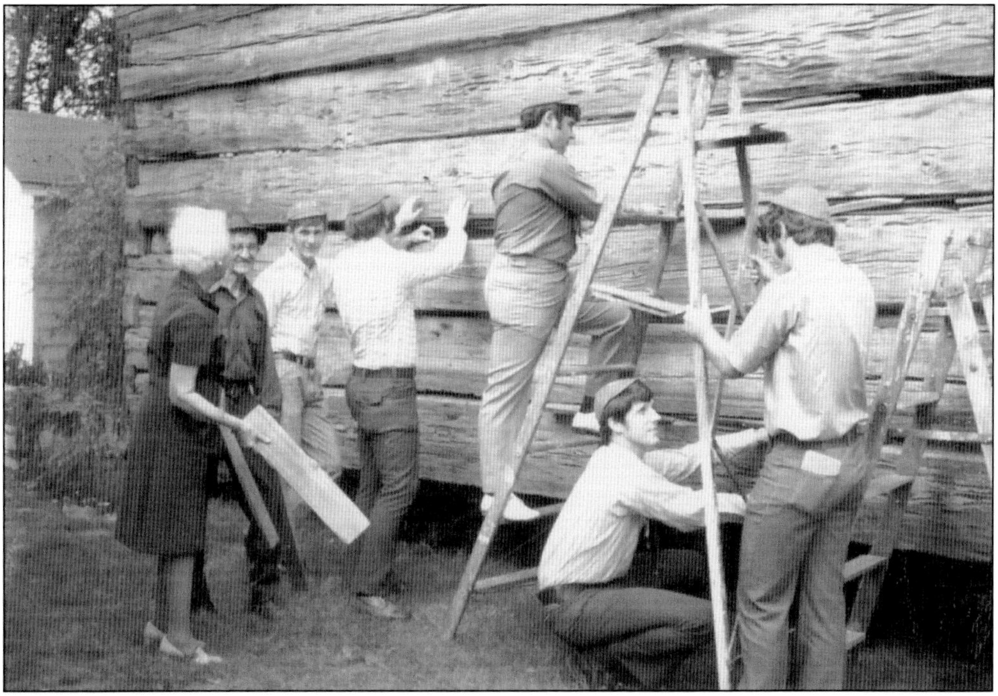

Members of a 1960s fraternity pledge class help to restore the 1819 log cabin on the Drew County Museum grounds. (Courtesy of Drew County Historical Society.)

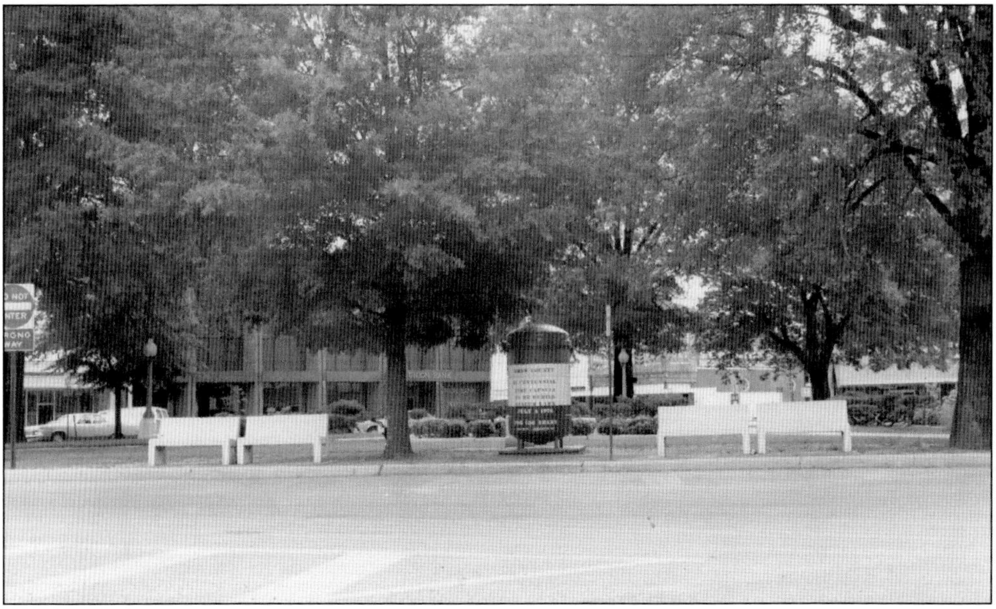

Monticello held many elaborate events to celebrate the nation's bicentennial in 1976. The Heritage '76 Committee organized a time capsule, which is pictured here on the square. The capsule was filled with pictures, publications, and letters from Monticello and buried on July 3, 1976, in the front lawn of the Drew County Museum. Following the ceremony, the Drew County Archives building was dedicated and officially opened to the public. (Courtesy of Drew County Historical Society.)

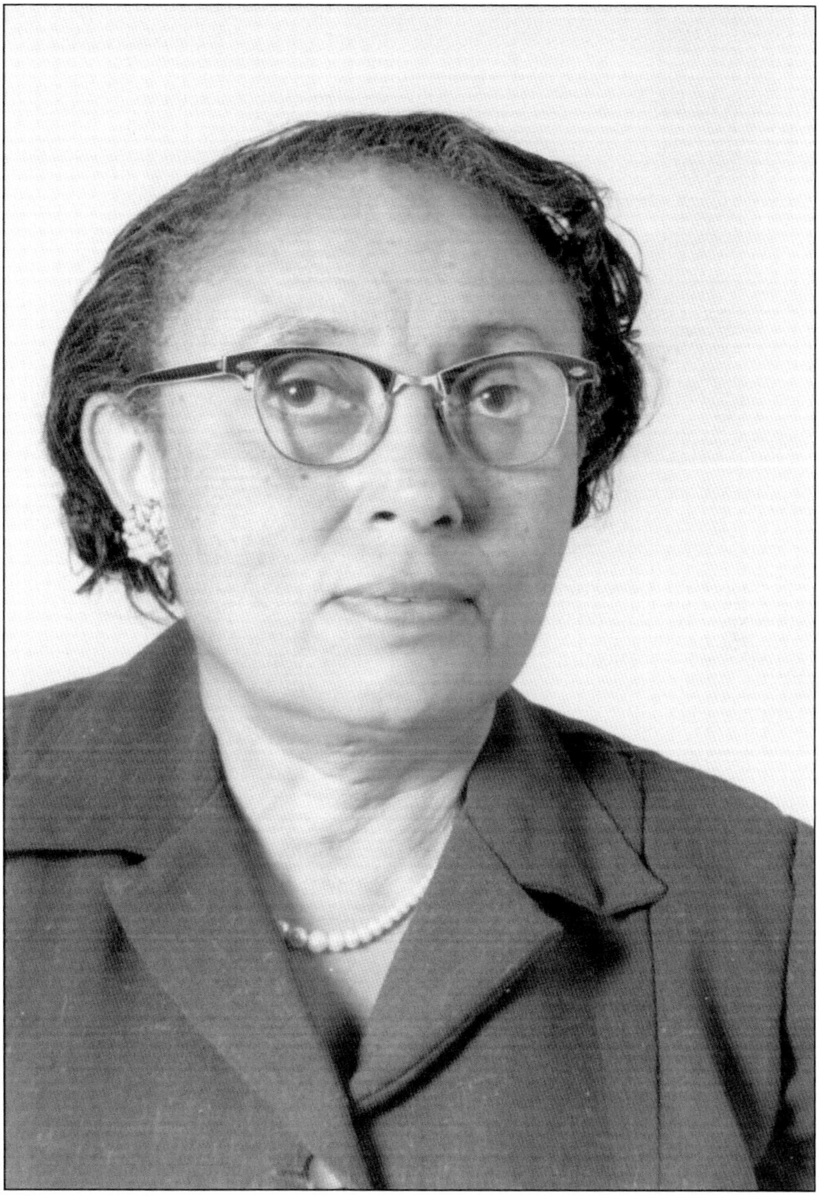

Sadie T. Johnson was born in Monticello in 1903. Her mother, Sarah Gilchrist Thomasson, was one of the first African American teachers at the Monticello Presbyterian Academy, which was established in the 1890s. Johnson attended segregated public schools in Monticello, which, in her time, provided instruction to African American children up to only the seventh grade. Her parents sent her to an all-girls high school in West Point, Mississippi. While teaching full time in Monticello during the school year, she spent 15 years attending summer sessions at Arkansas Agricultural, Mechanical & Normal College in Pine Bluff and graduated in 1939. Johnson received her master's degree in education from the University of Arkansas at Fayetteville in 1958. Many credit Johnson, who served as principal of the Drew Training School from 1927 to 1968, with helping Monticello avert a desegregation crisis like the one that occurred in Little Rock in 1957. On August 11, 12, and 13 in 1978, over 300 of Johnson's former students came from 16 states to pay tribute to her positive influence on their lives. (Courtesy of Drew County Historical Society.)

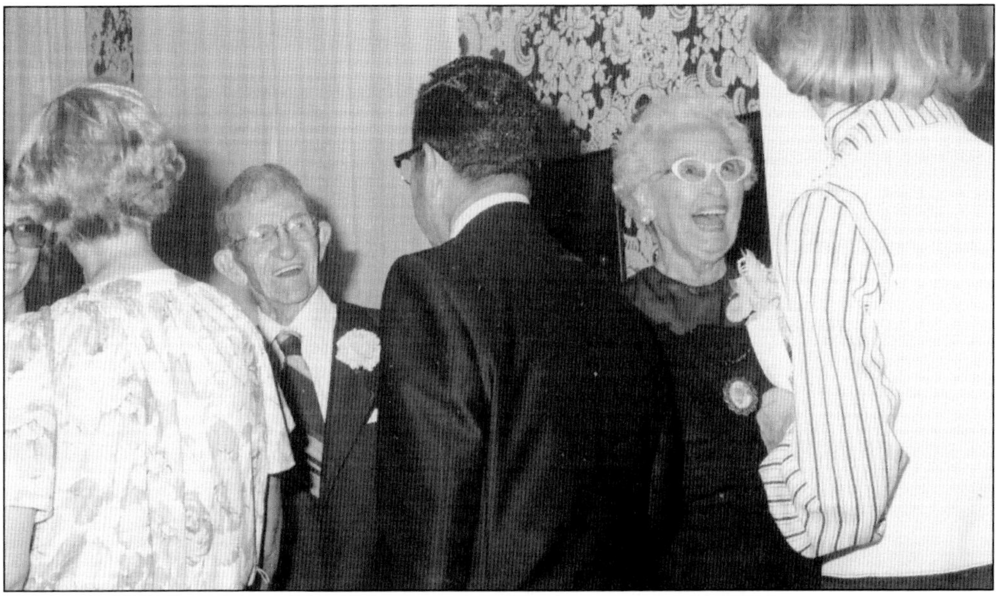

Eric and Lurene Hardy, pictured here in April 1978, were instrumental in establishing the Drew County Museum and Historical Society. (Courtesy of Drew County Historical Society.)

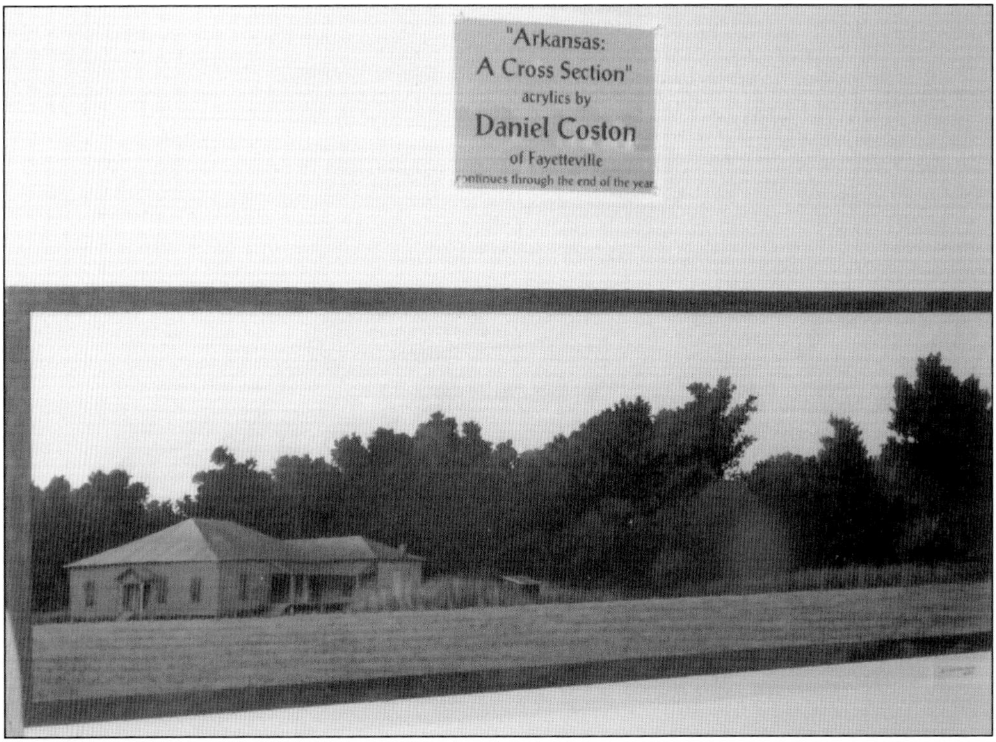

Monticello High School graduate Dan Coston is a professional artist and the son of Dan and Aileen Coston. On June 28, 1980, Union Bank of Drew County celebrated the opening of a new branch with the publication of a book of his drawings. These pen and ink drawings depicted historic images of Monticello. Pictured here is an acrylic painting of an Arkansas farmhouse. (Courtesy of Aileen Coston.)

Lee Greenwood, the country music star known for songs like "God Bless the USA" and "I Don't Mind the Thorns (If You're the Rose)," entertained UAM faculty, staff, and students in 1986. (Courtesy of UAM Library.)

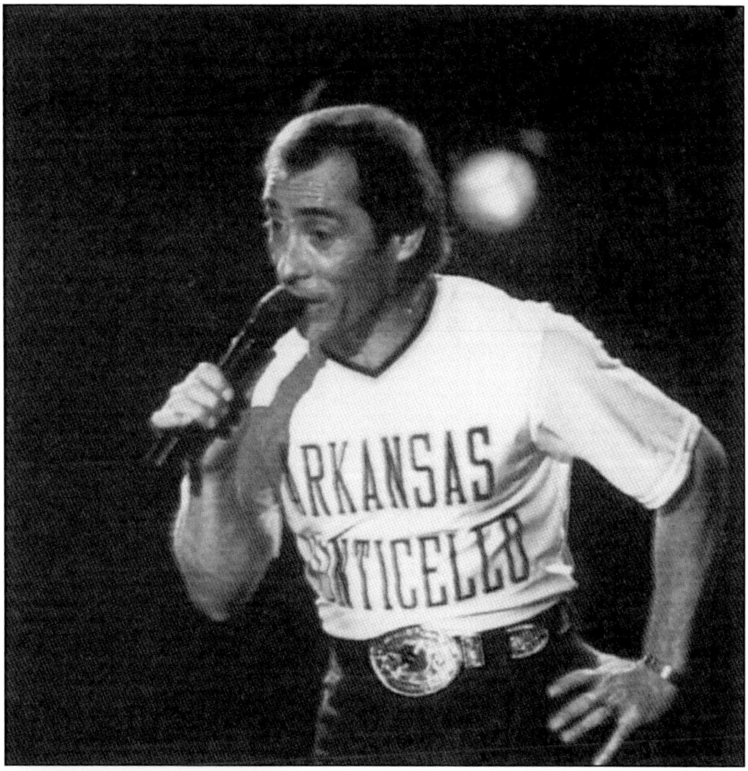

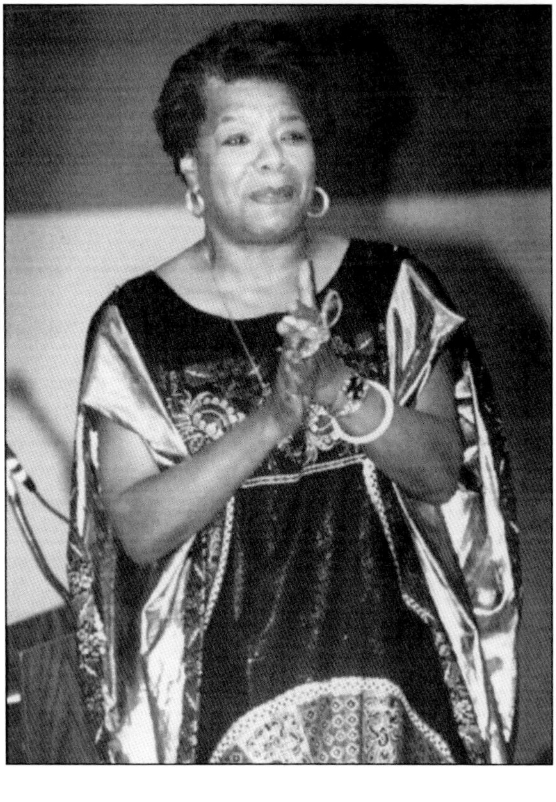

Maya Angelou, one of America's greatest writers of the 20th century and a product of segregated public schools in Arkansas, spoke at the UAM campus in 1991. (Courtesy of UAM Library.)

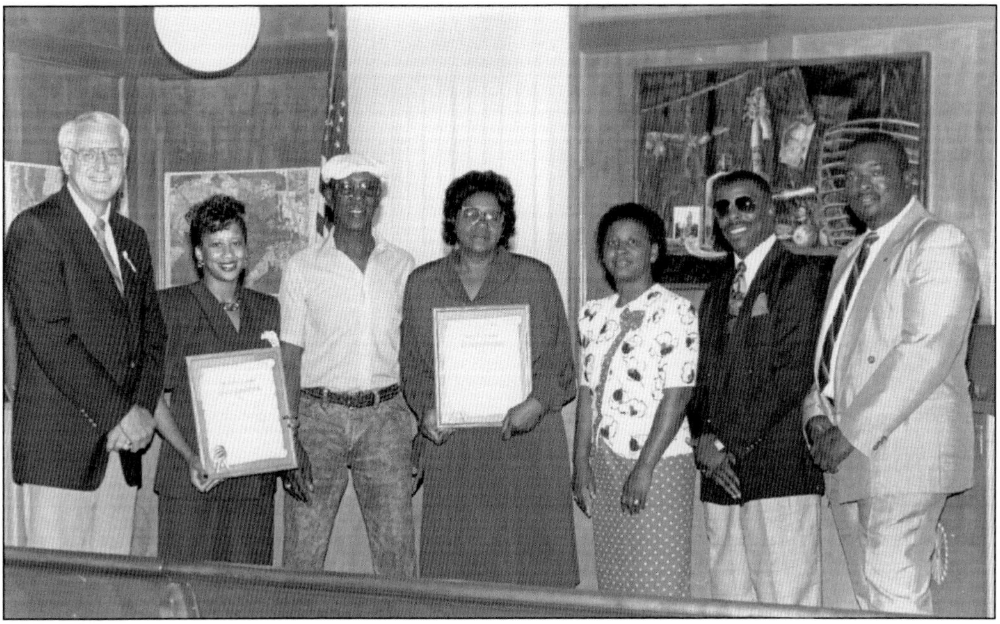

The Hank Thompson Field, located east of town, was dedicated in 1990 in memory of local baseball player Hank Thompson. Pictured here from left to right are Mayor Harold West; Thompson's wife, Linda; his father, Shelvis Thompson Jr.; his mother, Mary Vern Thompson; Sherrie Gillespie; Shay Gillespie; and Clarance Brooks Sr. (Courtesy of Drew County Historical Society.)

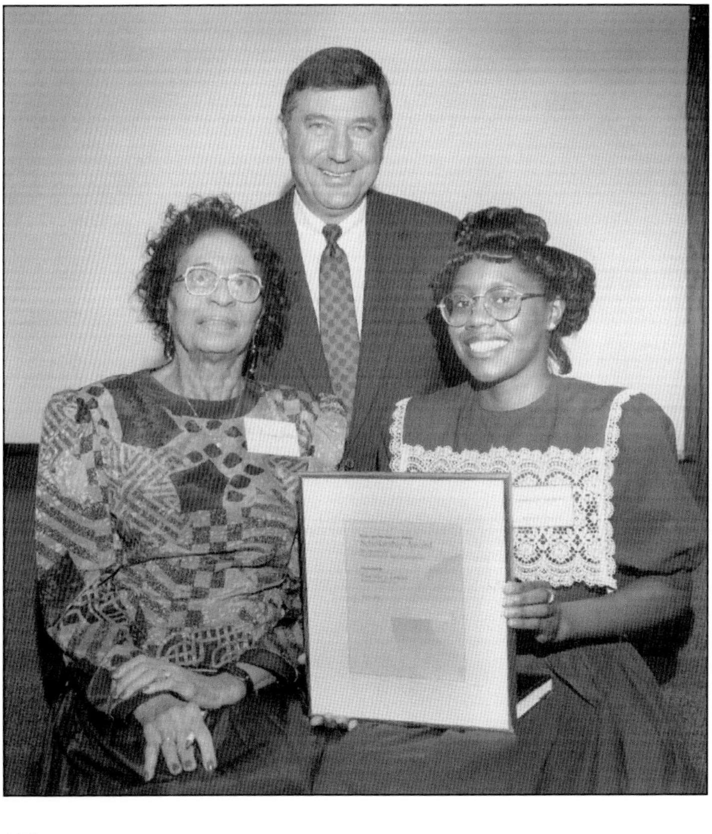

In May 1991, Monticello High School student Demetrius Lambert received the "Daisy and the late L.C. Bates Scholarship Award" from Southwestern Bell Foundation. Pictured here are Bates, Lambert, and an unnamed elected official. Civil rights activist Daisy Bates mentored the Little Rock Nine, a group of African American students who integrated Little Rock's Central High School in 1957. (Courtesy of Drew County Historical Society.)

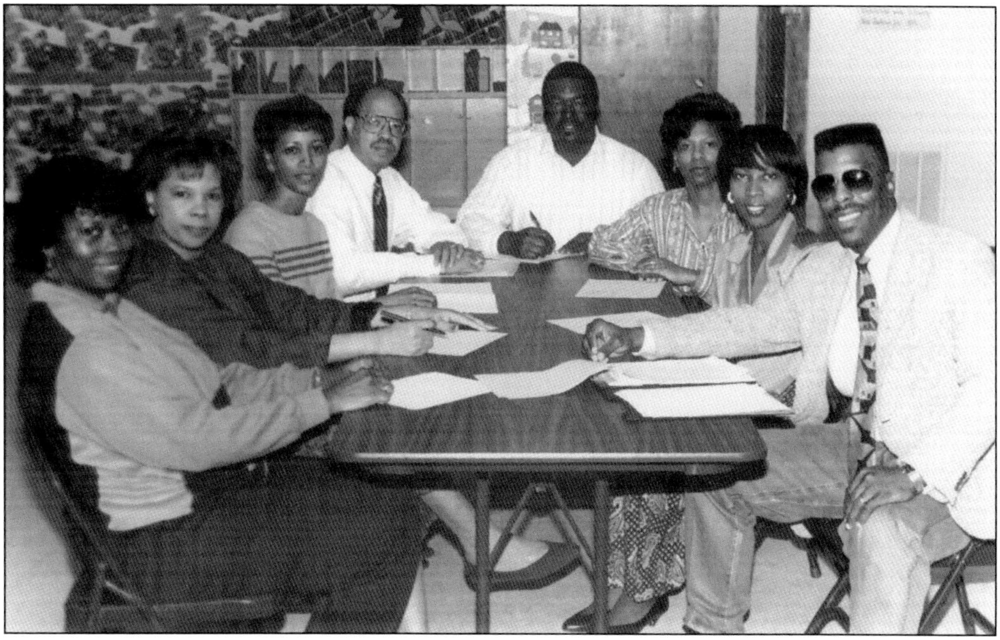

Pictured here in the 1990s are members of a planning committee for the community's celebration of Dr. Martin Luther King Jr.'s birthday. The committee members are, from left to right, Linda Bassett, Bettye Gragg, Verlenda Harris, Michael Binns Sr., Clarance Brooks Sr., Barbara Benton, Shelia Jacob, and Shay Gillespie. (Courtesy of Drew County Historical Society.)

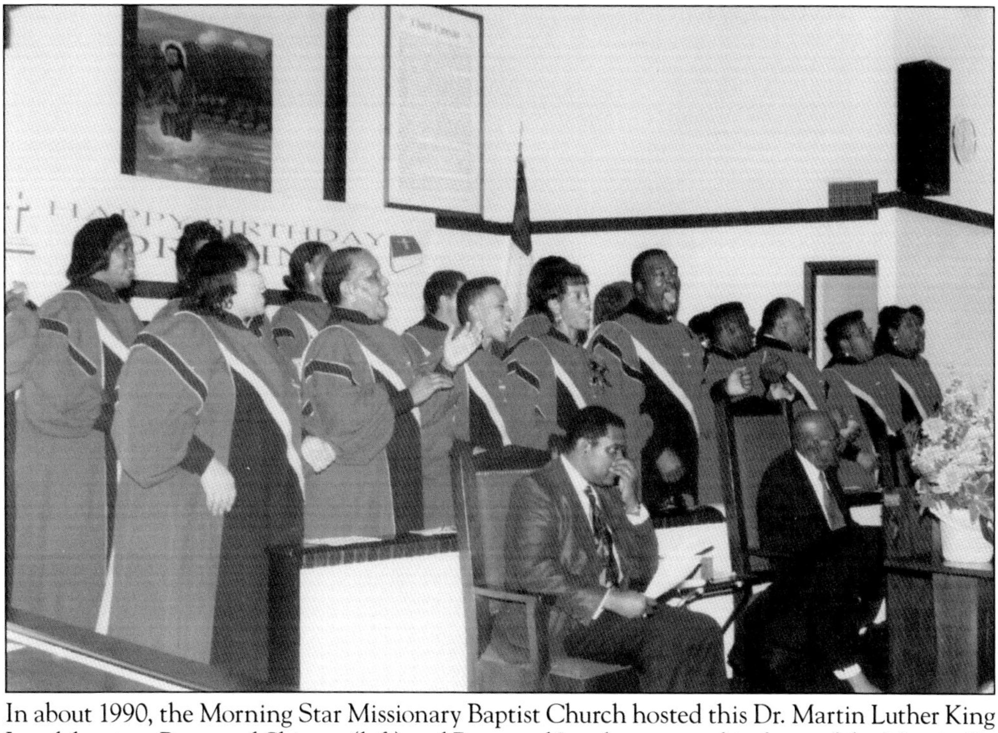

In about 1990, the Morning Star Missionary Baptist Church hosted this Dr. Martin Luther King Jr. celebration. Reverend Skipper (left) and Reverend Lamb are seated in front of the Monticello Community Choir. (Courtesy of Drew County Historical Society.)

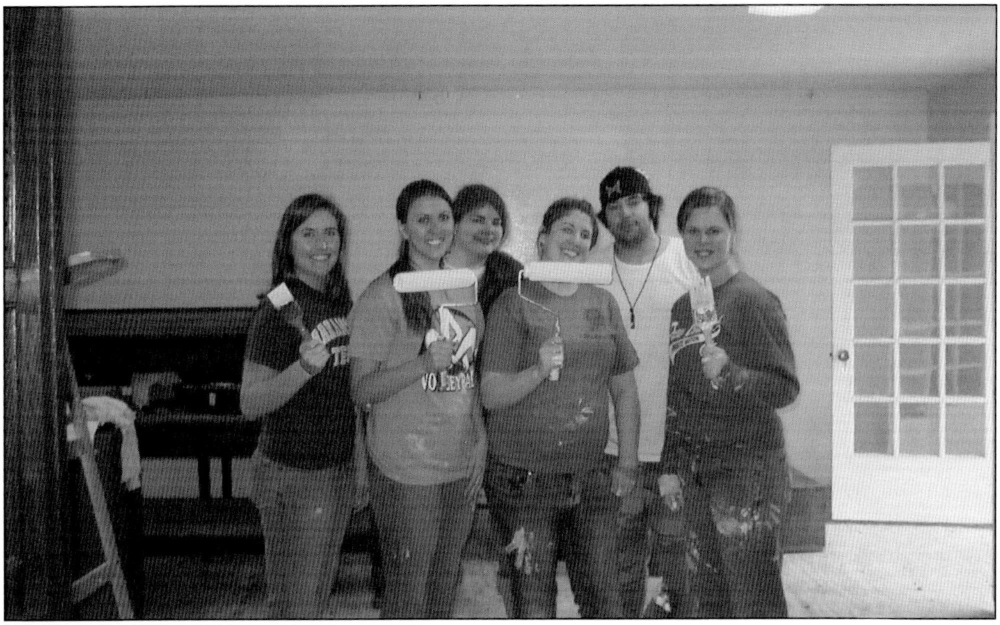

The local chapter of the Phi Alpha Theta history honor society was established in 2007. In 2009, members of the society worked with students from the Alpha Chi honor society to repaint the interior of the Drew County Museum's "Country Store." (Courtesy of Kyle Day.)

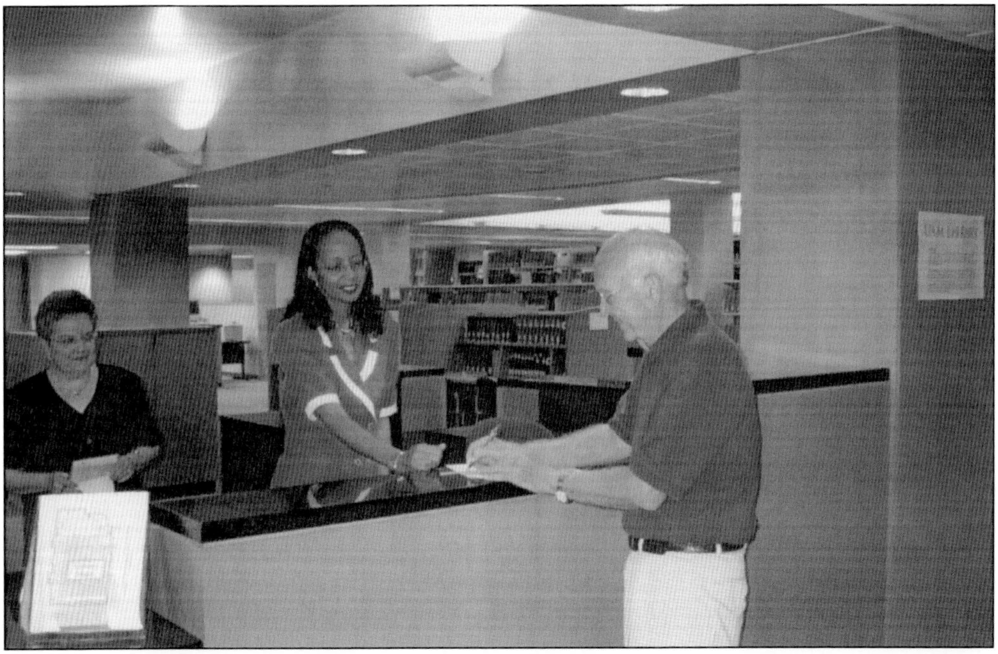

Chancellor Fred Taylor served UAM from 1977 to 2004. Upon his retirement, the UAM library was named the Fred J. Taylor Library and Technology Center. Taylor Library occupies a modern facility, with collections consisting of over 500,000 items. Dr. Taylor is pictured here at the library circulation desk shortly after his retirement; library director Sandra Dupree Campbell (center) and associate librarian Helen Giessen Guenter (left) assist him. As of 2011, both librarians have served UAM for over 25 years. (Courtesy of UAM Library.)

Robert Kennedy Jr., son of the late Sen. Robert Kennedy and the nephew of Pres. John F. Kennedy, spoke at UAM in 2007 about his work as an environmentalist. Kennedy's visit was funded by the Winthrop Rockefeller Distinguished Lecture Series. (Courtesy of UAM Library.)

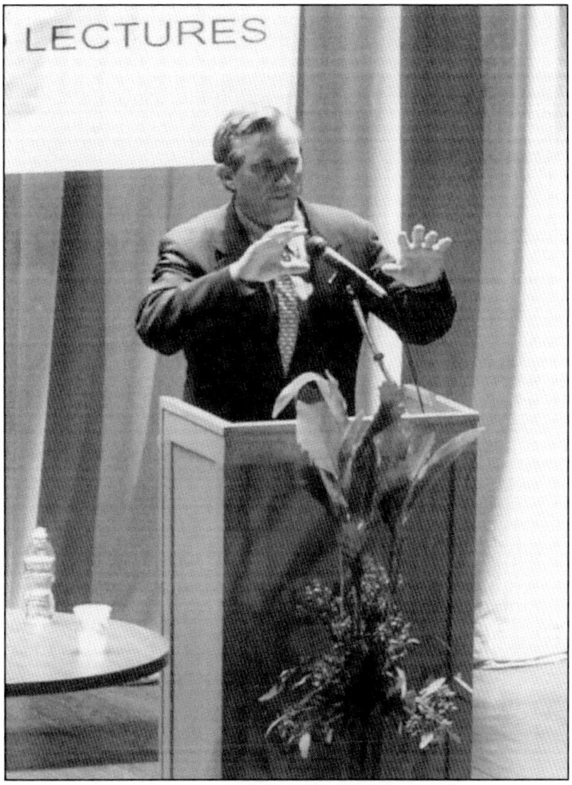

In 2008, UAM hosted Julian Bond, the chair of the National Association for the Advancement of Colored People, as a Winthrop Rockefeller Distinguished Lecturer. Bond spoke of his participation in the civil rights movement of the 1960s and 1970s and the continuing challenges for Americans of color. (Courtesy of UAM Library.)

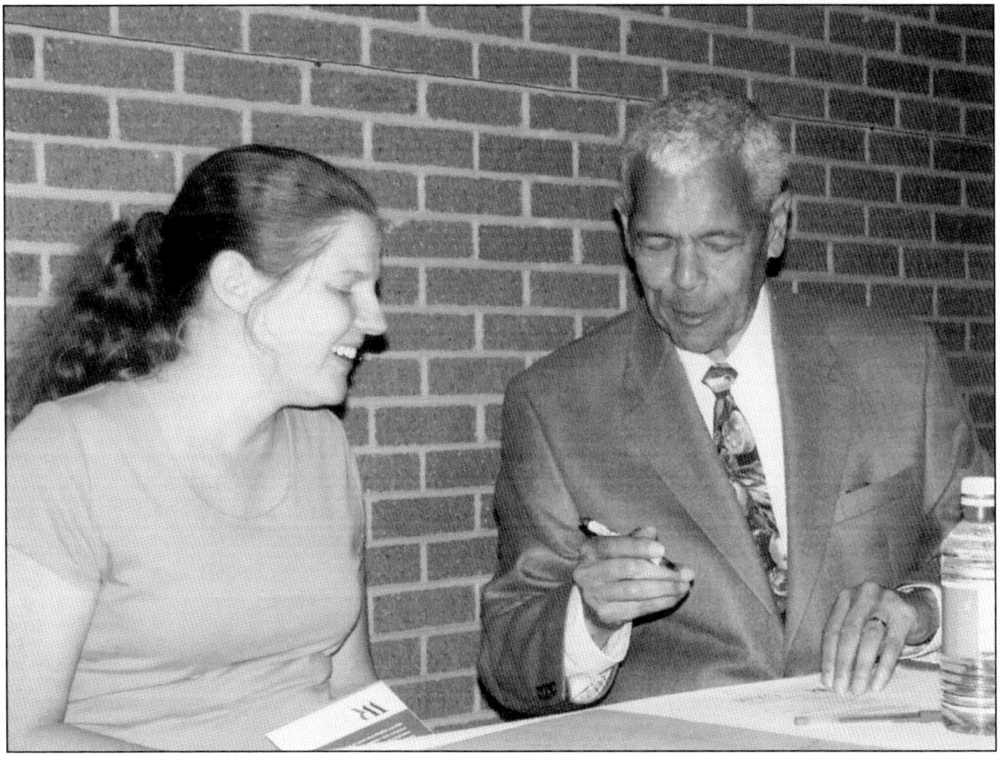

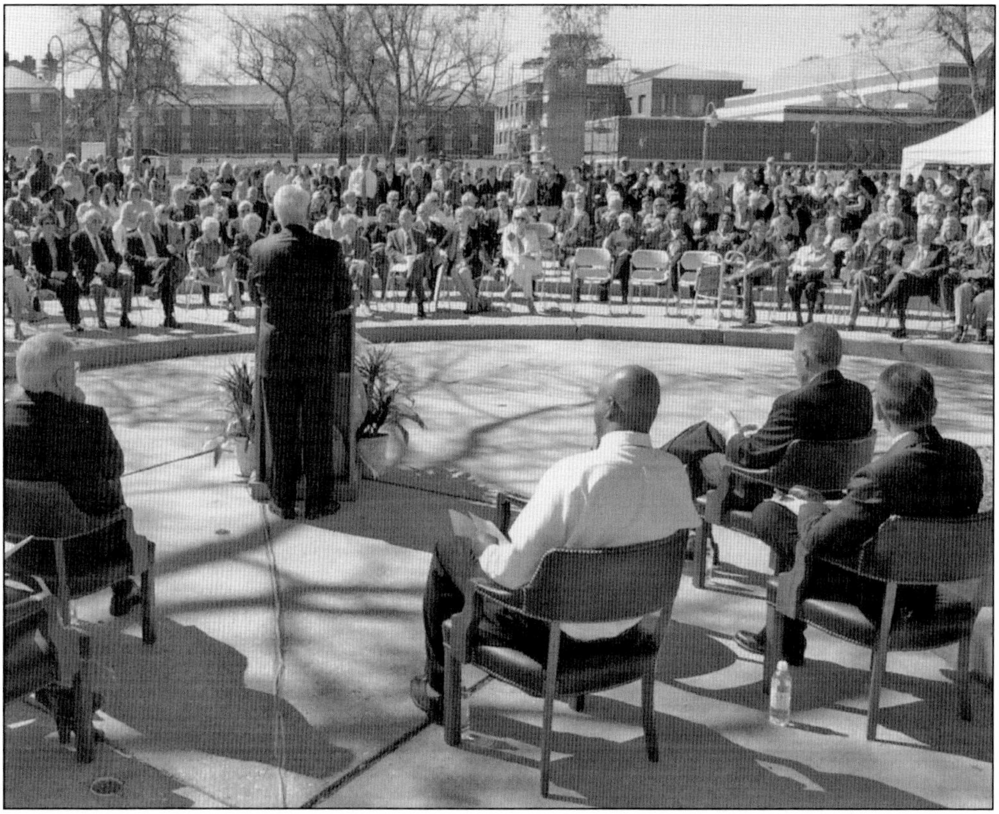

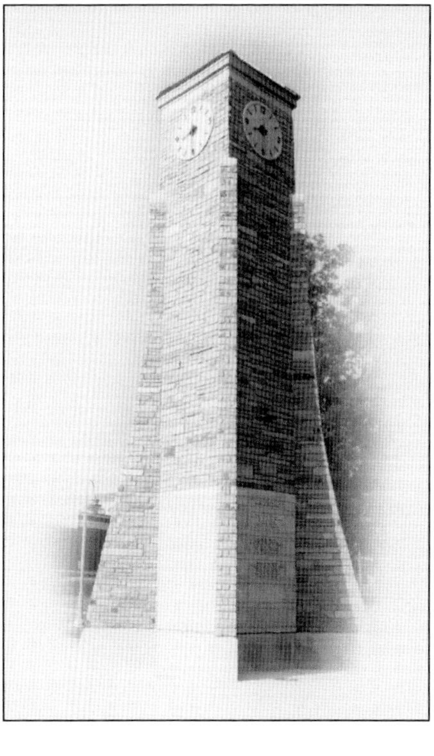

UAM kicked off its centennial celebration on April 1, 2009. Chancellor Jack Lassiter is shown welcoming visitors to the Centennial Convocation. Other centennial events included the burial of a time capsule during homecoming; publication of the first book-length history of UAM, by Dr. Donald Holley; and the performance of a play written by UAM students in which significant historical facts, legends, and myths were dramatized. The construction of the clock tower in the center of campus was completed just in time for the celebration of "100 Years of Opportunity." As an open-admission institution, UAM, like Monticello, represents the opportunity for an individual to strive for a better life regardless of his or her background. (Both, courtesy of UAM Media Services.)

In May 2010, members of the Arkansas Archeological Survey and the Arkansas Archeological Society spent two days excavating a small area of the town square that they had determined was the location of the southeast corner of the clock tower of the "French castle" courthouse, which was razed in 1932. After meticulously digging more than a foot into the soil, the archeologists uncovered several artifacts, including bricks, nails, wire, and possible tile gutter. The limited excavation suggested that additional remnants related to the courthouse, such as its foundation and two wells, are probably underground. The excavation was made in anticipation of planned renovations and improvements to the square. These downtown revitalization projects were in progress in 2011. In the top photograph, UAM Station Archeological Assistant Jessica Howe maps the brick floor of the clock tower corner. Below, Arkansas Archeological Society member Kenny Bragg sifts soil for artifacts. (Both, courtesy of Jessica Howe and Don Bragg; photographs by Don Bragg.)

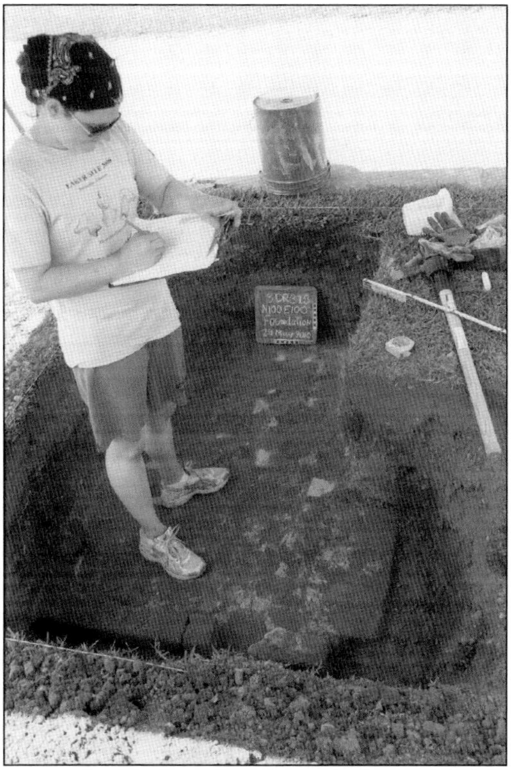

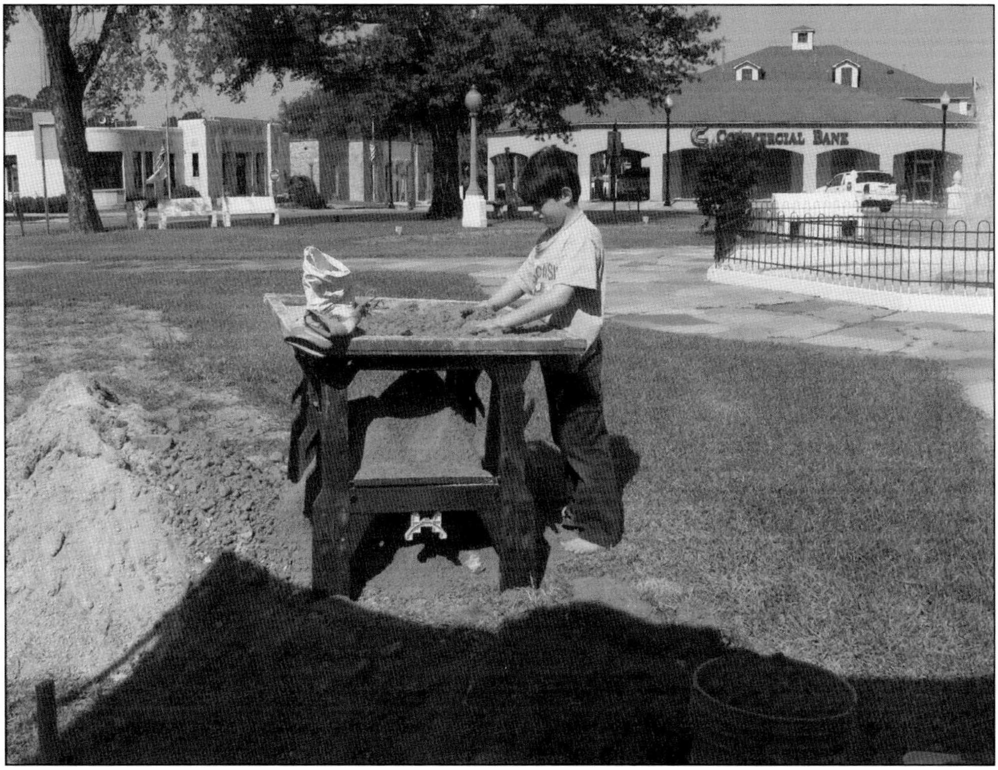